D0457872

THE CHALLENGE OF THE MEDIEVAL TEXT

Studies in Genre and Interpretation

PN
681
.J3
1985

The Challenge
of the
Medieval Text

Studies in Genre and Interpretation

W. T. H. JACKSON

Edited by
JOAN M. FERRANTE
ROBERT W. HANNING

New York   COLUMBIA UNIVERSITY PRESS   *1985*

WITHDRAWN

HIEBERT LIBRARY 65699
Fresno Pacific College - M.B. Seminary
Fresno, CA 93702

Library of Congress Cataloging in Publication Data

Jackson, W. T. H. (William Thomas Hobdell), 1915–83
    The challenge of the medieval text.

    1. Literature, Medieval—History and criticism—
Addresses, essays, lectures.   I. Ferrante, Joan M.,
    1936   .   II. Hanning, Robert W.   III. Title.
        PN681.J3 1985   809'.02   84-22981
            ISBN 0-231-05970-1

Columbia University Press
New York   Guildford, Surrey
Copyright © 1985 Columbia University Press
All rights reserved

Printed in the United States of America

*Clothbound editions of Columbia University Press books are
Smyth-sewn and printed on permanent and durable acid-free paper.*

Contents

Introduction

THIS COLLECTION OF ESSAYS, planned to honor William Thomas Hobdell Jackson on his retirement from Columbia at the end of 1983, was sadly transformed by his death in May of that year into a memorial volume. It seems an appropriate way to celebrate him, nonetheless, since it gathers some of his most important essays on a variety of genres and national literatures. Like the great medieval comparatists of an earlier generation, Curtius, Auerbach, and Spitzer, Jackson was well-trained in the classics and his interests ranged from medieval Latin rhetoric, drama, allegory, poetry, and parody, to Middle High German lyric, epic, romance, and drama, to Middle French and Provençal. The essays in this volume give some indication of his scope, though they cannot of themselves suggest the extent of his contributions to medieval studies, not only as scholar and critic, but also as lecturer and teacher.

W. T. H. Jackson was educated in Sheffield, England, where he was born in 1915, and later in the United States, where he lived from 1948. He began his studies at High Storrs Grammar School, a school he called "abashedly academic," which selected top students from the city of Sheffield by examination and gave them a strong traditional training; from there he went to the University of Sheffield, where he read Classics, earning a B.A. with First Class Honours, in 1935, and an M.A. (a status degree), in 1938. He taught in English public schools from 1935 to 1940. He spent the next six years in the army, five of them as an officer of the Royal Artillery, Captain Adjutant, Queen's Own Dorset Yeomanry, and Staff Captain. He studied German at the Staff College at Camberly, and eventually became the Education Officer for secondary schools and universities in the province of Hanover, Germany, during the Military Government. There he met his wife, Erika Noltemeyer, whom he married in 1945. At the urging of his wife's cousin, a doctor in the American army who lived in Seattle, Jackson came to the University of Washington. Finding no program in Classics there, but an active one in German, he took a Ph.D. in German in 1951, writing a dissertation on the German poems of the Carmina Burana. Carl Bayerschmidt, chairman of the German department at Columbia University, was a visiting professor at Washington while Jackson was a student, and later asked him to come to Columbia. In the interim, Jackson taught at Coe College in Cedar Rapids, Iowa, from 1950 to 1952.

In 1952, Jackson came to Columbia, where he taught for the next thirty years. Although he had been invited to teach German, he was offered other medieval courses as they became available. First he was asked to take on Medieval Latin, when the instructor died, and he taught both the elementary and the advanced courses, turning the latter into a literature course, and eventually adding a semester of Paleography. Then Roger Sherman Loomis retired, and Jackson began to teach a survey of the major genres of medieval literature from a comparative perspective, and later he gave a doctoral seminar on specific topics of medieval literature. Of this course he said: "It would be hard to overstate the pleasure I derived from those seminars and the knowledge I gained from those who participated in them. Comparative medieval literature became a reality and those who took part in the seminars have made sure that the word has been spread."

This sense of the seminars, and indeed of all his medieval courses, is one most of his students shared. His strength as a teacher, and also as a scholar, lay not in the espousal of a particular concept or system, but in the catholicity of his interests and the range of his perspectives, in his willingness to confront each work on its terms, rather than on his, something he tried very hard to pass on to his students. He also conveyed the excitement of studying medieval literature as literature, even in the Medieval Latin and Paleography courses, which had once been simply technical studies, but which he enriched with rhetoric and classical sources, with an appreciation of the material's literary techniques, intellectual content, and humor. The survey of medieval literature introduced generations of nonspecialists, as well as specialists, to the pleasures and intricacies of medieval texts, as literature, not as philological or anthropological artifacts. The doctoral seminars took up all the important genres and texts of continental medieval literature, in allegory, drama, epic, lyric, and romance, in Latin, German, French, and Provençal, and spawned many dissertations, books, and articles from among the participants. Jackson encouraged his students to pursue their own interests, as long as they did close and careful readings of their texts, and did not distort the texts to support their theses. He instilled in his students a sense of community, encouraged in them intellectual generosity and human responsibility, so that many continued to work together after they left the seminars, to write together, to share their ideas and their criticisms, to support each other in their activities.* That is a legacy for which many of us will always be grateful.

Because of the popularity of the survey course he taught for so long, Jackson was frequently called upon to examine students who decided to offer a minor subject in medieval comparative literature on their Ph.D. qualifying (oral) examination. One would have thought that quizzing such nonspecialist students for twenty minutes, on medieval texts many had read only in translation, could offer little challenge (or pleasure) to a scholar of Jackson's stature. In fact, he showed himself on these occasions to be a superb examiner, using well-formulated questions to lead the candidate to deeper levels of understanding of the material. As a result the examination became for the student, and indeed the other examiners, a pleasurable learning experience rather than a trial. Students majoring in modern British or American literature frequently said after their orals that their brief dialogue with Jackson was the high point of the occasion.

A man of wide general cultivation, Jackson could be counted on to supply a student or colleague with needed information on a broad range of topics, always without pretension or fanfare. His quiet confidence heartened those who studied with him almost as much as his frequent words of encouragement to them. His connoisseurship of food and wine, complemented by his wife Erika's culinary expertise, gave further pleasure to many, especially those who dined at the Jacksons' home on Morningside Drive.

Jackson's work as a teacher was not confined to Columbia. He also gave courses at Rutgers University, regularly from 1961 on, and was a visiting

---

* Six of his students wrote a book together on courtly love (*In Pursuit of Perfection*), which they dedicated to him.

professor at Chicago in 1955, Princeton in 1958, Duke in 1965, Yale in 1966, CUNY in 1975, 1976, and 1977, Fordham in 1977, and SUNY in 1979. He was Phi Beta Kappa Visiting Scholar in 1965–66. He lectured widely at conferences and universities (frequently at West Point), and participated in the publication of series for the nonspecialist (as editor of the Medieval and Renaissance section of Scribner's *European Writers*); he wrote encyclopedia articles for the *American Encyclopedia,* for Wilson's *European Authors,* and the *Encyclopedia of Poetry and Poetics,* as well as for more specialized audiences, like those in the ACLS-sponsored *Dictionary of the Middle Ages* (on Medieval German Romance, on Gottfried von Strassburg, Eilhart von Oberge, Hugo Primas, the Archipoeta, Andreas Capellanus, the Alexander Romances, and Beast Epic). He was the General Editor of the Columbia University Press' Records of Civilization series from 1962, and was thus responsible for making many important texts available in careful translations with full scholarly commentary. He also served as a member of the editorial boards of *Germanic Review* (of which he was the editor from 1954 to 1964), *Medievalia et Humanistica,* and *Columbia Monographs in Classical Civilization.*

Jackson was well-known in the scholarly community: he was a councillor of the Medieval Academy from 1968 to 1971, and was elected a Fellow of the Academy in 1975; he became the second vice-president in 1983 and would have been president in 1985. He was a Guggenheim Fellow in 1957–58 and again in 1967–68, and was awarded an ACLS grant in 1958 and in 1972. He served on the Executive Council of the Modern Language Association from 1960 to 1964, and became a trustee of the Columbia University Press in 1980. Despite his various obligations in the outside world, he also managed to be chairman of the German department at Columbia from 1961 to 1967, and of the Interdepartmental Committee for Comparative Literature from 1970 to 1982.

In his major scholarly works, Jackson made significant contributions to a general appreciation of medieval literature, particularly in *The Literature of the Middle Ages* (Columbia, 1960), which has also been published in German as *Die Literaturen des Mittelalters. Eine Einführung* (Heidelberg: Winter 1967), and in *Medieval Literature: A History and a Guide* (New York: Macmillan, 1966). In *The Anatomy of Love* (Columbia, 1971), he presented the poem he considered the greatest work of the Middle Ages, Gottfried's *Tristan,* with skill and love, setting it in its context with contemporary medieval literature and with other Tristan poems, discussing its major ideas, but particularly analyzing the poetic structure and language, the art of the poet, an aspect of literature that especially interested him. In *The Interpretation of Medieval Lyric Poetry* (Columbia and Macmillan, 1980), he brought together a collection of essays by a number of medieval scholars, each analyzing a particular lyric from a particular perspective, a different but no less effective way of revealing the technical and substantive riches of medieval poetry. In his last book, *The Hero and the King; An Epic Theme* (Columbia, 1982), he drew on a lifetime of interest in classical and medieval epics, attempting a definition of the genre by the dominant theme he saw in the works, the conflict between the older king and the young hero.

Combining a knowledge of the classics with a sharp sense of humor, Jackson was particularly alert to parody and to irony, aspects of medieval literature which modern readers have been increasingly aware of. Himself a master of occasional verse, in Latin as well as in English—a poem in praise of *Brevis onda* was read on the BBC for the twenty-fifth anniversary of their World Services Program, "Outlook"—he was particularly sensitive to word-plays and nuances in the poetry of all the medieval languages he worked in, as several of the essays in this collection will attest.

We have divided the essays republished here into four categories. The first, "Courtly Love," includes two pieces that show Jackson at his commonsensical best, eschewing extravagant claims for the status of courtly love within medieval literature and society, and concentrating instead on the playfulness and irony with which particular texts used routines and rituals of love. The essays in the second section, on lyric, combine the scholar's knowledge of literary sources and topoi with the linguist's ability to move comfortably between Latin, Provençal, and German, and the critic's feeling for content and poetic techniques. The third grouping, "Epic and Drama," contains pieces scrutinizing conventions of character, time, space, and structure in these important medieval genres. Jackson shows himself attentive both to characteristics which define a genre and to techniques which make particular texts distinctive within it. Similar concerns unite the essays in the last group, on allegory and romance. These range from definitions of the genres, and the relationship of particular works to others of the same type, to those elements of a work which go beyond the genre, such as romance in the *Roman de la Rose*, lyric in *Tristan*, allegory in *Parzival*.

J.M.F.
R.W.H.

Publications

BOOKS

The Literature of the Middle Ages. New York: Columbia University Press, 1960. German translation: *Die Literaturen des Mittelalters: Eine Einführung,* Heidelberg: Winter 1967.

Essential Works of Erasmus. New York: Bantam, 1965.

Medieval Literature: A History and a Guide. New York: Macmillan, 1966.

An Anthology of German Literature 800–1750. Englewood, N.J.: Prentice Hall, 1968, Peter Demetz and W. T. H. Jackson, eds.

The Anatomy of Love: The Tristan of Gottfried von Strassburg. New York: Columbia University Press, 1971.

The Interpretation of Medieval Lyric Poetry. New York and London: Columbia and Macmillan, 1980.

The Hero and the King: An Epic Theme. New York: Columbia University Press, 1982.

Joachim Bumke, *The Concept of Knighthood in the Middle Ages.* New York: AMS Press, 1982, W. T. H. and Erika Jackson, trans., introduction by W. T. H. Jackson.

ARTICLES

"The Medieval Pastourelle as a Satirical Genre." *Philological Quarterly* (1952), 31:156–170. Appeared in German as "Die mittelalterliche Pastourelle als satirische Gattung." *Mittellateinische Dichtung,* Karl Langosch, ed. Darmstadt: Wissenschaftliche Buchgesellschaft, 1969.

"The Role of Brangaene in Gottfried's *Tristan.*" *Germanic Review* (1953), 28:290–296.

"The German Poems in the Carmina Burana." *German Life and Letters* (1953), 7:36–43.

"The Interpretation of Carmina Burana 147." *Medievalia et Humanistica* (1954), 8:3–5.

"Der Streit zwischen miles und clericus." *Zeitschrift für deutsches Altertum und deutshe Literatur* (1955), 85:293–303.

"Pyrgopolinices Converted: the Boasting Soldier in Medieval German Literature." *Germanic Review* (1955), 30:92–100.

"The Composition of Meier Helmbrecht." *Modern Language Quarterly* (1957), 18:44–58.

"The *De Amore* of Andreas Capellanus and the Practice of Love at Court." *Romanic Review* (1958), 49:243–251.

"The Progress of Parzival and the Trees of Virtue and Vice." *Germanic Review* (1958), 33:118–124.

"Gottfried von Strassburg." *Arthurian Literature in the Middle Ages,* Roger Sherman Loomis, ed. Oxford: Clarendon, 1959.

"Tristan the Artist in Gottfried's Poem." *PMLA* (1962), 77:364–372. Appeared in German as "Der Kunstler Tristan in Gottfrieds Dichtung," *Gottfried von Strassburg.* Alois Wolf, ed. Darmstadt: Wissenschaftliche Buchgesellschaft, 1973.

"Allegory and Allegorization." *Research Studies* (1964), 32:161–175.

"The Stylistic Use of Word-Pairs and Word-Repetition in Gottfried's *Tristan.*" *Euphorion* (1965), 59:229–251.

"Medieval German Literature." *The Medieval Literature of Western Europe,* John H. Fisher, ed. New York and London: New York University and University of London, 1966.

"The Epic Center as the Structural Determinant in Medieval Narrative Poetry." *Studies in Germanic Languages and Literature.* Robert A. Fowkes and Volkmer Sander, eds. Reutlingen: Heutzler, 1967.

"Faith Unfaithful—the German Reaction to Courtly Love." *The Meaning of Courtly Love.* F. X. Newman, ed. Albany: State University of New York, 1968.

"Alliteration and Sound Repetition in the Lyrics of Oswald von Wolkenstein." *Formal Aspects of Medieval German Poetry.* Stanley N. Werbow, ed. Austin: University of Texas Press, 1969.

"The Literary Views of Gottfried von Strassburg." *PMLA* (1970), 85:992–1001.

"Problems of Communication in the Romances of Chrétien de Troyes."

Medieval Literature and Folklore Studies: Essays in honor of Francis Lee Utley. Jerome Mandel and Bruce A. Rosenberg, ed. New Brunswick: Rutgers Press, 1970.

"Contrast Imagery in the Poems of Friedrich von Hausen." *Germanic Review* (1974), 49:7–16.

"The Nature of Romance." *Approaches to Medieval Romance,* Peter Haidu, ed. *Yale French Studies* (1974), 51:12–25.

"Persona and Audience in Two Medieval Love-Lyrics." *Mosaic* (1975), 8:147–159.

"The Politics of a Poet: The Archipoeta as Revealed by his Imagery." *Philosophy and Humanism, Renaissance Essays in Honor of Paul Oskar Kristeller,* Edward P. Mahoney, ed. New York and the Hague: Columbia and Brill, 1976.

"The Structural Use of the Arrival-Challenge Motif in the *Nibelungenlied*." *Germanic Studies in Honor of Otto Springer,* S. J. Kaplowitt, ed. Pittsburgh: K & S Enterprises, 1978.

"The Arthuricity of Marie de France." *Romanic Review* (1979), 70:1–18.

"Time and Space in the *Ludus de Antichristo*." *Germanic Review* (1979), 54:1–8.

REVIEWS

Barber, Charles C. *An Old High German Reader.* Oxford: Basil Blackwell, 1951. In *Germanic Review* (1953), 28:309–311.

Kuhn, Hugo. *Minnesangs Wende.* Hermaea: Germanistische Forschungen, Neue Folge, I. Tübingen: Max Niemeyer, 1952. In *Germanic Review* (1953), 28:309–311.

Schröbler, Ingeborg. *Notker III von St. Gallen als Übersetzer und Kommentator von Boethius de Consolatione Philosophiae.* Hermaea: Germanistische Forschungen, Neue Folge, II. Tübingen: Max Niemeyer, 1953. In *Germanic Review* (1955), 30:147–149.

Stratman, Carl J. *Bibliography of Medieval Drama.* Berkeley and Los Angeles: University of California Press, 1954. In *Germanic Review* (1956), 31:148–149.

Webster, Kenneth G. T. *Ulrich von Zatzikhoven, Lanzelet. A Romance of Lancelot Translated from the Middle High German.* Revised and provided with additional notes by Roger Sherman Loomis. New York: Columbia University Press, 1951. In *Romance Philology* (1956–57), 10:61–62.

Langosch, Karl, ed. *Verfasserlexikon der deutschen Literatur des Mittelal-*

ters. Vol. IV, fasc. 1. Berlin: de Gruyter, 1951. In *Germanic Review* (1957), 32:147–148.

Suchier, Walter, ed. *Adrien und Epictetus, nebst verwandten Texten (Joca Monachorum)*. Tübingen: Max Niemeyer, 1956. In *Romanic Review* (1957), 48:140–141.

"Some Recent Publications in the Medieval Field." In *Germanic Review* (1957), 32:215–218.

Curtius, E. R. *La Littérature européenne et le moyen âge latin*. Jean Bréjoux, tr. Paris: Presses Universitaires de France, 1956. In *Romanic Review* (1958), 49:203–205.

Rickard, P. *Britain in Medieval French Literature, 1100–1500*. Cambridge: Cambridge University Press, 1956. In *Romanic Review* 49(1958):57–59.

Burger, Michel. *Recherches sur la structure et l'origine des vers romans*. Genève: Droz, 1957. In *Romanic Review* (1959), 50:203–205.

Bumke, Joachim. *Wolframs Willehalm. Studien zur Epenstruktur und zum Heiligkeitsbegriff der ausgehenden Blütezeit*. Heidelberg: Winter, 1959. In *Germanic Review* (1961), 36:308–311.

Lebendiges Mittelalter: Festgabe für Wolfgang Stammler. Hrsg. von der philosophischen Fakultät der Universität Freiburg/Schweig. Freiberg: Universitätsverlag, 1958. In *Journal of English and Germanic Philology* (1961), 60:126–127.

Adolf, Helen. *Visio Pacis, Holy City and Grail: An Attempt at an Inner History of the Grail Legend*. University Park, Pennsylvania: Pennsylvania State University Press, 1960. In *Journal of English and Germanic Philology* (1963), 61:177–179.

Tax, Petrus W. *Wort, Sinnbild, Zahl im Tristanroman. Studien zum Denken und Werten Gottfrieds von Strassburg*. Philologische Studien und Quellen, Heft 8. Berlin: Erich Schmidt, 1961. In *Journal of English and Germanic Philology* (1963), 62:177–179.

"Some Recent Works in the Medieval Field." In *Germanic Review* (1963), 38:191–193.

Braun, Werner. *Studien zum Ruodlieb. Ritterideal, Erzählstruktur und Darstellungsstil*. Quellen und Forschungen zur Sprach und Kulturgeschichte der germanischen Völker, N.F., 8. Berlin: de Gruyter, 1962. In *Journal of English and Germanic Philology* (1964), 63:277–279.

Vries, Jan de. *Heldenlied und Heldensage*. Bern: Francke, 1961. In *Speculum* (1964), 39:136–137.

Bezzola, Reto R. *Les Origines et la formation de la littérature courtoise en occident (500–1200); Troisième partie, la société courtoise: littérature de cour et littérature courtoise*. 2 vols. Paris: Champion, 1963. In *Romanic Review* (1965), 56:284–286.

Steinmeyer, Karl-Josef. *Untersuchen zur allegorischen Bedeutung der Träume in altfranzösischen Rolandslied.* Langue et parole, Heft 5. Munich Huber, 1963. In *Romanic Review* (1966), 57:56.

Weber, Gottfried. *Das Nibelungenlied: Problem und Idee.* Stuttgart: Metzler, 1963. In *Germanic Review* (1966), 41:72–78.

Kolb, Herbert. *Munsalvaesche: Studien zum Kyotproblem.* München: Eidos, 1963. In *Germanic Review* (1967), 42:229–33.

Speckenbach, Klaus. *Studien zum Begriff 'edelez herze' im Tristan Gottfrieds von Strassburg.* Medium Aevum Philologische Studien, 6. Munich: Eidos, 1965. In *Speculum* (1967), 42:408–411.

Gellinek, Christian. *König Rother. Studie zur literarischen Deutung.* Bern and Munich: Francke, 1968. In *Germanic Review* (1970), 45:229–231.

Huby, Michelle. *L'adaptation des romans courtois en Allemagne au XIIe et au XIIIe siècle.* Paris Klincksieck, 1968. In *Cahiers de Civilisation Mediévale* (1970), 13:382–384.

Georgi, Annette. *Das lateinische und deutsche Preisgedicht des Mittelalters.* Berlin: Erich Schmidt Verlag, 1969. In *German Quarterly* (1971), 44:564–566.

Bumke, Joachim. *Die Wolfram-von-Eschenbach-Forschung seit 1945: Bericht und Bibliographie.* Munchen: Fink, 1972. In *Germanic Review* (1972), 47:310–312.

Dronke, Peter. *Poetic Individuality in the Middle Ages: New Departures in Poetry 1000–1150.* Oxford: The Clarendon Press, 1970. In *Speculum* (1972), 47:529–532.

Jung, Marc-Rene. *Études sur le pòeme allégorique en France au Moyen Âge.* Romanica Helvetica, 82. Berne: Francke, 1971. In *Romanic Review* (1972), 63:222–224.

Picozzi, Rosemary. *A History of Tristan Scholarship.* Canadian Studies in German Language and Literature, no. 5. Frankfurt: Lang, 1971. In *Germanic Review* (1972), 47:310–312.

Steinhoff, Hans-Hugo. *Bibliographie zu Gottfried von Strassburg.* Bibliographien zur deutschen Literatur des Mittelalters, Heft 5. Berlin: Schmidt, 1971. In *Germanic Review,* 47 (1972), 310–312.

Gay-Crosier, Raymond. *Religious Elements in the Secular Lyrics of the Troubadours.* University of North Carolina Studies in the Romance Languages and Literatures, no. 111. Chapel Hill: The University of North Carolina Press, 1971. In *Romanic Review* (1974), 65:117–118.

Cartier, Norman R. *Le Bossu désenchanté. Étude sur "Le Jeu de la Feuillée."* Publications Romanes et Françaises, 116. Genève: Librairie Droz, 1971. In *Romanic Review* (1974), 65:118–120.

Endres, Marion. *Word Field and Word Content in Middle High German:*

The Applicability of Word Field Theory in Gottfried von Strassburg's 'Tristan.' Göppinger Arbeiten zur Germanistik, Nr. 47. Göppingen: Alfred Kummerle Verlag, 1971. In *Monatshefte* (1974), 66:172–173.

Freytag, Wiebke. *Das Oxymoron bei Wolfram, Gottfried und andern dichtern des Mittelalters.* München: Fink, 1972. In *Germanic Review* (1974), 49:172–173.

Kratz, Henry. *Wolfram von Eschenbach's "Parsival." An Attempt at a Total Evaluation.* Bern: Francke, 1973. In *Germanic Review* (1976), 51:155–157.

Rossman, Vladimir R. *Perspectives of Irony in Medieval French Literature.* The Hague: Mouton, 1975. In *Romanic Review* (1977), 68:140–143.

Uitti, Karl D. *Story, Myth and Celebration in Old French Narrative Poetry 1050–1200.* Princeton: Princeton University Press, 1973. In *Romanic Review* (1977), 68:143–144.

Beer, Jeanette M. A. *A Medieval Caesar.* Geneva: Librairie Droz, 1976. In *Romanic Review* (1978), 69:336–337.

Nagel, Bert. *Staufische Klassik: Deutsche Dichtung um 1200.* Heidelberg: Lothar Stiem Verlag, 1977. In *German Quarterly* (1978), 51:355–358.

Rossman, Vladimir R. *Les Concepts médiévaux du testament.* Paris: Jean-Pierre Delarge, 1976. In *Romanic Review* (1978), 69:337–338.

Scholler, Harold, ed. *The Epic in Medieval Society: Aesthetic and Moral Values.* Tübingen: Max Niemeyer, 1977. In *Olifant* (1978), 6:129–137.

Blumstein, Andree Kahn. *Misogyny and Idealization in the Courtly Romance.* Studien zur Germanistik, Anglistik und Komparastik, vol. 41. Bonn: Bouvier Verlag Herbert Grundmann, 1977. In *Germanic Review* (1979), 54:35–37.

Jaeger, C. Stephen. *Medieval Humanism in Gottfried von Strassburg's* TRISTAN UND ISOLDE. Germanische Bibliothek, Reihe 3. Heidelberg: Carl Winter, 1977. In *Germanic Quarterly* (1979), 52:534–35.

Erzgräber, Willi, ed. *Europaische Spätmittelalter.* Neues Handbuch der Literaturwissenschaft, 8. Wiesbaden: Akademische Verlagsgesellschaft Athenaion, 1978. In *Speculum* (1981), 56:128–131.

Kästner, Hannes, *Harfe und Schwert: Der höfische Spielman bei Gottfried von Strassburg.* Untersuchungen zur deutschen Literaturgeschichte, 30. Tübingen: Max Niemeyer, 1981. In *Speculum,* 58 (1983), 193–94.

Plummer, John F., ed. *Vox Feminae: Studies in Medieval Woman's Songs.* Studies in Medieval Culture, 15. Kalamazoo: Western Michigan University, 1981. In *Speculum* (1983), 58:216–18.

ONE
COURTLY LOVE

I

The *De Amore* of Andreas Capellanus and the Practice of Love At Court

IT HAS BEEN the fate of Andreas' work *De amore* to be linked with the doctrine, real or imagined, of courtly love.[1] There are good reasons for the connection. Andreas was probably a chaplain at the court of France at a time when the sophisticated amusement of courtly love, in the social sense of courtly, was widely practiced. He names personages in his work who are invariably associated with the finest flowering of courtly poetry. His treatise lays down some rules for the elaborate game which was to be played. In these respects Parry was justified in translating the alternative title *De arte honeste amandi* by *The Art of Courtly Love*.[2] Unfortunately, however, the term "courtly love" acquired during the nineteenth century a meaning quite different from that just described. Instead of meaning "love as practiced at court" it came to mean "spiritual, idealized love," such as that sung by the troubadours and *Minnesänger,* or "adulterous love," such as that of Tristan and Isolde or Lancelot and Guinevere. Although the troubadours in the *canzon* sang of *fin amors,* a spiritual, nonsensual love, and although the loves of the heroes of the romances were often anything but spiritual, it has been assumed by many critics that there was a generalized type of courtly love which was practiced or at least sung by all authors in all genres and that it was somehow a part of the chivalric code. Such a belief is in complete defiance of the works of literature as we have them. The mood of love in the *canzon* is quite different from that in the *alba* and the love of Parzival for Condwiramurs has no resemblance to that of Tristan for Isolde. Married love is important and indeed sacred in *Erec,* as it is in *Parzival* and *Willehalm.* No one conception of love will cover all the relations between the sexes in medieval lyric and epic, and it is unprofitable to seek for such a definition, especially if we regard this love as a spiritual or even an intellectual phenomenon. We may attempt to trace the influences which color the expression of love in the *canzon* or *Minnesang;* we may justifiably ask what causes brought about the startling change of attitude to woman in society and how widespread this change of attitude was. Finally, and this is the purpose of this essay, we may ask what were the externals, the social graces of love-making which were current in a small, highly sophisticated part of medieval society, which were reflected in literature, and which, because they are often mistakenly connected with a preconceived code of "courtly love," have frequently been misinterpreted.

It is here that Andreas can help us. For his work is not an intellectual treatise on the ideas of love (although he tried to make it sound like one and would have been highly flattered at the masses of notes which have accumulated at the foot of his pages), nor a blast at the courtly manners of his time (even though he tacks on a third book which looks like an attack, for symmetry and safety), but a simple manual for those who wanted to love *honeste,* that is, like gentlemen.

Why should a court chaplain write such a book? Any answer is naturally conjectural but the position of the chaplain as tutor to the family and especially to its female members gave him a privileged position as adviser in matters literary and a person with the address and skill which Andreas displays in the first two books of the *De amore* would have little difficulty in establishing himself as a kind of *arbiter elegantiarum.* The *capellanus* was frequently in minor orders only and did not feel too closely restricted by the obligations of the priesthood. I have tried to show elsewhere that the literary disputes as to the superiority of priest or knight as lover may well have had a basis in fact. The love poetry written by men of clerical training was not all written in the tavern or in the cloister and there is nothing inherently improbable in the conjecture that a court chaplain may have been an active participant in the elaborate game of love as played at a sophisticated court and that he may have written a treatise on the subject for the enlightenment and edification of his fellow players.

This very question of the purpose and the audience of the work has been the point most neglected by critics. Andreas is not writing a systematic treatise on love, as we shall see when we examine his work in more detail. His work is a pratical one, designed for the courts which he knew and for the noble personages whom it was in his interest to flatter. Let us see how he approaches his subject.

The opening address to Walter is, of course, a typical introduction to a work of this kind. The pretense that it was written at the request of a person interested is part of the "humility formula," which is continued by the statement that the subject is not worthy of attention but that he, Andreas, will do his best out of consideration for the needs of his friend. The actual treatise begins, systematically enough, with an attempt to divide up the subject into subdivisions—the nature of love, those who can participate, its acquisition, increase, and decline. This general outline is preserved in the text but in proportions which are very significant. The great bulk of the book is in fact devoted to careful studies of the techniques involved in bringing about love-affairs between couples of differing social grades. The object is conquest by the man and satisfied acquiescence by the woman, but stress is laid on the persuasive techniques since these constituted the game and it was in their performance that artistry could be shown. It is no accident that so much of the first book is in dialogue form. It reflects accurately the situations for which Andreas was writing—the game of persuasion, of rhetoric, of declarations made without sincerity and ironically accepted in the spirit in which they were offered.

Andreas defines love. Even the most ardent proponent of a doctrine of courtly love could hardly call his definition spiritual or find much satisfaction in his point of view: "Amor est passio quaedam innata procedens ex visione et immoderata cogitatione formae alterius sexus, ob quam aliquis super omnia cupit alterius potiri amplexibus et omnia de utriusque voluntate in ipsius amplexu amoris praecepta compleri."[3] These are blunt words and no doubt reflect the actual situation at court. The definition makes no mention of any spiritual or intellectual aspects of love. There is no attempt here to differentiate *amor purus* and *amor mixtus*. Merely a blunt statement of the true end of love, sensual entirely, and a passion. Andreas' description is hardly original. He is using a definition common enough in philosophical treatises but one hardly suitable if he is attempting to describe a nobler type of love. Here, for purposes of comparison, is the definition of *concupiscentia* (not *amor*), given by Hugo of St. Victor:

Eodem modo concupiscentiam esse dicimus in irrationalibus inconsultam quandam et materialem ex naturali motu aut consuetudine in mutabilibus incontinenter ingenitam passibilitatem et irrationabilem corporis voluptatis continuitatem . . . nunc consequenter differentiam concupiscentia ostendit sive quando in spiritualibus et divinis nominatur. Corporalium quidem concupiscentiam definiens esse passibilitatem quamdam, sive passionem, id est dominantem affectionem, inconsultam quidem, quia ratione non fertur sed trahitur temerario appetitu in ea, quorum delectatione afficitur; et materialem, id est ex carne et ex sensu carnali surgentem, et carnalia et sensibilia apparentem, passibilitatem dico ingenitam aut ex naturali motu, quando scilicet secundum naturam est appetitus eius; aut ex consuetudine in ipsis mutabilibus incontinenter habita, quando extra naturam vel contra fertur desiderium illius.[4]

It is not difficult to see the essential resemblance between Hugo's definition of *concupiscentia* and Andreas' description of *amor*. In fact Andreas is merely giving a stock definition of *concupiscentia* which has little significance for the subsequent development of his theme. When he uses the word "amare," he merely means "to be a lover," "to have a love affair." His definition is given to impart an air of authenticity to his study; his demonstrations are drawn from the facts of love-making rather than from any theoretical considerations. It is pleasant to think that Andreas may have been aware of the contrast between his description of the lover, full of fear at being unable to please his lady and at the mercy of the passion inspired by *immoderata cognitione,* and the cold-blooded account of the methods of winning her which follows. In this he is truly the disciple of his master Ovid.

This dependence upon Ovid is also reflected in the following chapters on the persons who can love: poverty is harmful to one's prospects ("non habet unde suum paupertas pascat amorem"); the oversexed and over-adorned should be avoided. The early chapters are indeed full of these reminiscences and of truisms liberally spiced with the stock phrases of polite love ("potest amoris pertingi aculeis"; "personae aptae ad amoris arma ferenda").

It is in the long chapter "Qualiter amor acquiratur et quot modis" that Andreas approaches his real theme.[5] He has paid tribute to the ennobling power of love "qui tantis facit hominem fulgere virtutibus" and to its disturbing power ("saepe suos nautas valida relinquit in unda") without taking the trouble to distinguish between the types which produce such different effects. He will now show how the game of love is to be played. The ensuing dialogues demonstrate that, for Andreas, everything depended on the social status of the participants. Persons below the middle class are not even considered, except as far as a male of the upper classes may amuse himself with a peasant female, an occupation that Andreas views with some disgust and does not classify as love. The dialogue between the *plebeius* and the *plebeia* consists mostly of flattery and coyness, although Andreas often uses the lady's replies to keep the dialogue going. For example, her sudden and quite unmotivated interjection that she does not wish to have an old man for a lover is clearly inserted to take care of the theoretical possibility that the *plebeius* may be an old man of material substance but little charm. Much more revealing of Andreas' attitudes and interests is the dialogue *plebeius/nobili*. A cynical distinction is made between the noble lady who is *simplex*—naive—who can be treated and won over as if she were a *plebeia*, and the noble lady who is *prudens*. In the latter event, says Andreas, it is unwise to attempt flattery. He advocates rather an approach showing extreme humility (again expressed in Ovidian terms—the wound of love, etc.) but making the claim that love strikes all alike and that therefore mercy is deserved. The claim has little effect on the lady, whose entire concern is to stress the social barriers and ironically to point out that the world would indeed be upside down if such a love were possible. The man claims that *probitas* confers *nobilitas* and therefore removes social barriers between them, a claim rejected with scorn by the lady, on the ground that it would eliminate all ancient distinctions of nobility. Apparently the lady is unaware of Andreas' own statement to Walter: "Mulier similiter non formam vel cultum vel generis quaerat originem, quia nulla forma placet si bonitate vacet, morum atque probitas sola est quae vera facit hominem nobilitate beari et rutilanti forma pollere." If the man's argument ultimately triumphed, it would be possible to say that the lady's arguments are advanced only to be destroyed. But in fact quite the opposite is true. The man is on the defensive throughout and is finally dismissed with little hope. This lack of consistency between Andreas' general, theoretical statements and the practice which he indicates in the dialogues is characteristic of the whole work and is largely responsible for the widely varying interpretations of it which have appeared. More will be said on this topic when the question of the third book is discussed. It is sufficient here to remark that the general state-

ments are borrowed and are the pious sentiments of moralists and phi-
losophers, whereas the dialogues are, so far as we know, original and
probably reflect experience as well as Andreas' own inclinations.

It is unnecessary to appraise each of the dialogues in detail. In every
instance the stress is on rhetorical and verbal skill in presenting one's own
case. The lady is, in almost every instance, practical, often ironical, and
gifted with a lively sense of the ridiculous. It is the man who is fantastic
and often insincere. In almost every dialogue the male participant brings
up one of the accepted "topoi," only to have it attacked by the strictly
practical lady. There could hardly be a clearer case of the use of rhetoric
to give a man practice in an art. It should be noted that, while successful
love-making is the object of the instruction, the method shows the lady
in an entirely favorable light. The dialogues are designed to appeal to her
ego; she is the judge of the eligibility of man. He can appeal to her, persuade her, but not contradict her. She may prolong indefinitely the period of flattery, persuasion, and pursuit before she yields. In fact, Andreas never does show one of his ladies won over. The world for which
these dialogues are designed is one dominated by sophisticated women.
It is impossible to dismiss this major part of Andreas' work as merely
ironical, insincere, and not to be taken seriously as compared with the
third book. It is the most original and the most competent part of the
whole treatise and artistically the most satisfying. There can be no doubt
that Andreas wrote much of the dialogue tongue-in-cheek but this does
not mean that he regards the conditions he is describing as sinful nor
that he intends his readers to reject them. There is much irony in the
troubadours' treatment of spiritual love and no doubt all participants appreciated its elements of fantasy and exaggeration. They were an accepted
part of the game.

Before leaving the dialogues, we may examine a few aspects of the most
important one of all—that between the two higher nobles. As might be
expected, it is here that we find the rules for the highest type of love.
Very early in the dialogue the point is made that the woman is responsible socially for raising men to their greatest heights but that the performance of the duty may lead to conflict with the principles of Christianity.
The man answers this objection by admitting that the perfect Christian
would indeed find it hard to love in the way described, but because love
is something "natural," he does not think that God would punish the sin
very severely. "Credo tamen in amore Deum graviter offendi non posse,

nam quod natura cogente perficitur, facili potest expiatione mundari." Furthermore, adds the man, the spice of danger makes the pursuit more exciting. The lady's reply seems to indicate that she was merely making a point, not necessarily condemning love. In any case, she dismisses the subject and passes on to the question of generosity and fame.

Andreas' treatment of this important objection is typical. Clearly the whole structure of courtly love would fall to the ground if the lady's remark were taken seriously and further discussion would be unnecessary. But it is in fact treated as just one more argument in a chain of conventionalities. The remainder of the dialogue follows the same pattern, often with massive inconsistencies. On page 172 of the Trojel edition we find that the lady is a widow: "immo etsi alia cuncta mihi amare suadeant, viduitas tamen et optimi amissi mariti tristia omnia mihi solatia contradicunt." On page 175, on the other hand, she is a virgin: "Quamvis appetibile satis cunctis videatur amare, virginili tamen videtur plurimum obviare pudori. Nam, ut bene novistis, virgo cito perdit honorem et eius fama modico rumore brevique dissolvitur aura. Immo nec mihi plena suffragatur aetas, ut amoris ancoram debita possim industria gubernare. Fertur enim quod ante plenam cuiuslibet pubertatem amor non potest firma stabilitate durare." On page 204 again, the lady makes the point that she has already promised herself to another. Here Andreas is actually changing the character of one of his participants in mid-career, so as to be able to take account of all possible objections on the part of the lady. The man suffers the same type of change. On page 172 he remarks: "Confiteor me pulchram satis habere uxorem et ego quidem ipsam totius mentis affectione diligo maritali." He continues with the standard decision that true love cannot exist between man and wife. But on page 185, we again find a different situation. The discussion has ranged over the difference between *amor purus* and *amor mixtus*, the lady has rejected the former as impossible of attainment and she then remarks to the man that love can in any case mean nothing to him because he is a cleric ("vos tamen neutrius decet affectare militiam, clericus enim ecclesiasticis tantum debet vacare ministeriis.") The man admits that he is a cleric ("quamvis clericorum sim sorte coniunctus"). He defends love for clerics in terms very similar to those found in the poem "Phyllis et Flora" (Carmina Burana, No. 92) and in the *Conseil de Remiremont*—in other words in the terms already conventionally established in the popular *altercatio*.[6] The same may be said of the long discussions about the merits of the "amor superioris partis" and of the "amor inferioris partis," and of the long argument on the possible transfer of love.

Of the second part of Andreas' work, we need only note that the word *amor* means "love-affair." For all the precepts about the maintenance of love are directed to the affair, not the affection. Typically, it is pointed out ("qualiter amor diminuatur") that lack of resources will soon put an end to love. The whole attitude to love is social, not emotional. The examples are obviously taken from a common stock to illustrate attitudes and situations well recognized in the courts of love.

When we turn to the third part of the book, we are immediately struck by a change in manner, tone, and method of presentation. The life has gone out of the work. The opening excuse for the first two books ("I have told you everything you need to know in order to be proficient in the art of love-making—but only so that you will know what to avoid") is as lame an excuse as can be found in literature, if it is seriously intended. For, as we have seen, Walter has been instructed in a social art, not in emotions, and he would have no need of any such knowledge if he did not move in a small sophisticated part of society. Having made his excuse (tongue-in-cheek, I suspect), Andreas goes on to detail the reasons against making love. They are all based on conventional prohibitions and show the shocking things which are caused by love—poverty, sin, war, physical weakness, shortening of life, even death itself. Coupled with this are the standard antifeminist complaints of the viciousness, greed, lust, and infidelity of women: "Est quoque ad omne malum femina prona. Quodcunque maius est in hoc seculo nefas, illud omnis mulier sine timore pro levi occasione committit." The whole book lacks completely the skill and light touch of the first two. It consists of a string of precepts and little more. The final summation urges Walter to follow these precepts if he wishes to lead a good life.

How are we to reconcile the contradictions in the work? Any attempt to do so must, of course, be pure speculation, since we have no other works of Andreas to guide us and no knowledge of his private life. The late Father Denomy saw here an anticipation of the Averroistic doctrine of the double truth.[7] He realized, of course, that direct influence of the Arabic philosopher was highly improbable on chronological grounds but his conviction that the *De arte amandi* was essentially an unchristian work led him to categorize it with a system of reasoning later condemned as heretical. To assume, as Father Denomy did, that an Averroistic doctrine was being developed independently of Averroes is surely pushing speculation too far. Furthermore—and this is a very important point—there is little evidence in the work that Andreas was a philosophical thinker, even in a very low sense of the term. He quotes principally tags from the classics, especially Ovid, whom he clearly regards as his master, but there is no evidence of logical thinking or of the ability or desire to present a consequentially argued case. His arguments are presented in dialogue form with more regard for the rules of rhetoric than of logic and, as we have seen, with little attempt at consistency. He uses any arguments which come to hand, even though they do not suit his case particularly well, and a definition of love which accords ill with his subsequent presentation.

For these reasons, I am unable to agree with Robertson that the first two books are intended to be ironical and that the third represents Andreas' true point of view.[8] Surely, if this were so, he could have done better than a mere listing of the sad results of love-making, when he had depicted the other side of the coin so artistically.

Andreas' work can, in my opinion, be read only within the social context for which it was intended. The sure fact is that Andreas was a chaplain closely connected with the French court at a time when that court's principal amusement was sophisticated love-making. He is writing a not too serious text-book for certain members of that court—and in particular, a book for the ladies of that court. The whole tenor of the book shows its feminist bias. The lady is the center of attraction. She sets the standards, she gives the judgments. The man is always in the position of pleading. The dialogue form is no accident, for it represents, from the ladies' point of view, the most important part of the art of love-making—the pleading, the flattery, the mock worship, the refinement of what was undoubtedly an otherwise very crude world. The core of Andreas' book is in these dialogues and decisions. They are not intended seriously, in the sense that the whole art they represent was not serious but an elaborate game. Too much has been made of the "spiritual" side of the medieval lyric. Undoubtedly some poets were spiritual in a sense (and these more commonly German than French) but most were using flattering "unphysical" terminology. Andreas' work represents, in my opinion, a collection of the things he had heard in sophisticated court circles, put in a handbook. It is not an attempt at an intellectual study of courtly love, nor should it be used as a guide to what modern critics call "courtly love" in literature. It represents much more what might be called current practice rather than theory, social conditions rather than those in literature.

But if Andreas was writing for a sophisticated court circle, why did he add the utterly contradictory third book? The answer, I think, lies in the attitude so well described by Huizinga in the *Waning of the Middle Ages,*[9] the attitude which could combine the coarsest sensuality with the sharpest asceticism, the strictest moral code with the crassest deviations from that code. The representation of two sides of life, or of any problem, is one of the most marked features of all types of medieval literature. All of the love lyric of the High Middle Ages depicts a tension, a struggle between two emotions or points of view. The romance is capable of the same type of analysis. It should not surprise us that Andreas felt the need to express both sides of the question he was discussing. His audience probably felt no incongruity in his treatment. I have no doubt that the ladies for whom he wrote were perfectly capable of the sincerest protestations of repentance in church after their games of love and just as capable of a light-hearted return to the games afterwards. Such attitudes are not, after all, entirely unknown in our own day. It may be added also that the third book is a kind of *Remedium amoris* in the tradition of master Ovid.

As I have already said, any statements about Andreas' intentions must remain conjecture. But we would do well to remember when reading the *De amore* that it is a reflection of the behavior of a small segment of the culture of the time, not a milestone along the road of the history of ideas. Andreas was not overserious and there is no reason why we should be.

NOTES

1. Andreas Capellanus, *De amore libri tres,* E. Trojel, ed. (Copenhagen, 1892). All subsequent references are to this edition.

2. Andreas Capellanus, *The Art of Courtly Love,* J. J. Parry, ed. and tr. (New York: Columbia University Press, 1941).

3. *De amore,* p. 3.

4. Hugo of St. Victor, *Expositio in hierarchiam coelestem S. Dionysii,* Book III, *Patrologia latina,* CLXXV, 981.

5. *De amore,* p. 14.

6. *Carmina Burana,* A. Hilka and O. Schumann, eds. (Heidelberg), Vol. I,

Part 2 (1941), pp. 94 ff; *Das Leibeskonzil von Remiremont,* W. Meyer, ed., Nachrichten der königlichen Gesellschaft der Wissenschaften zu Göttingen, phil.-hist. Klasse, 1914.

7. "The *De amore* of Andreas Capellanus and the Condemnation of 1277," *Medieval Studies* (1946), 8:107–49.

8. D. W. Robertson, Jr., "The Subject of the *De amore* of Andreas Capellanus," *Modern Philology* (1953), 50:145–61.

9. Johan Huizinga, *The Waning of the Middle Ages,* F. Hopman, tr. (New York: Doubleday, 1954).

2

Faith Unfaithful—The German Reaction to Courtly Love

THE LITERATURE OF GERMANY in the High Middle Ages is largely a reaction to contemporary literature in France. Some French critics—Jeanroy is a good example—prefer to regard it as a mere continuation, an imitation or adaptation of French literature, but this is not so. It is a reaction, sometimes little more than a feeble reworking but more often an attempt to express the thought and style of French literature in new terms. It must be borne in mind that the reaction was to French literature as the German poets understood it, and this understanding was sometimes faulty. Just as for an understanding of classicism it is important to know what an eighteenth-century European believed the Greeks to be, rather than what they actually were, so we must recognize that many German authors failed to perceive the ironical overtones in French literature and reacted to a system of values which they believed to be there. It is interesting that many of their more recent countrymen have done the same.

There is little point in reviving the controversy started by Ehrismann in 1919 and continued by Curtius and Neumann,[1] except to point out that they all assume some consistency of attitude in the German authors they are discussing. Most people would agree with Curtius that there is little evidence to link Aristotle with an assumed moral philosophy which is present in the "courtly code." Yet it must be remarked that even Curtius seems to believe that there was such a code, even if it was not formal or written. Ehrismann had advanced the thesis that the German authors derived their code from Wernher von Elmendorf, that is, from philosophical rather than literary sources. The implication would seem to be that the Germans observed a code largely independent of that supposedly derived from the French works they used as models—a scarcely tenable thesis.

There can be little doubt that the German authors saw in the French works they read evidence of a code of ideal behavior for a secular knight. Hartmann von Aue makes it clear that he knows of such a code when he describes, in *Der arme Heinrich,* the man who has every virtue to give him social grace and distinction but lacks humility and charity.[2]

We are fortunate to be able to make direct comparisons between many major German narrative works and their French originals—the two romances of Hartmann von Aue and Wolfram's *Parzival* are based directly on the works of Chrétien de Troyes, even if additional material is used by both authors, and Gottfried von Strassburg acknowledges Thomas of Britain as his model. Konrad von Würzburg and Rudolf von Ems make extensive use of extant French works. In lyric poetry there is no acknowledgment by the Germans but a great deal of obvious borrowing, both of style and content. We might expect, therefore, that the German works would follow their French models closely in their depicting of the love phenomenon. Yet quite the opposite is the case. Each author chose works which suited his purpose and modified the treatment of love which he found there.

It is not surprising that Hartmann should have chosen the *Erec* and the *Yvain*. The two works, particularly *Yvain*, seem to present a neat formulation of the love-adventure problem, so neat, in fact, that the literary histories have found them complementary, two works showing adventure neglected for love and love neglected for adventure. The formulation is too simple, for Chrétien does not present love in *Erec* as he does in *Yvain*. Enide is a simple, unsophisticated girl who is unaffected by courtly trappings, while Laudine is a widow whose moves are calculated in accordance with her social position. If we are to assume that it is characteristic of courtly love that the lady be won by unremitting service, then neither *Erec* nor *Yvain* shows evidence of the phenomenon. Enide is won by the usual method employed by medieval suitors who were not in Arthurian romances. Erec says that he would like to take her to the tournament where he intends to compete for the prize of the sparrow-hawk; if her father agrees, Erec will return the favor by marrying her. It is a business arrangement. Erec never says at this stage that he loves Enide, nor does he ask whether she cares for him; nevertheless, Enide is "honored" to accept the proposition. After all, she is living in fairly straitened circumstances with her father but if she marries Erec, she will be a queen. Chrétien is careful to point out the difference between the unspoilt Enide and the artificial and calculating ladies of Guenevere's court. Enide's reaction to the rumors about Erec's idleness and its effect on his men is therefore entirely natural. She does not want her husband to look bad in the eyes of his peers. Guenevere does not care how bad Lancelot looks, so long as she can demonstrate her power over him. Erec appreciates Enide's love when he hears her reject the overtures of the Count of Limors under circumstances which could not possibly be feigned. But even after this experience he does not perform love-service for her. He serves a greater cause and she is his champion. The concluding "Joie de la Cort" episode makes very clear the difference between the servile bondage of a knight to a lady's whim and the free association of lovers in a purposeful life. The association of Erec and Enide begins without sighs or complaints and it ends in a loving companionship. By no stretch of imagination can the term "courtly" be applied to it, except in the very limited sense that Enide is a noble creature who inspires Erec.

Hartmann von Aue has even less to say about the early meetings of Erec and Enide than Chrétien has. In his version Enide does not even say that she will be honored to accept. It is clear that Chrétien and Hartmann following him were thinking in terms of *mutual* love between the sexes. As Furstner has pointed out,[3] such mutuality is not a characteristic of many so-called courtly works, least of all of the love found in lyric poetry. That love is rather admiration of specific qualities in the lady, qualities which are carefully enumerated and described. It is this assessment of qualities rather than love for the lady as a person which brings about the effect commented on by so many critics: that the lover does not appear to be in love with a lady at all or, if he is, it is with the same lady who has been eulogized by many other lyric poets. In the last analysis such love consists in the recognition of the presence of abstract qualities and does not call for any corresponding recognition from the lady. It is not love but worship.

Yvain's love, on the other hand, is of the courtly order. Chrétien makes this clear by several stylistic devices. The first is the use of the internal monologue, which shows the hero analyzing the reasons why he loves and weighing the obstacles to that love in pseudo-rational fashion. Another device is the personification of love as a power which exercises dominance in the most unlikely situations, which wounds and cures the wounds it makes. There are also the required fervid descriptions but here they are ironical, leading as they do to the interview with Laudine in which Yvain's protestations of eternal fidelity and complete subservience to his lady cause him to be employed as defender of the fountain. Laudine does not say that she loves him at this point; the relation is one of service. Only when she permits him to go on adventure does she show any signs of affection by giving him a ring which will prevent him from being wounded. When he is received back, she again fails to show any signs of affection. On the contrary, she says that she has been deceived into taking him back and that only the oath she has sworn forces her to accept him. All she allows is peace between them. Chrétien's version of the Yvain story demonstrates with full irony the difference between service and love.

The irony is not so clear in the version of Hartmann von Aue. He follows Chrétien closely, even to the point of literal translation of some passages, but he expands the scenes in which Iwein's love is depicted and he dilates more than does Chrétien on the power of love. It is in the final scene, however, that Hartmann proves that he has misunderstood his source. Quite gratuitously he adds to Chrétien's ironical conclusion a scene in which Laudine falls at Iwein's feet and begs his forgiveness for all the trouble she has caused him.[4] The action is utterly out of character. It is Iwein who raises Laudine to her feet and is all magnanimity. Hartmann has achieved his happy ending and made love conquer all, but he has misunderstood Chrétien's purpose. Clearly Hartmann believed that there was such a thing as courtly love and that it brought lovers together into harmony. In appreciating each other's virtues, they loved. The thought is touching, but it was not what Chrétien believed nor, as we shall see, did Hartmann's great German contemporaries follow him.

Wolfram von Eschenbach denies that he owes anything to the *Conte del Graal* of Chrétien de Troyes, although he mentions Chrétien's name in a manner which makes it seem likely that he would expect his audience to assume that he had used the French author as a source. It is, in fact, perfectly clear from a comparison of *Parzival* and the *Conte del Graal* that Wolfram has taken much of his material from the French poem but has modified it wherever he felt that it failed to express his views or where, more important, he felt that views were advanced, particularly about women, which conflicted sharply with his own. It is almost impossible to say what Chrétien intended to do with his heroine Blanscheflur. She appears only in one scene and that a very conventional one. She is the lady besieged—by potential lovers whom she dislikes—and Perceval arrives in the nick of time to rescue her. Presumably it is feminine intuition which tells her that the newly-arrived Red Knight can save her from her enemies, for she goes to great lengths to win him to her. The situation is not precisely one in which the knight volunteers his services. He is in his room, retired for the night, when she comes to him and exerts her charms to win him to her side. Perceval may be a boor, crude and unpolished, but innocent he is not. Even at the earliest stage of his knightly career he was able to appreciate the difference between the kisses he forced from the lady in the tent and those of his mother's serving maids. There can be little doubt that Perceval enjoyed his night with Blanscheflur and that not allegorically. How courtly can such a situation be? If aloofness is the mark, we do not have it here. Nor is there any love-service, only the promise of practical support. Further relations between the two are on a sensual level. After Perceval leaves Blanscheflur he remembers her, so far as we are informed, only on the occasion of his seeing the blood in the snow. She plays no further part in his progress. The situation is quite different in Wolfram's poem, as we shall see.

Wolfram frequently addresses his audience in the first person, but by far the most important instance of such communication is that which, significantly, appears between the second and third books of *Parzival*. Wolfram has just completed the introduction to his poem, an introduction which owes nothing to Chrétien or indeed to any known work, and is about to embark on his main theme, which, as he was well aware, followed Chrétien's poem very closely. Here was the point at which he should make his intentions clear. He might be following the story, but he was not following the morality. And in particular he wished to make it perfectly clear that he did not accept the attitude toward women which he found in earlier works. His statements on the subject are worth analyzing. He claims that he has nothing against women and is glad to hear their praises, but one woman has aroused his ire and with her he can never be reconciled. He accuses her of unfaithfulness and states that she has enlisted the support of other women against him. There is no clear indication of the identity of this woman, and earlier commentators thought of her as an actual person who had proved unfaithful to the poet. More recently scholars have tended to believe that the lady referred to is Isolde

and that the whole passage is a reference to the continuing and fundamental disagreement between Wolfram and Gottfried von Strassburg.[5] This
is very probably true, but it does not alter the much more fundamental
point that Wolfram is opposed not to Isolde alone but to the feminine
society which, in his opinion, she represents. His reference to the large
number of women makes this clear. He also leaves no doubt of the characteristic which makes him despise them—*untriuwe,* faithlessness. It may
seem strange that he should single out this quality when the courtly writers themselves emphasize that faithfulness in love is highly desirable. The
difference lies in the object of that faithfulness. Isolde was faithful to Tristan
but that does not absolve her from guilt in Wolfram's eyes; for him there
is only one kind of faithfulness, that between husband and wife. Wolfram
makes this last point abundantly clear by his careful gradation of women.
It is not hard to show parallels between the most important women of
the Parzival story and those of the Gawan adventures. One or two of the
female characters appear in both parts with different characteristics. Parzival meets Sigune much earlier in the work than Perceval meets his unnamed cousin, and it seems likely that his was an intentional change on
Wolfram's part, for Sigune and Jeschute are clearly contrasted. Schionatulander, Sigune's lover, is killed by Orilus because of Sigune's absurd
demand that he demonstrate his *Minnedienst* by undertaking adventure in
her name. It is the same Orilus who is capable of believing that Jeschute
is unfaithful to him. His brutal treatment of her is ended only by his defeat at the hands of Parzival, a defeat, incidentally, which fulfills his unthinking promise to avenge Sigune when she first tells him of her loss.
Thus both Sigune and Jeschute have lost their lovers, the latter through
a blunder by a boy who thought himself courtly and through the vulgar-
ity of a man who was professedly a courtly lover, the former through a
mistaken belief in "adventure." It is courtliness which is responsible for
both tragedies. Both these incidents appear in Chrétien's work, but the
treatment is different. In the "Lady in the Tent" scene, Chrétien's emphasis is entirely on the blunders of Perceval. Wolfram emphasizes the
luscious beauty of the lady and in doing so is careful to make clear that
his hero is untouched by it. There can be no reference to the sweetness
of the lady's kisses. Later, when Jeschute is being driven in rags through
the forest, Wolfram has plenty of time to dwell upon those charming parts
of her body whose well-turned beauty cannot be hidden by her inadequate clothing. Her reconciliation with Orilus is described entirely in

physical terms and it is brought about by physical methods. Quite the opposite is true of Sigune. As the story progresses, her concern for the affairs of this world grows less and less. Her spiritual progress is actually in advance of that of Parzival. She assures herself that Schionatulander was actually her husband, even though they were never officially married. It is, of course, impossible to tell what Chrétien would have made of the character of Perceval's cousin if he had completed his romance. There is little evidence, however, that he had any intention of depicting the spiritualized figure who appears in Wolfram's work. Both Jeschute and Sigune show the disastrous effects of an aspect of courtly love which Wolfram mentions in the remarks to which we have already referred—the desire on the part of the knight to demonstrate that only one lady, his own beloved, can be considered "fair." Wolfram makes a mockery of the suggestion by showing what happened to two very different ladies whose lovers practiced such a creed.

The picture of the demanding lady is made even more absurd by the contrast between Orgeluse and Condwiramurs. We should note that Orgeluse has a part in both the Parzival story and the Gawan adventures. It is she who has caused Amfortas to lose his kingship by his pursuit of unchaste love. She fails to persuade Parzival to follow the same path. Her relations with Gawan are almost a parody of the *Minnedienst* situation. She orders him to perform deeds which are obviously designed to bring about his death, so that service to her is virtually fatal, and any other knight but Gawan (or, of course, Parzival) must inevitably have perished. And all this is accompanied by scorn and disgust. Surely, one would say, we have here a parody of the courtly lady, a Guenevere on an even lower plane, who tests her knight not by making him lose tournaments but by sending him to his death. Yet she has her reasons. Like Sigune, she has lost her lover in the courtly game, lost him to a man who, like Orilus, is not a murderer but an unthinking participant in a system which demanded that men kill or be killed in defense of their lady's fame—not her honor in any moral sense. Sigune lost Schionatulander in this way and Orgeluse lost Zidegast. Her fatal influence impinged upon the Grail story in her luring of Amfortas from his dedication to the pure love of the Grail. Thus her conduct toward Gawan takes on an altogether different aspect. She was avenging herself, not on Gawan himself, but on a system which had deprived her of her lover and she was doing so by pushing that system to its logical end—by insisting that as a potential lover he should undertake tasks entirely because she told him to do so, without promise of reward and entirely as a matter of service. It is only when he does these things without flinching and meets with Gramoflanz, her lover's killer, that she breaks down and confesses her reasons.

Now all these events are to be found in the version of Chrétien de Troyes, and I have little doubt that he intended to make an ironic commentary on the courtly system. He does so in all his works. But because his poem is unfinished we cannot tell whether he intended the contrast which Wolfram makes so pointedly. Sigune's reaction to the death of her lover is to turn to the spiritual life. It is a personal devotion rather than participation in the spiritual fellowship of the Grail company, but it is clearly oriented to religion, as can be seen in her successive appearances—first as a fresh girl, emaciated and sad after Parzival has left the Grail castle, then in a hermit's cell as Parzival approaches Trevrizent for the discussion which is the turning point of his career, and finally dead in her cell as Parzival makes his way again to the Grail castle. She rejects the secular for the spiritual, but there is no evidence that her nameless counterpart in Chrétien's work would have done the same. Chrétien's lady sorrows over her dead lover, but far from taking refuge in the spiritual, wishes that her lover's killer could himself be killed. The explanation for the difference between the two works lies in the fact that Chrétien does not envisage a separate, spiritually oriented Grail community as an alternative to a secularly oriented Arthurian world. His criticism of that world remains, in his extant work, criticism and no positive alternative is offered.

Wolfram's criticism of the idea of love-service is quite explicit. He has no time for the kind of man who overpraises his lady and regards her as the only one worthy of consideration. He does not consider that it is a knight's duty to maintain such a belief, nor should the lady expect it. If she wants him, she should do so on the basis of his knightly conduct in general rather than his service to her in particular. Thus Wolfram clearly states that service to the lady is not the most important part of knightly duty and that knightly combat is not intended for the winning of ladies but for higher objectives. Gawan may spend his time in this fashion but, as we have seen, Gawan is on a much lower level than Parzival—and even he marries his lady before winning her love. It is not too much to say that all knights who are obsessed with the idea of love-service prove defective in one way or another—Orilus is a fine example—until they bow to circumstances and marry their ladies. But Parzival goes much further. His service to women is of a very different order. At no point does he set out to win any woman's love by service. He does reject Orgeluse, whom Gawan serves. His wife comes to him for help and that help is granted, not out of any belief that it would win her love, but because she is a helpless creature opposed by overwhelming forces. Wolfram goes to great lengths to emphasize the unimportance of *Minne* in their relationship. He changes even small details of Chrétien's narrative of the visit of Blansche-flur to Perceval in order to stress the chastity of the meeting of his own characters. He is careful to have them married, as Chrétien's lovers are not, and even after they are married, he shows them postponing the con-summation of the marriage for three days. Wolfram has no patience with love as a mere expression of physical desire, as he tells us in his own per-son, and he has even less with those women who use their charms to allure men to do their bidding. In this respect he is closer to the attitude of the Church than he is to that of the romance.

Parzival leaves his wife in order to search for his mother. He does not see Condwiramurs again until his second visit to the Grail castle. The only occasion on which there is any lengthy reference to her before this is when he is fascinated by the drops of blood in the snow and is reminded of the beauty of his beloved. Hers is an abstract, magical beauty whose form is close to the conventional imagery applied to the Virgin. Although he found the incident in his source, Wolfram had no objection to it since it did not represent any physical appearance by Condwiramurs during the pe-riod of Parzival's trial. For Parzival's struggle for the Grail kingdom con-centrates on that alone, and this concentration constitutes the sharpest contrast between his behavior and that of Gawan. Gawan's fight is for love. All the combats in which he engages after his first meeting with Orgeluse are directly or indirectly designed to further his attempt to win her. Knightly adventure is, for him, subordinated to the pursuit of love, the very point which Wolfram attacks so sharply in the prologue to Book III and which, incidentally, he was to make the main aim of the pagan, as contrasted to the Christian, pursuit of religion in his other major nar-rative poem, *Willehalm*.

Wolfram makes very clear what he believes to be the function of the female in knightly endeavor. Condwiramurs meets Parzival again when he attains the Grail castle for the second time—and she brings with her two children. Her marriage has already assured Parzival that he will have not only a son to succeed him but another who can carry out the other major function of the Grail knights, the aiding of distressed persons, particularly rulers. The stress on the family and its continuation is as evident here as it is throughout Wolfram's work. But the women have another function. They, not the men, are the true guardians of the sacred vessel. It is kept in the women's quarters and attended entirely by them. Parzival is connected with the Grail through Herzeloyde, his mother, and it is clear that Wolfram considers that the spiritual qualities are to be sought in the female rather than in the male. Yet his Grail guardians are far from being Vestal Virgins. They can and do marry and leave the Grail castle, but their offspring return to the service of the Grail.

No better example of Wolfram's attitude toward *Minnedienst* could be chosen than the story of Parzival's brother Feirefis. When he encounters Parzival he is indeed seeking his father but he is also maintaining the supremacy of his lady, Sekundille, queen of "India," to whom he is married. Thus, although he has never been to Arthur's court or, so far as we know, been instructed in the niceties of courtly love, he is following the standard and, in Wolfram's view, ridiculous, practice of seeking adventure to prove his love. All this obsession fades as soon as he sees Repanse de Schoye, the chief guardian of the Grail, who is Parzival's aunt and quite literally old enough to be Feirefis' mother. But the Grail has kept her young. All thoughts of Sekundille disappear in a flash. He desires Repanse de Schoye alone and he attains her by being baptized a Christian. Wolfram makes no secret of the fact that it is to win a lady that Feirefis is baptized, but for Wolfram there exists no essential difference between Christian and pagan except the fact of baptism. By the act of becoming a Christian, Feirefis abandons love-service in the courtly sense; he exchanges a lower for a higher form both in religion and in love.

Thus Wolfram makes clear his criticism of the ideas of love which he had received from his sources. He rejects the two basic constituents of courtly love, the right of a woman to demand unquestioning service in whatever triviality she fancies, and the need for a knight to gain honor for his lady by embarking on a series of otherwise pointless adventures, adventures which often result in the death of innocent persons and lifelong grief to others with whom the knight has no personal quarrel, nor even grounds for quarreling. We have already noted that Chrétien is critical of courtly love, but his criticism takes the form of ironical comment, not of fundamental rejection. The fact is that Wolfram is writing for life.

He emphasizes the didactic sense of his work and its application to the conduct of his audience. Yet he is reacting to a literary courtly ideal which he must have recognized in the works he had read and which, unless he crassly misunderstood his source, as I sometimes suspect, he did not find in the works of Chrétien de Troyes. Wolfram, in other words, saw in the current ideals of love-service a clear danger to his own standards of morals.

Wolfram von Eschenbach and Gottfried von Strassburg found little on which they could agree and indeed went out of their way to make unobliging remarks about each other. But on one thing they were in complete accord—they both disliked the ideas of courtly love which they found in current literature. So far as our knowledge goes, there could have been very little written in German at this time to call forth their ire. Only Hartmann von Aue, Heinrich von Veldeke, and perhaps Ulrich von Zazikhoven had written anything of any significance and both Wolfram and Gottfried are loud in their praise of Hartmann. They must have been reacting principally to the French literature of their day. Gottfried's reasons for disliking courtly literature are quite different from those of Wolfram and he is even more explicit about them.

Gottfried's approach is intellectual rather than moral or social. He is concerned with love as a phenomenon, not as something which may affect contemporary life for good or evil. In fact, it becomes very clear in his work that he is perfectly well aware of the enormous potentiality for evil which love may have. Gottfried sets forth his thesis in the prologue to his *Tristan,* and although the language is deliberately ambivalent, the thesis itself is clear. Most authors regard love as one of the world's pleasures. They are concerned with it only as an element in the leisure time of a knight. Their purpose is to describe only the joys of love, not its full nature. Gottfried says that he has no objection to these people, since they are doing their best but he asks indulgence if he decides to take a different point of view. That point of view will be that there is no certainty in love, that its nature is shifting and imprecise, affecting different people in different ways but showing one characteristic in all cases—its immense power. It should be noted at once that we are not discussing here whether love is sensual or spiritual, whether it is *amor purus* or *amor mixtus.* Gottfried assumes that there will be a sensual element in all love. Otherwise it would not exist. His interest lies rather in the relation of love to the totality of existence. In earlier works in which love at court had been shown, the situation was fairly simple. The love of a woman was sought by a knight. His service to her might take the form of defending her honor, of winning tournaments in her name, of maintaining her beauty and other qualities before all comers, even, in the lyrics, of praising her in verse. These are his services to her. They show the knight's love as a form of homage, a homage for which he should receive his reward. In the romances he does receive that reward, and it is certainly not true that in narrative poetry courtly love means unrequited love. The *canso* has as a convention that the lady is beyond the lover's reach, but the convention does not apply to the romances. Gottfried never concerns himself with this "unattainability" convention, since love cannot exist if it is not mutual. He is concerned, however, with the service-reward relationship and with the reasons why people fall in love.

Curious as it may seem, French narrative poetry gives little attention to the reasons why people love. In *Cligès* and *Yvain* we are shown the deadly effects of the sight of the beloved upon the knight and in *Cligès*—but not in *Yvain*—of the knight on the lady. The process of falling in love is brought about by sight, by the image, but further details are usually lacking. Again there is none of the analysis we find in lyric poetry, especially in later Italian. The interest of the love story lies in the later justification of the love through adventure and service. In *Lancelot, Erec,* and *Perceval* there is not even a preliminary description of the devastating effects of the lady's eyes. Lancelot is already in love at the opening of the poem, Erec wins his bride originally because he needs her for adventure, and Perceval (in the French version) enjoys his love as part of the defense of his lady's lands. Falling in love is an abstraction leading to homage through adventure. The lover thinks that his lady is the most beautiful and virtuous lady in the world—but what lover does not? We are never told precisely what it is that makes lovers attractive to one another.

Gottfried takes a very different view of the problem. He is concerned that his readers should know what steps lead to love on the various levels at which it may be conceived. Hence his work begins not with the story of Tristan but with that of his father, Riwalin. Blanscheflur, the sister of King Mark, is attracted to Riwalin when she sees him riding at Tintagel and later in a tournament. This attraction is conventional, brought about by the eyes, a fact which Gottfried emphasizes by the nature of his descriptions. Here we have the clichés of courtly love, and they are reinforced by the description of the perfect May weather of the tournament, the ideal landscape, and the glory of the court. When Riwalin is gravely wounded in battle, there is much neat play on the wound of love-cure of love topos, but oddly enough, when Riwalin recovers, he is quite prepared to terminate the affair with suitable protestations of sorrow. The situation is that of the *Aeneid*, with one important difference. Blanscheflur is expecting a child, and at this disclosure Riwalin's honor is affected. He cannot leave Blanscheflur to be publicly disgraced, since his own honor would be impugned, and he therefore offers to take her with him. Later the two are married and Tristan, at least according to the law in some countries, was born legitimate. It will be noticed that the child is the only reason for Riwalin's taking of Blanscheflur with him. Otherwise this "typical" courtly romance would have come to an abrupt end. As the flowers of May fade, so does love. There is no basis for love here except physical attraction expressed in visual terms. Nor is there any thought of permanence. Gottfried shows us that Tristan's birth is the result of a union whose aim was pure joy, and that the partners in the liaison had no thought of love beyond self-gratification. Sorrow was indeed present, because Riwalin was wounded in the tournament, but sorrow was not an essential part of their love.

The description of the *enfance* of the hero is common enough in the romances, but Gottfried's description of Tristan's education goes far beyond the normal. It concentrates on the aesthetic attainments, on the development of a cultured personality, and dwells on two aspects of Tristan's training in particular, his skill in languages and his power in music. I use the word "power" advisedly, for Tristan does not merely possess a high degree of performing skills. He is technically accomplished and thereby gains admiration, but his music wins over men to such a degree that they have no power over themselves and are no longer capable of rational thought. They can do nothing but respond to the music he plays. Gottfried makes this clear on several occasions, but the most important by far is Tristan's use of music to gain entrance to the court of Ireland. The common people are drawn by the charm of his music, Isolde's tutor by its great technical skill. It is this music which brings him to Isolde.

It is worth examining the description of their first meeting with some care: "And so they sent for his harp and the young Princess, too, was summoned. Lovely Isolde, Love's true signet, with which in days to come his heart was sealed and locked from all the world save her alone, Isolde also repaired there and attended closely to Tristan as he sat and played his harp. And indeed, now that he had hopes that his misfortunes were over, he was playing better than he had ever played before, for he to them played not as a lifeless man; he went to work with animation, like one in the best of spirits."[6] There are several noteworthy points about this meeting. The first is that Tristan does not react to Isolde's presence at all, nor does she to his. He sees her as any lover in the romances sees his lady, but there is no overwhelming impact, no love at first sight. The most enduring love affair in medieval literature begins with no sign of affection on either side. But there is a second and perhaps more significant aspect. We have noted the stress on the visual in falling in love, courtly fashion. Herbert Kolb, in his monumental work *Der Begriff der Minne*, rightly devotes a long chapter to the discussion of "Die Mystik des Auges und des Herzens,"[7] for in all lyric poetry from Guillaume de Poitiers to Petrarch, love is a matter of sight. Not so in Gottfried's poem. Tristan himself says that he will be cured "through his music," and it is through music that he moves to love. In the highly detailed description that Gottfried offers of the instruction of Isolde, the stress is always on sound—on language and on music. It is through them that she learns, as Tristan had, to move the hearts of men and render them incapable of rational thinking. The "moraliteit" which he teaches her is, as I have pointed out elsewhere,[8] closely connected with music, with the forming of character by musical means. Isolde moves on the same level as Tristan, she is prepared for a kind of love different from that found in the earlier romances and, let us observe, different from that of Riwalin and Blanscheflur, whose attraction was visual and physical.

Although the practice of music establishes a kind of harmony between Tristan and Isolde which is to be found between no other characters in the poem, it does not make them fall in love. The most diligent search fails to reveal any indication of love at this stage. Tristan is, after all, Tantris and hence not noble, so far as the Irish court knows. The invention of a wife as an excuse for leaving is an ironical comment on courtly love. The irony becomes more marked when Tristan returns to Ireland to woo Isolde for Mark. He knows that Isolde can be won by an act of service—killing the dragon—and Gottfried stresses this fact. The whole incident in Ireland is a mockery of the service-reward cliché of courtly love. Tristan kills the dragon, cuts out its tongue, and is promptly rewarded for his pains by being poisoned. The reason is, of course, that he cannot go around with a dragon's head in his hand, and his plans are uncertain because he cannot declare himself as Mark's envoy. He is, to use an expression appropriate to Tristan, playing it by ear. The seneschal who cuts off the dragon's head has no such problems. To him the equation is simple: a seneschal (inevitably of noble birth) plus one dragon's head equals a suitor for the hand of Isolde. There would be nothing remarkable about this if he had really killed the dragon. Courtly romance is full of such incidents. Isolde despises the seneschal, and the thought of marrying him disgusts her, but she and her mother realize that there is no escape unless it can be proved that he is a liar. Tristan saves Isolde when he is able to show that it was he who performed the service. In the version of Thomas of Britain, Tristan uses this very point to stop Isolde from killing him in the bath—"kill me and you will have to marry the seneschal"—but for Gottfried this was too crass. His hero appeals to Isolde's honor. As a lady, she cannot kill a defenseless man. All this should not blind us to the fact that no one disputes the seneschal's right to marry Isolde. Love or no love, he has performed his service and is entitled to his reward. And dragon-slaying was definitely a recognized form of service. Nor should we fail to notice that Isolde is to marry Mark for the same reason—Tristan has performed the service of killing the dragon and now has the right to dispose of Isolde's person. He could marry her himself, but his loyalty to Mark causes him to delegate his rights to his sovereign. No wonder Isolde complains. She has escaped the seneschal only to be handed over to a foreign king whom she has never seen. "You have won me by guile from those who brought me up, and are taking me I know not where! I have no idea what fate I have been sold into, nor what is going to become of me!"[9] Tristan's reply is to offer her social advantages, and she is unmoved. Yet Tristan's actions have in fact followed the rules of courtly love—he has performed the right actions to win his lady, but he has not won her for himself. It is Mark who will enjoy the fruit of his *Minne-dienst* and that fruit will be his purely sensual enjoyment of Isolde. This is something less than true love, particularly since Mark's first experience with his "wife" is really Brangaene, and Mark is utterly unable to distinguish between the two.

Tristan and Isolde come to love each other on the ship. There are no special circumstances which bring about their love except that the close conditions on shipboard throw them together. The ground has long been prepared, and Isolde has already given evidence that she is in love with Tristan, although the reverse cannot be said to be true. If the love-potion means anything, it is that a wave of conscious physical attraction sweeps over them both. They are aware of love and, each for different reasons, struggle against it. Love does indeed conquer all but not in the trite fashion of conventional romance. It is an overmastering desire which is far removed from the self-conscious agonies of Alexander in *Cligès*, from the sensual daydreams of Lavinia and Aeneas, from the maunderings of Yvain at his first sight of Laudine. It is, perhaps, closest to the feelings of Lancelot but with the important difference that the idea of making Tristan serve her as Lancelot serves Guenevere never enters Isolde's head. Quite the contrary. When he is in exile and wins for her a little dog, Petitcriu, whose bell will delight her with its music, she tears the bell from its neck so that she will not have pleasure while Tristan suffers pain.

Each of the lovers has only one thought—to be with the other. Neither considers that there is any obligation of service between them. Yet it is perhaps inevitable that the early stages of their love should follow a pattern of courtly intrigue and that Brangaene in a positive sense and Melot in a negative sense should regard their love affair in this light. Other authors, Eilhart and the authors of the prose versions, do in fact so regard it. Only very slowly do the lovers themselves come to realize what "Tristan-love" involves, and it is something very different from courtly love. The scene in the grotto of love is the key to Gottfried's *Tristan,* as the scene in the hermit's cave is to *Parzival.* It is distinguished by several important features. The first is the separation of the grotto from civilized life. It is utterly cut off from the court by mountains and dense woods. The grotto itself is set in a *paysage idéal,* strongly reminiscent of, but by no means identical with, the landscape of Mark's court at the meeting of Riwalin and Blanscheflur. Second, it is pagan. The cave is specifically said to date from pre-Christian times and to have been made in honor of the pagan goddess of love. Yet the symbolism used is similar to the conventional allegorization of the Christian church building in terms of the *Ecclesia Dei.* Thus it is at once a temple for the worship of love and a shrine within the heart of every lover in which love can dwell. Perhaps most important of all is the fact that the lovers are alone there. Their life is concentrated entirely on love, which means on each other. Moreover their love is mutual in the sense that neither is regarded as the active or passive partner. Gottfried emphasizes this mutuality by his description of their playing instruments and singing, each in turn taking the part of instrumentalist and vocalist. Such a scene is unparalleled in works which profess to treat of courtly love or are presumed to do so. When Erec devotes himself entirely to his wife, he is accused of uxoriousness, of neglecting his knightly duty, and the remainder of the romance is devoted to his rehabilitation. In other words, courtly love is a social matter. Whatever our view of the existence of a courtly code, of a type of love called courtly, there is no denying that the French romances and many of their German imitators see love as part of a system of social behavior. It bestows dignity and honor on a man, it gives respect to a woman. Without it both knight and lady are incomplete members of society. Further, it influences the knight's total behavior, his use of prowess, and the kind of adventure on which he embarks. All these aspects of love in the romances are denied by Gottfried's *Tristan*. Love is entirely individual; it exists between lovers only. The opinion of other members of society is immaterial and should be considered only in so far as flouting it may create difficulties for the lovers. Adventure is not made more purposeful by the fact that love inspires it. Bluntly, courtly society is inimical to true love. Many members of that society are of too base a clay to be able to appreciate it—Melot and the seneschals are good examples—but even those who, as persons, are noble and kind, such as Mark and Brangaene, are unable to understand. Gottfried's poem raises the fundamental question about true love—is it, in fact, compatible with society at all? If Gottfried's poem had been completed we should presumably have his answer. As it is, we can say only that it appears that either society or love must break in the struggle and that it would have been the lovers who were crushed.

Gottfried thus denies the essentially comic (in the medieval sense) outcome of love at court. The happy ending, which comes from the individual's learning to adjust to the needs of courtly society and from the modification of courtly attitudes because of the hero's achievements, is impossible in his story. Love is fundamentally incompatible with courtly life. There is, in fact, no such thing as courtly love, for such an expression would be a contradiction in terms. The court is an artificial organization which is conducted by a series of shams. Gottfried says in his prologue and continues to say throughout the poem that there are many decent and well-meaning people in courtly society and that they should be honored as such. But the system, represented by the seneschals and their like, restricts even the good.

We should at this point note one essential difference between Wolfram and Gottfried. Wolfram did not regard himself as primarily a writer. He thought of himself as a knight. His remarks on love may be taken to express his personal beliefs and to be didactic in the sense that contemporaries could follow them in their daily lives. This is not Gottfried's sense of his own mission. He is an artist who is examining the phenomenon of love, of noble love. Inevitably, his milieu is that of the court—no other would have been conceivable in his day—but he is not didactic. His characters are exemplary, they are martyrs of love but they belong to the literary and artistic world.

The histories of German literature often divide later German writers of romance into the successors of Wolfram and the successors of Gottfried. In fact they had no successors. Whatever superficial resemblances of style or treatment are to be found, the later writers did not treat love in the same way as either of these two authors. Even the continuators of Gottfried were unable to finish his poem in the sense in which he had written. Konrad von Wurzburg, Rudolf von Ems, and their like sentimentalize love, and this is the fate we would expect of a system whose principal constituent was slavish devotion.

The German reaction to love in French and Provençal lyric poetry is really a different subject from that we have been discussing. One of the great disadvantages of a term like "courtly love" is the ease with which it can be stretched to cover many different types and genres. The German love lyric is courtly only in the sense that the men who wrote it were at least technically noblemen who had connections at court. At the end of the twelfth century the only alternative to this would have been that they should be clerics. For the early imitators of Provençal and French poetry, love is indeed ennobling but there is no theoretical reason, implied or stated, that only those of noble birth can participate in it. Heinrich von Morungen feels as strongly as Guido Guinizelli that it is the noble heart that loves a noble lady and that it is character not birth which decides nobility. Those elements in Provençal poetry which might conceivably be called courtly, particularly the formal panegyric of an actual lady, even though she be concealed under a *senhal,* are conspicuously absent. Even when reference is made to a specific lady, the interest is concentrated on the love felt by the poet. It is not too much to speak of the persona of the lady and the persona of the poet set in a situation of tension with each other. Yet it cannot be denied that the essential element of courtly love, *Minnedienst* or love-service, is stressed by all the poets before Walther von der Vogelweide and many after. In the work of Heinrich von Morungen, the relation is expressed by a series of images, though not without ironical overtones, while Reinmar von Hagenau anticipates the *dolce stil nuovo* in his rational language and analytical approach. Yet in both there is an absence of metaphysical concepts. The analysis is of the feelings, the emotions, the reasons for continuing to serve a lady with song, even though any reward seems remote.

The approach was sterile. In a few years all its possibilities had been exhausted. No amount of discussion could provide a reason for a love relationship which in the last analysis rested not on an emotion or even a noble heart but on a feudal concept of service. The Italian poets realized this and turned to metaphysical analysis. Walther von der Vogelweide realized it and removed the essential features of courtliness from his best love poems.

Walther's great service to German love-poetry is his recognition of the futility of *Minnedienst*. To him, true love was mutual and natural. Consequently his lovers meet in a spring landscape which is not the formal description derived from classical rhetoric but a modification of it in which each element is alive. His lady is fresh and young. She is not a lady who must be served but a person who is to be loved naturally and who must return this love. There is no service element in this love, but the existence of the service concept gives many opportunities to contrast natural love with the artificial concepts of *Minnesang*. An excellent example is this passage from the poem "Muget ir schouwen":

> Daz mich, frowe, an fröiden irret,
> daz ist iuwer lîp.
> An iu einer ez mir wirret,
> ungenædic wîp.
> Wâ nemt ir den muot?
> Ir sît doch genâden rîche:
> tuot ir mir ungnædeclîche,
> sô sît ir niht guot.

The strophe is full of references to the clichés of love-service, but they are there only to be mocked. Walther, like his great contemporaries, knew of the existence of a courtly convention but he ceased to believe in it after his apprenticeship, even though in later life he occasionally wrote songs in the mode.

What, then, are we to understand by courtly love in German literature? Firstly, we should think of it in a literal sense, as love-at-court. To this degree German literature, like all literature of the High Middle Ages not written by clerics, is in some sense courtly, because it was written for audiences at courts which thought of themselves as possessing a superior culture. But if we are to think of courtly love as a special kind of love—spiritual, unfulfilled, nonsensual, and all the other epithets commonly attributed to it, then in German as in French literature we are faced with very difficult problems. It is clear that German authors regarded the love they found in the works of their French models as characterized by love-service. This is natural enough, since it appears in one form or other in most if not all French romances. That they did not always recognize the irony in Chrétien's treatment is not surprising. A large number of modern critics have failed to recognize it also. This element of service, the most telling evidence of the influence of feudal society on the love concept, was regarded as a thoroughly bad characteristic by the greatest of the German authors. It is in this sense that they recognized "courtly love" and in this sense that they rejected it. There is no German version of Chrétien's *Lancelot*. All the poetry of these authors is a reaction to courtly love and, in the best authors, it is a rejection. The ideal of love based on service and admiration of specific qualities is to be replaced by mutual attraction. Each in his own way, Wolfram, Gottfried, and Walther told of a love that was shared and in turning his back on the concept of service opened new ways for the consideration of the love phenomenon.

NOTES

1. Gustav Ehrismann, "Die Grundlagen des ritterlichen Tugendsystems," *Zeitschrift für Deutsches Altertum und Deutsche Literatur,* (1919), 56: 137–216; Ernst Robert Curtius, "Das ritterliche Tugendsystem," *Deutsche Vierteljahrsschrift für Literaturwissenschaft und Geistesgeschichte* (1943), 21: 343–68; Eduard Neumann, "Der Streit um das ritterliche Tugendsystem," *Erbe der Vergangenheit,* Festgabe für Karl Helm (Tübingen: Niemeyer, 1951), pp. 137–55.

2. Hartmann von Aue, *Der arme Heinrich,* Fedor Bech, ed. (Leipzig: Brockhaus, 1891), lines 47 ff.

3. Hans Furstner, *Studien zur Wesenbestimmung der höfischen Minne* (Groningen: Wolters, 1956).

4. *Iwein,* Fedor Bech, ed. (Leipzig: Brockhaus, 1873), lines 8121 ff.

5. Karl Kurt Klein, "Wolframs Selbstverteidigung," *Zeitschrift für Deutsches Altertum und Deutsche Literatur* (1954–5), 85:150–62.

6. Gottfried's *Tristan,* A. Hatto, tr. (Baltimore: Penguin Books, 1960), p. 145.

7. Herbert Kolb, *Der Begriff der Minne* (Tübingen: Niemeyer, 1958).

8. *PMLA* (1962), 77:364–72.

9. Gottfried's *Tristan,* p. 193.

TWO
LYRIC

3

Contrast Imagery in the Poems
of Friedrich von Hausen

FRIEDRICH VON HAUSEN belongs to that group of German poets who, so far as extant work allows us to judge, were the first to be influenced deeply by the lyrics of the *langue d'oïl* and through them by the Provençal troubadours. The account of his death at Philomelium in 1190 makes it clear that he was a well-known and respected nobleman, far more famous as a soldier than as a poet. It is a reasonable assumption that he was an amateur in both senses of the word, a man who wrote poetry because he liked it, with no thought of establishing a professional reputation or of pleasing a patron. Such a poet would be likely to show two characteristics: he would work within the form and framework of imagery already established by the professional poets in the Romance languages but would express his personal feelings more directly. More accurately, perhaps, he would allow his personal feelings to show more obviously than the form of the *canzon* would normally allow.

If we assume that most of his work was written in the decade 1180–1190, a fair assumption in view of the fact that he is extraordinarily fond of crusading motifs, he would have been able to use as models the earlier masters of the *canzon* in Provençal but not those whose work becomes highly complex and obscure, in other words, Bernart de Ventadorn and Folquet de Marsile but not Arnaut Daniel and Peire Cardenal. We can be reasonably sure that he knew several of the poets of the *langue d'oïl,* particularly Conon de Bethune, since there are echoes of their work in his verse. But we must ask one important question: in what does their influence consist? Certainly not in the verse forms. Friedrich's verse forms do admittedly follow the *fronte/coda* form of the Provençal *canzon* in some but by no means all of his poems but there is not a trace of the more sophisticated elements, of *coblas doblas, coblas unisonans,* or *coblas capcaudadas.* Clearly Friedrich von Hausen, like other German poets, had no desire to pursue this line of technical virtuosity. He follows another path. In the Provençal *canzon* he discovered the problem of love. The emphasis should be on the word "problem," for it is to a large degree an intellectual exercise with which he is concerned. Stated in an oversimplified form, it is this: any woman who is really worthy of my love is too far above me to accept it. The value of the *canzon* lies not in its sentiments but in its methods of expressing them, and we are probably entitled to assume that it was these methods which were the principal object of study by their German imitators. A study of the work of Friedrich von Hausen, an early Minnesänger, may give us some indication of what the German poets thought was the chief artistic merit of the romance writers and what the methods of their poetic mentors were.

The study of imagery in both the *canzon* and the *Minnelied* has been to some extent distorted by the tendency of scholars for the last twenty years to see it in terms of topoi. There can be no doubt that many, perhaps most, of the images used by lyric poets can be shown to have a long history, a tradition in the schools of rhetoric which goes back to classical Latin and even to classical Greek. The images which express love in terms of war or of health and sickness are easily demonstrated to be topoi. It is not the existence of such images but the use which is made of them which must be of concern to the critic.

Friedrich von Hausen and his Romance predecessors who wrote the *canzon* saw love in terms of polarized situations—of extreme desire and extreme rejection, of intense love by the man and frigid indifference in the woman, of spring warmth and winter cold, of generous sacrifice and lack of grace. The most expressive way of expressing such polarization was by means of contrast imagery, by setting one image, with all its reverberations and associations, against another equally powerful in the opposite sense. This contrast imagery is one of the most marked characteristics of the poetry of Friedrich von Hausen and an examination of his poetry from this point of view throws considerable light on his technique of poetic creation.

Many of the contrast images had, of course, become so conventionalized even by the time of Friedrich that there would be little point in noting their mere existence if they were not used as part of a more comprehensive scheme. Let us examine, for example, *Des Minnesangs Frühling*, 49.13ff.:[1]

> Mir ist daz herze wunt
> und siech gewesen nu vil lange
> (deis reht: wan ez ist tump),
> sitz eine frowen erst bekande,—
> der keiser ist in allen landen,
> kust er si zeiner stunt
> an ir vil roten munt,
> er jaehe ez waere im wol ergangen.
>
> Sit ich daz herze han
> verlazen an der besten eine,
> des sol ich lon enphan
> von der selben diech da meine.
> swie selten ich ez ir bescheine,
> so bin ichz doch der man
> der ir baz heiles gan
> dan in der werlte lebe deheine.
>
> Wer möhte mir den muot
> getroesten, wan eine schoene frouwe,
> diu minem herzen tuot
> leit diu nieman kan beschouwen?
> dur not so lide ich solhen rouwen,
> wan sichz ze hohe huop.
> wirt mir diu Minne unguot,
> so sol ir niemer man voltrouwen.

The first image is only too familiar—the heart wounded by love, a tired metaphor. But the reader's attention is promptly recalled to an absurdity in the tradition. Why should a heart be wounded because of a lady? The poet supplies the answer. His heart is *tump*, naive, untutored. Such a remark immediately calls the whole tradition in question. Sophisticated poets had talked for centuries about the wound of love. But Friedrich's heart is *wunt* because of its lack of sophistication. The poet thus creates from a tired metaphor an air of sincerity, for it may be presumed that a heart which is naive will blurt out the truth. But the sequence is not yet over, for there follows a highly speculative proposition: if the emperor were to kiss her, he would be in fine condition. The contrast is between the emperor—the lord of all—and the naive persona of the poet, between the effect of the lady's red mouth on the emperor and the mere sight of the lady on the poet's heart. There is no chance, apparently, of the poet's kissing the lady's mouth, but we may assume that if he did, the result would be the same as or greater than that effected on the emperor. Thus the pain inflicted on the heart by the sight of the lady would be cured by the lady's kiss. The wound of love would be cured by the same agency which caused it. We are back at the wound-of-love/cure-of-love topos but in a different and ironical form. For the naive poet suffers from the mere sight of the beloved—this is actuality—but can only speculate that the greatest of men would be stimulated by a kiss. A compliment to the lady, perhaps. Or is it? It may be that only emperors are admitted. There is sharp contrast between the actual misery of the poet, caused by the lady, and the potential happiness of the emperor. Suffering is actual, for the poet, health is hypothetical, for the remote figure of the emperor. Moreover, the heart, the seat of true affection, is contrasted with the outward signs of love. The "herzen wunt/roten munt" rhyme is not an accident.

This use of old metaphors for new purposes is continued in the third strophe. Here the topos is sorrow which is really joy and vice versa, the *liebe/leid* contrast. The paradox is expressed with unusual clarity. It is illogical but quite in accordance with the *canzon* tradition that only a lady who causes sorrow can soothe the poet's spirit. The unusual feature of the use of the topos lies in the statement that it is a sorrow which is invisible to others. Again there is the same contrast between appearance and reality which we saw in the use of the "wound-of-love" image. The images of pain and sorrow continue to the end of the poem and the paradoxical "wirt mir diu Minne unguot." It is not *Minne* who is unkind but the lady, and the lady should not be trusted. The last line could mean this too.

The most basic of all contrast images is that of light and darkness, and it is interesting to see how Friedrich von Hausen uses it. In *MF* 48.23 the persona of the poet narrates his experience, but, even more significantly, the experience itself is a dream. The night is thus the period in which the lady appears; she is a part of the unreality of the darkness, something which will not stand against the light of day. When day, the time of reality arrives, the lady disappears and her whereabouts cannot be determined. The roles of day and night have thus been reversed. Yet it is from this lady that the poet's joy is supposed to come. In what sense does he mean "supposed"? The answer is revealed in the crowning paradox, which takes one of the principal figures of the *Minnesang*, the damage done to the persona of the poet by his eyes. This damage is due to the effect of the light from the lady's eyes on the poet's own eyes and the subsequent entanglement of his heart. The heart is thus involved as a result of the light and its effect on the senses, and the poet can, within the rationale of the *Minnesang*, justly blame his eyes for this sorrow. In this poem Friedrich von Hausen does use exactly this kind of imagery, but its effect is completely different. The only joy he can feel comes from vision without eyes, the dream vision. His eyes may have been originally responsible for the identification of his lady and even for his falling in love with her, but his realization of love comes not from light and actuality but from darkness and dream. He wishes to be without eyes, not for the conventional reason that they have done him harm but because he can realize his love only through the inner vision. There is thus a total contrast with conventional imagery. But the poet goes further. His imagery raises serious questions about the very existence of the lady. To be without eyes, to rely on dreams, to be given to darkness is to be divorced from reality. The poet may, in fact, never have "set eyes" on the lady and she may be and probably is as much a figment of the poet's imagination as is the poet's own persona. In other words, both the poet's persona and the lady have been created by the poet himself. Friedrich von Hausen thus aligns himself, like Heinrich von Morungen, with those who raise the question of whether their love is in fact love for a person or whether it is nothing more than a state of mind which the lover himself has induced and in which the role of the lady, if indeed there is a lady, is incidental. If this short poem is read without reference to the image tradition, it is a bald and not very interesting work. Only the reverberations of the imagery give it point and meaning.

A study of Friedrich's poetry reveals that it consists very largely of the setting together of familiar *Minnesang* or *canzon* images with the object of showing the essentially contradictory nature of love and thus revealing the effects on the poet-lover. There is nothing remarkable or even new about this. The writers of the *langue d'oc* had done the same thing. In his best poems, however, Friedrich von Hausen carries the technique a stage further. Let us examine, for example:

> Si darf mich des zihen niet,
> ichn hete si von herzen liep.

des mohte si die warheit an mir sen,
und wil sis jen.
ich quam sin dicke in solhe not,
daz ich den liuten guoten morgen bot
engegen der naht.
ich was so verre an si verdaht
daz ich mich underwilent niht versan,
und swer mich gruozte daz ichs niht vernam.

Min herze unsanfte sinen strit
lat, den ez nu mange zit
haldet wider daz aller beste wip,
der ie min lip
muoz dienen swar ich iemer var.
ich bin ir holt: swenn ich vor gote getar,
so gedenke ich ir.
daz ruoche ouch er vergeben mir:
ob ich des groze sünde solde han,
zwiu schuof er si so rehte wol getan?

Mit grozen sorgen hat min lip
gerungen alle sine zit.
ich hate liep daz mir vil nahe gie:
dazn liez mich nie
an wisheit keren minen muot.
daz was diu minne, diu noch mangen tuot
daz selbe klagen.
nu wil ich mich an got gehaben:
der kan den liuten helfen uzer not.
nieman weiz wie nahe im ist der tot.

Einer vrouwen was ich undertan,
diu ane lon min dienest nam.
von der enspriche ich niht wan allez guot,
wan daz ir muot
zunmilte wider much ist gewesen.
vor aller not so wande ich sin genesen,
do sich verlie
min herze uf genade an sie,
der ich da leider funden niene han.
nu wil ich dienen dem der lonen kan.

Ich quam von minne in kumber groz,
des ich doch selten ie genoz.

> swaz schaden ich da von gewunnen han,
> so friesch nie man
> daz ich ir spraeche iht wan guot,
> noch min munt von frouwen niemer tuot.
> doch klage ich daz
> daz ich so lange gotes vergaz:
> den wil ich iemer vor in allen haben,
> und in da nach ein holdez herze tragen.
>
> (*MF* 45:37 ff.)

The poem opens with an entirely conventional utterance but the next two lines provoke attention, for the poet introduces the expression "warheit sen" and thus raises the question of what the truth is and whether the lady can see it. For the rest of the poem reverts to a familiar *canzon* cliché—the disorienting effects of love which render the persona incapable of such elementary distinctions as that between day and night. It becomes clear that the poet is using familiar figures to draw a sharp distinction between appearance and reality, between what the lady sees and what she actually could see, between the truth of his love and the deceptive forms of his behavior. The important rhyme words at the end of the first strophe, *verdaht, versan, vernam,* make this clear. They indicate the perversion of all normal sense perception. The poet appears mad, but the lady should see that this state is due to love.

Two familiar images dominate the first part of the second strophe. *Strit,* the struggle with the lady to convince her of the poet-persona's true love, and *dienen,* his service to her. In feudal terms the two expressions are incompatible, since one cannot serve a lord and fight him, but they are not incompatible in terms of the *Minnesang,* since the service consists in the writing of poetry by the poet-persona, poetry which is intended to convey the struggle for her love. The two images continue the main theme of the contrast between appearance *(strit)* and reality *(dienen)*. But at the end of the *Aufgesang* of the second strophe a new element is introduced which is crucial for Friedrich's poetry. The words "swar ich iemer var" show that the poet-persona (and, incidentally, the poet, as we know from other sources) is going on a journey. The idea of physical and spiritual separation had been an important theme of the *canzon* at least since the poetry of Jaufré Rudel. But here the matter is different. Although the word "Crusade" never appears, there are enough allusions in the poem to make it clear that the contemplated journey will be undertaken "for

God" and may therefore be assumed to be a crusade—in the course of which Friedrich was destined to die at Philomelium.

This introduction of the idea of service to God starts a new series of contrast images in which those associated with God are contrasted with those associated with the lady. "Service" is of predominant importance here, since, by definition, service to the lady must be, quite literally, wholehearted and hence would have no place for the service of God. Friedrich's first solution is that God may be kind enough to forgive him, since he created the lady and is, so to speak, responsible for her. But this is a facile solution, as the poet realizes, for it takes little account of the figure, essential to the whole *canzon* concept, that the poet-persona serves without reward. Although he hopes for reward, he knows that he will not receive it. For the true Christian, on the other hand, the reward is given without labor. His service will be pleasing to God, but it is not necessary to ensure that God gives him the greatest reward of all, the salvation of his immortal soul. The poet-persona has tormented himself with affairs which vex his earthly person but such a struggle is, in fact, folly—it has prevented him from turning to *wisheit,* true wisdom, Christian wisdom. The rest of the poem is taken up with a series of contrasts, not between different love-poetry images but between an image as used in connection with the love of a lady and that same image when it refers to the love of God.

A lady has accepted the service of the poet without any assurance that she will reward him (46.30), even though he has put himself in her power. The poet's only criticism of her at this point is that she is "ungenerous." In other words, she shows no grace, in spite of the fact that the poet has quite literally thrown himself on her mercy. How different would be the reception his service would find in God! The implication is quite clear. The *total* service which the poet-persona has heretofor given to the lady must now be given to God. Such service would be true *wisheit.* The lady has totally failed him and the image in which this is expressed is linked with the crusading spirit:

> vor aller not wande ich sin genesen
> do sich verlie
> min herze uf genade an sie . . .

The words refer to the lady, but they are exactly those which could be used of God, with the word "genesen" understood in its spiritual sense.

The last strophe again opens with a well-worn image—love has caused him much trouble but he will not complain. The poet observes a convention of love poetry but in doing so he raises a serious criticism—because of his love for the lady he has forgotten God. This is, of course, the fault of the poet-persona, not that of the lady, but even so she is as much the cause of his loss of salvation as God would be the cause of salvation itself. In both cases the consent of the sinner is needed. The last two lines of the poem express the new attitude. As he was "holt" to the lady in 46.14, now he has "ein holdez herze" for God. This poem is thus a study in contrast imagery; figures of devotion to the lady are also used of devotion to God and it soon becomes apparent how shallow is devotion to love service and how poor are its rewards when compared with the external reward to be gained by service to God. It is also clear how dangerous service to the lady can be if it diverts the heart from God.

A poem such as the one we have just discussed has an air of finality, of rejection of devotion to love in favor of devotion to the cause of the crusade. It would hardly seem possible for the poet-persona to retreat from or even modify such a position. Yet what are we to say of 47.9? Was it written earlier? Possibly, but not much earlier, since the circumstances are the same. It is an even more remarkable demonstration of the ambivalence of the poet-persona.

> Min herze und min lip diu wellent scheiden,
> diu mit einander varnt nu mange zit.
> der lip wil gerne vehten an die heiden:
> so hat iedoch daz herze erwelt ein wip
> vor al der werlt, daz müet mich iemer sit,
> daz si ein ander niene volgent beide.
> mir habent diu ougen vil getan ze leide.
> got eine müeze scheiden noch den strit.
>
> Ich wande ledic sin von solher swaere,
> do ich daz kriuze in gotes ere nam.
> ez waere ouch reht deiz herze als e da waere,
> wan daz sin staetekeit im sin verban.
> ich solte sin ze rehte ein lebendic man,
> ob ez den tumben willen sin verbaere.
> nu sihe ich wol daz im ist gar unmaere
> wie ez mir an dem ende süle ergan.

Sit ich dich, herze, niht wol mac erwenden,
dun wellest mich vil trureclichen lan,
so bite ich got daz er dich ruoche senden
an eine stat da man dich wol enpfa.
owe wie sol ez armen dir ergan!
wie torstest eine an solhe not ernenden?
wer sol dir dine sorge helfen enden
mit solhen triuwen als ich han getan?

Nieman darf mir wenden daz zunstaete,
ob ich die hazze diech da minnet e.
swie vil si geflehet oder gebaete,
so tuot si rehte als ob sis niht verste.
mich dunket wie min wort geliche ge
als ez der summer vor ir oren taete.
ich waere ein gouch, ob ich ir tumpheit haete
für guot: ez engeschiht mit niemer me.

This poem is an extemely complex study in contrast imagery and its
highly ambivalent effects depend entirely on the opposition between the
use of words in the *Minnesang* and the use of those same words in the
tradition of Christian imagery. The contrast between heart and body is a
distinction made long before Christianity, but in Christian imagery that
distinction is between the spiritual and the physical, between matters of
the soul and matters of the senses. The heart is higher than the body,
often indeed encumbered by it. In the language of the *Minnesang* the distinction is a different one. The heart is the part of a human being most
affected by love but it attains that state because of the impression made
on it by the senses. The sight of the lady through the eyes of the body
gives the initial impulse. The heart is not a representation of spiritual love,
although it represents the highest emotion of which the lover is capable.
The heart can be—figuratively—separated from the body because it is
possessed by the lady. She has won it, it is in her keeping and the lover
controls it no longer. A similar image occurs frequently in Christian mys-
tical writings.

Now this is a crusading song, as is made perfectly clear by the third
line, and the separation of heart and body had already become a cliché of
the genre—the body went to the Holy Land, the heart stayed with the
lady. Within the imagery of the genre, this was acceptable. But Friedrich
von Hausen does not make the statement in this form. The word "wel-

lent" indicates a determination on the part of his body and heart to separate and thus introduces the essential element of *voluntas*. Yet it is not the heart, the seat of the spirit, which has decided to go on the crusade but the body. The heart has a previous commitment to the lady. Thus the normal Christian order is reversed—the sensual pursues the interests of God on the Crusade, the spiritual stays with worldly love, a fact which is emphasized by the sound reminiscence *wellent/erwelt* and even more by the ambivalent expression "vor al der werlt" (in front of everyone? in preference to anything worldly?)

The final lines of the strophe complicate the matter still further. For the poet-persona must express his own distress at the behavior of these two apparently independent entities. He cannot, he implies, control their actions, and thus his own *voluntas* is ineffective, nor can he reconcile the two. Yet he is affected by their actions. The expression "mir habent diu ougen vil getan ze leiden" takes on new significance. Its normal meaning in *Minnesang* usage is here contrasted ironically with the effect on the poet-persona. Normally he would complain of the misery caused to his heart by the image of the lady. But the heart in its independence is now bringing his immortal soul into danger. In its devotion to the lady it has forgotten its devotion to God. Thus the statement that He alone can settle the quarrel between heart and body becomes bitterly ironical. What else can God do but decide in favor of the body, since it is the body which is determined to serve Him? We are thus confronted with the paradox that the body and God are allied against the lady and the heart.

This theme is amplified by the second strophe. The poet-persona states explicitly that his crusading activities will be carried out without the support of his heart. His *staetekeit (constantia),* normally a virtue both of lovers and of Christians, is here an obstacle to his salvation. He cannot hope to be a *lebendic man,* that is, be saved, if his spiritual part is divorced from his crusading activities, and the obstinacy of that part will be the death of him. Again there is the ambiguity of "an dem ende"—in the end or at the Day of Judgment?

In these two strophes there is a strong implied opposition between God and the lady. The poet-persona is helpless in this struggle but, as it is portrayed, the lady is the more powerful. The crusade will be undertaken in spite of her, but the essential element, the heart, will be missing and without it the spiritual benefits of the crusade will be lost.

The third and fourth strophes are largely without contrast imagery. The idea of converting the heart does, of course, recall Christian imagery, but the idea of God's sending the heart, now separated from the poet-persona, to a place where it will be well treated as it has been by the poet-persona is forced, since it implies that God will aid a rebellious heart in its struggle against Him. Yet the last three lines of the strophe imply that the poet has recognized the heart's difficulty in its constancy to the lady and would wish God to help it.

It is hard to understand the last strophe, normally attached to the poem, as a suitable conclusion. It shows none of the stylistic subtlety of its predecessors and it is hard not to agree that it should be regarded as a separate strophe. The use of imagery can sometimes be a clear indication of the integrity of a poem or its reverse.

Contrast imagery is an essential, perhaps the essential feature of Friedrich von Hausen's style. He uses the associations already firmly established by French poets to provide reinforcements of his statements about love but much more frequently he juxtaposes these images to provide contrasts, often ironical contrasts, which cause the audience to reassess their views and ideals of love. This type of contrast imagery is most effective when the standard verbal imagery of love is used in a Christian as well as in a secular sense, so that the whole problem of devotion to the lady, with its dubious or non-existent rewards must be compared with the certain rewards of the devotion of the Christian soul to God. The problem is deliberately left unresolved. The imagery leaves us with the impression that the lady may yet prove to be more powerful.

NOTE

1. I have used the text of *Des Minnesangs Frühling*, Karl von Kraus, ed., although I have consulted both the text and the commentary of D. G. Mowatt, *Friderich von Husen: Introduction, Text, Commentary, and Glossary* (Cambridge: University Press, 1971).

4

Persona and Audience
in Two Medieval Love-Lyrics

CRITICS HAVE LONG since abandoned the idea that the German *Minnesang* is a mere offshoot of Provençal lyric. In spite of the conventions, the imagery, and many formal characteristics which the German lyric borrows from the Romance, it is clear that there are major differences in attitude and that the German poets, while using the forms of their predecessors, are often asking different questions and answering those questions in different ways. Yet little attempt has been made at direct comparison between poems, and it would perhaps be useful to compare a Provençal poem with a German lyric in order to see whether any conclusions of general value can be obtained. By comparing the two poems, it may be possible to throw some light on such considerations as the relationship between the external audience for the poem and the internal audience of the poet-persona and on the power of the genre-form to shape the poet's approach to the love-theme. In approaching these problems I shall distinguish between the lover-persona, the figure within the poem who loves and suffers, and the poet-persona, whose task it is to express that love in a form which will help the lover and overcome the lady's resistance. It is thus the poet-persona, not the lover-persona, who performs love-service. Not all *canzon* and *Minnelieder* distinguish between these two personae, but the distinction can very frequently be observed and many apparent contradictions in the poems and still more apparent breaks in the sequence of thought can be best explained by assuming such a double persona. It is particularly important to observe that the service which is so integral a part of the genre means different things to the two personae, their aims are often differentiated and their audiences are not the same. It is these aims and audiences which I shall explore.

Bernard de Ventadorn

Lo tems vai e ven e vire
per jorns, per mes e per ans,
et eu, las! no·n sai que dire,
c'ades es us mos talans.
Ades es us e no·s muda,
c'una·n volh e·n ai volguda,
don anc non aic jauzimen.

Pois ela no·n pert lo rire,
e me·n ven e dols e dans,
c'a tal joc m'a faih assire
don ai lo peyor dos tans,
—c'aitals amors es perduda
qu'es d'una part mantenguda—
tro que fai acordamen.

Be deuri' esser blasmaire
de me mezeis a razo,
c'anc no nasquet cel de maire
que tan servis en perdo;
e s'ela no m'en chastia,
ades doblara·lh folia,
que: "fols no tem, tro que pren."

Ja mais no serai chantaire
ni de l'escola N'Eblo,
que mos chantars no val gaire
ni mas voutas ni mei so;
ni res qu'eu fassa ni dia,
no conosc que pros me sia
ni no·i vei melhuramen.

Si tot fatz de joi parvensa,
mout ai dins lo cor irat.
Qui vid anc mais penedensa
faire denan lo pechat?
On plus la prec, plus m'es dura;
mas si'n breu tems no·s melhura,
vengut er al partimen.

Pero ben es qu'ela·m vensa
a tota sa volontat,
que, s'el' a tort o bistensa,
ades n'aura pietat;
que so mostra l'escriptura:
causa de bon'aventura
val us sols jorns mais de cen.

Ja no·m partrai a ma vida,
tan com sia sals ni sas,
que pois l'arma n'es issida,
balaya lonc tems lo gras.
E si tot no s'es cochada,
ja per me no·n er blasmada,
sol d'eus adenan s'emen.

Ai, bon' amors encobida,
cors be faihz, delgatz et plas,
frescha chara colorida,
cui Deus formet ab sas mas!
Totz tems vos ai dezirada,
que res autra no m'agrada.
Autr' amor no volh nien!

Dousa res ben ensenhada,
cel que·us a tan gen formada,
me·n do cel joi qu'eu n'aten!

Heinrich von Morungen

Owe, war umbe volge ich tumben wane,
der mich so sere leitet in diu not?
ich schiet von ir gar aller fröiden ane,
daz si mir trost noch helfe nie gebot.
doch wart ir varwe liljen wiz und rosen rot,
und saz vor mir diu liebe wol getane
geblüejet rehte alsam ein voller mane.
daz was der ougen wunne, des herzen tot.

Min steter muot gelichet niht dem winde:
ich bin noch alse si mich hat verlan,
vil stete her von einem kleinen kinde,
swie we si mir nu lange hat getan
alswigend ie genote uf den verholenen wan,

swie dicke ich mich der torheit underwinde,
swa ich vor ir stan, unde sprüche ein wunder vinde,
und muoz doch von ir ungesprochen gan.

Ich han so vil gesprochen und gesungen
daz ich bin müede und heis von miner klage.
ich bin umb niht und umb den wint betwungen,
sit si mir niht geloubet daz ich sage,
wie ich si minne, und ich so holdez herze ir trage.
deswar mirn ist nach werde niht gelungen.
het ich nach gote ie halb so vil gerungen,
er neme mich hin zim e miner tage.

In the first two stanzas of Bernard's poem it is the lover-persona who appears. He is reflecting on the relationship with his lady, and his thoughts refer to two defeats in the game of love, incidents which are part of a continuing tension between the lady and the two personae. This reference to a game is most significant, for a game has rules, and there is no agreement between poet and lady on what those rules are. Nevertheless, there has been communication, for the lady and the poet-persona "sat down" to the game. The poet-persona's task, therefore, is to discover a method of presentation which will beat the lady at her game or of devising some set of rules for the game by which he can win. Only thus can he bring to fruition the continuing love of the lover-persona. The lover-persona muses on these things and hopes that through the poet-persona he can arrive at the *acordamen*.

The lover-persona is still speaking in the third stanza, but there is preparation for a transition. The service which the lover has given to the lady can only be the song composed by the poet-persona and the devotion expressed in that poetry. In other words, the lover-persona can claim his due only because of the efforts of the poet-persona, and these efforts, vain up to now, will continue and redouble unless the lady finally convinces the lover-persona of the folly of his efforts. The ineffectual struggle of the poet-persona is made clear in the fourth stanza. He declares that none of his poetry produces any effect and that the only service which he can use to win the lady is not only useless now but has no prospect of becoming more effective in the future. The singer is concerned to express the joy of love and the delight it brings, but such a song is designed to please the lady (and an audience), not to express the true feelings of the lover-persona. If the poet is not rewarded for his services, he will give up.

The poet-persona may give up but the lover-persona does not. He explicitly rejects the idea of separation because he hopes that the lady will move from cruelty to pity. Even though the lover-persona may, in effect, be robbed of life, he will still await the confession of love which must come. It will be noted that the lover-persona's attitude is completely opposed to that of the poet-persona. It is totally passive, totally dependent on the lady, totally unable, perhaps unwilling, to take action to win her. The poet-persona, on the other hand, performs active service and when that service does not succeed, he is ready to renounce it and try elsewhere. It is the poet-persona who can play the *game* of love, because he is performing, but it is the lover-persona who suffers from lack of success in the game.

The final full stanza of the poem is a combination utterance of these two personae, a hymn of praise which recognizes the feelings of the lover-persona as expressed by the poet-persona, the last effort of the poet-persona to gain his ends, the eternal feeling of the lover-persona. The *tornada* sums up this feeling. The poet-persona, in other words, is again playing the game of love, the lover-persona is resuming or rather continuing the suppliant attitude he showed in the first two stanzas. Bernard is here using a technique of which he is very fond—playing off one persona against the other and comparing the active poet-persona with the passive lover-persona.

In Heinrich von Morungen's poem the problem of the persona appears less complicated for the simple reason that the poet-persona does not overtly appear in an active role. It is the lover-persona who describes his memories of the lady. These memories are not even ostensibly objective. The first line in the poem reveals that the poet-persona is seeing his relation to the lady through "tumbem wane," a recognition on his own part that he is not objective and that the state of mind in which he finds himself is not normal. Heinrich thus reveals his technique—the lover-persona is describing his experience with a lady whose person and reactions exist in his own fancy and not necessarily in actuality. Even if she does exist, what we know of her is seen through the distorting-glass of the lover-persona's "wan." We do not know and cannot know what she is actually like, still less what her true attitude to the lover-persona is.

The first stanza is carefully constructed to show the reactions of the lover-persona. It moves from describing her merely by the pronouns "ir" and "si" to a description of her complexion, "ir varwe liljen wiz und rosen rot." The visual impression is vivid but it is hardly an original piece of imagery. The lady appears as the embodiment of the rhetorical and love-lyric figure of innocence and passion. She is being described by the lover-persona in the terms he knows best, those of the Provençal, French, and German love-lyric, themselves derived from the rhetorical tradition of Greece and Rome and tinged with religious symbolism. He knows them best because the poet-persona uses them when he sings a song before an audience, praising a lady. His recollections are not of a lady but of the description of her given by the poet-persona. The remaining epithets in the stanza are of the same class and have the same reverberations. The visual memory of the lady is therefore composed of poetic associations, not of truly remembered impressions. The last line confirms this, for the lover-persona's emotions are portrayed through a cliché of the lyric—the wounding of the heart by the impression gained through the eyes. The meaning of "tumber wan" now becomes clear. It is the point of view which sees the lady in the distorting glass of *Minnesang*.

It is still the lover-persona who is speaking in the second stanza and he is using *Minnesang* imagery to express his relationship to the lady. He concentrates on a quality so frequently discussed in the love-lyric, the constancy of the lover, even when rejected. *Staete* is one of the greatest virtues a lover can display, the virtue which makes a triumph out of rejection. There is, however, no great triumph here. The constancy is expressed negatively—it does not change direction, it is not like the wind, which bloweth where it listeth. The lover's mood has not changed since he last saw the lady—not, be it noted, since she failed to respond to his love-pleas. The image of *staete* is severly damaged by the next line, where it is described as being the same since the lover-persona was a child. It appears that the constancy of the lover-persona is a matter of inherent character rather than an attachment to the lady and even a result of naiveté. However great the lady's cruelty, however much she may neglect him, his constancy is not affected. It is quite clear that the lover-persona has never merged with the poet-persona, for the poet-persona is more easily discouraged. The lover-persona has kept silent about his love. He has yielded to the *verholener wan* which possesses him, he has even found words to express that love ("sprüche ein wunder finde"), but when he appears before the lady he can say nothing. He goes away without expressing his love.

In this second stanza Heinrich makes clear the fact that he has never told his love. He is his own audience and he uses the imagery of the *Minnesang* to create his love within himself. He is not proclaiming that love but spinning it from the images in which earlier love-poets had flattered their ladies. It is equally clear that such a love can exist only for him. The lady has no part in it, even to the extent of rejecting it. Her "cruelty" is thus a figment of the poet's imagination. He has not won her, but equally she has not rejected him. The expressions used by the Provençal poets of the rejection of the poet-persona by the lady are thus being used by the German lover-persona to show that he would be rejected, if the poet-persona were to proclaim his love.

This failure to express his love before the lady is still further explained in the third stanza. In the first four lines it seems as if the poet-persona is finally speaking. But is he? Certainly there has been a great deal of "speaking and singing," so much that the speaker is hoarse with complaining. Yet the next line shows that this complaint has nothing to do with singing before the lady. She does not allow him to do so.[1] We must therefore assume that any songs of complaint that the poet sings are performed before an audience which does not include the lady. He may tell others of his love but not her. The poet-persona, if he exists at all, has been deprived of his *raison d'être*. He cannot perform the one service which may win the lady, namely praise her to her face and confess the love felt by the lover-persona. He is, indeed, wasting his time ("ich bin umb niht und umb den wint betwungen").

The failure of the poet-persona is, according to the last three lines of the poem, responsible not only for the failure of the lover-persona but also for the misdirection of the lover-persona's loyalty. If he had made half so much effort "nach gote," he would have been accepted "e miner tage." The point is, of course, that God has no need of service but only of faith, and therefore a man needs no poet-persona to present his case to God. The lover-persona protests that his true worth is unknown to the lady and for a good reason—the poet-persona has had no opportunity to function before the lady and thus win her by service. Only God can appreciate worth if it is not expressed.

Heinrich's poem thus seems to proclaim a split between the two personae in the poem. It is the lover-persona who is lamenting his lack of success and for this, by implication, he blames the poet-persona. In the *canzon* and the *Minnelied,* the usual complaint is that the lady hears the lover's plea but is unaffected by it or actively hostile to it. But she at least recognizes that it is there. In this poem the lady does not reject the plea because the poet-persona is unable to make it, partly because she will not listen, partly because of his own ineptitude. Clearly the problem in this poem, however we read the opening lines of the third stanza, lies in the failure to communicate, not in the actual cruelty of the lady. It is therefore impossible for the lover-persona to estimate the reaction of his lady to his love, since the poet-persona never succeeds in presenting it. The love remains an unexpressed "wan."

The lover-persona is thus turned completely on himself. His love may be genuinely directed toward his lady but in the absence of any reaction from her, it remains quite literally a figment of his imagination ("volge ich tumbem wane"). His constancy is not to a lady but to a dream which he has maintained over the years, and his love is secret because it exists in his inward being, not because the lady's honor must be guarded. The social convention of the *canzon* has become the emotional reality of the *Minnelied.*

To both poets the question of time is of major concern, but they treat it very differently. Bernard carefully presents a vista of long time-spans, stretching into years, during which the lover-persona has experienced no change in the attitude of his lady. The purpose is to demonstrate his constancy in adversity, but the effect, no doubt intended, is to show the timelessness of love and the total loss of a sense of time-divisions. Past tenses are rare in the poem and when they occur, it is in describing something which has already happened twice, the game of love for example, and which will certainly happen again. Most of the tenses are "present," that is, tenses of habitual action, and future or conditional. They show a set of actions which can and will occur as long as time lasts. The statements by the poet-persona that he "will not" sing or plead are pointless, since his actions are a part of time itself. The line "Ja no·m partrai a ma vida" thus takes on a special significance. His love is synonymous with time but it is the time of the endurance of his power as a man. Love is thus ever-present and does not itself change. The situation with the lady who is its object does not change either. The lover-persona loves her while time lasts: it is the poet-persona who is the element of mutability, for he attempts to change her mood by singing, is defeated and, because of his lack of success, ceases to sing in disgust at his failure, and later returns to repeat his effort. The poet-persona is thus responsible for any appearance of past, present, and future in the love-lyric, since his attitude is determined by the incidents of presentation which represent his attempt to bring the love he celebrates to a specific place at a specific time. For him there is a past—the last occasion on which he attempted to persuade the lady—and the future—his next attempt to persuade her. For the lover-persona there is only the continuum of love. Bernard's poem thus operates on two time-levels, that of the poet-persona, which is determined by changes in his activity, and that of the lover-persona, which is as unchanging as the love he bears the lady. What is left unspoken is the time-level on which the lady's attitude operates. We have only the poet-persona's word for this and it is determined by his own attitude. If his plea were ultimately successful, he would, of course, bring the lady's love to the lover-persona's time-continuum.

If this time dichotomy appears complicated, it should be remembered that a medieval writer was accustomed to think in terms of the *saeculum* and *aeternum,* of the temporal reflection of an eternal idea and of that idea itself, of earthly life and eternal life. There is no reason why this dichotomy should not be presented in terms of the love-lyric as it is in terms of the romance by Chrétien de Troyes, Wolfram von Eschenbach, and particularly by Gottfried von Strassburg.

We have already pointed out that in Heinrich's poem it is the lover-persona who is speaking in the first stanza. The lover-persona states his continuing problem in the first two lines but all the other tenses in the stanza are past. They are, in fact, the recollection of visual impressions gained at one or another of the many meetings with the lady and they are expressed here in terms of the *Minnesang.* Yet the past tense is deceptive. As the poet says in the second stanza, the attitude is independent of time, for he is ever constant. His constancy, however, is to an image whose features are determined by a poet-persona, who up to now has not spoken. The lover-persona's eternal view of his lady is thus conditioned by the terminology of a genre whose function is praise of the lady but whose service in this instance she rejects. The sentiments of the second stanza are expressed from the point of view of the continuing "present," and again they recall an indefinite number of occasions on which the poet-persona failed, and reiterate the charge that he is not only unable to convince the lady but even to present the lover-persona's case. The lover-persona regards his love and the inability to present it as coterminous with time itself. For him there is no different form of time for the poet-persona, as there is in Bernard's poem. This concept of time continues in the third stanza. There is no beginning and no end to pleading and hence no reward. Only God would have set a point in time ("e miner tage") at which to reward service to Him and by doing so God would have conferred upon the lover-persona true eternity.

Bernard's method of treating time is very different. His conception is ultimately secular, since it is governed by the presentation of love by the poet-persona. Although the feeling of love in the heart of the lover-persona is eternal, it is the occasions on which the poet-persona celebrates that love which are the principal concern of Bernard. His lyric describes the preparation for the game of love, the actual game or presentation to the lady, the despair which follows the loss of the game, the slow recovery and the preparation for the next game. Love may be unchanging and eternal, but the activity of the poet-persona is cyclic and his object is to find rules for the game of love—or a way of winning which will change this cyclic activity to a presentation of love as unvarying as the love itself, in essence make the poet-persona and the lover-persona one.

No such reconciliation is envisaged by Heinrich von Morungen because there is no game to play. The time-continuum is the same for the lover-persona as for the poet-persona because a presentation of love never has and never will take place. The point of view of the lover-persona is that of a man without an audience who will forever conduct a monologue of love. It is clear that in the German poem the lady never hears the pleas and is therefore never part of the audience for the poem. No word is addressed to her, even in apostrophe, and the poem thus becomes a statement to a third person of the lover-persona's sorrow. We are, of course, speaking of the audience of the poet-persona, not that of Heinrich himself. Yet there is some doubt of the existence even of this "theoretical" audience. The poet-persona never addresses it directly. There is not the slightest indication of any reaction from it. The only possible clue is given in the first line of the stanza "ich han so vil gesprochen und gesungen," but this is not proof that the poet-persona has actually sung his sad tale, for he may have been singing to himself. If there was an audience we have no idea how it felt about his song, and certainly the lover-persona does not care. He seems to be framing his thoughts for himself, in the language of the *Minnesang* but without the *Minnesang* audience. The song, like the love, exists only in the "wan" of the lover-persona.

The situation is quite different in the poem of Bernard. As we saw earlier, the first three stanzas are the musings of the lover-persona on his situation and the failure of the poet-persona to affect the lady on his behalf, but the next two stanzas equally clearly indicate that the poet-persona presents the lover-persona's case to the lady herself ("on plus la prec, plus m'es dura"), and also to a neutral audience, for only to such an audience could he say "vengut er al partimen" and only of such an audience could he ask "qui vid anc mais penedensa/ faire denan lo pechat." The poet-persona tells of his presentation of the joys of love, that is, of his celebration of the power of love, independently of his attempt to persuade the lady to accept his service and in doing so he is presenting his case to an audience which he hopes will agree with him and perhaps even influence the lady. The audience is urged at least to place the blame for his lack of success where it belongs and not expect the poet-persona to do penance for sins he did not commit. The poet-persona is depicted as bound to his audience because he pleads the lover-persona's case to them. This audience has another function. It listens to the praise of the lady which constitutes the poet-persona's service, the service through which he hopes to influence the lady in favor of the lover-persona. This audience is vital to the poet-persona's cause, for without it there would be no service to the lady and hence, in the terms of this poem, no possibility of the lover-persona's success, as that success depends on the lady's being influenced by the praise of her which the audience hears. What that service is appears in the last stanza. Here the poet-persona expresses the lover-persona's feelings and at the same time performs the service to the lady for which he lives and for which he hopes to be rewarded.

The audience has no such function in Heinrich von Morungen's poem. Since his lady does not listen, he rejects the idea of an audience altogether—to him the lady is the only audience. He does not mention and does not appear to be interested in the service which he would perform for the lady. His poem consists entirely of a complaint and there is no element of praise nor indeed of any participation by the poet-persona in his capacity of mouthpiece of the lover-persona or as servant of the lady. In Heinrich's poem the concept of service has been abandoned.

The two poets thus present their two personae in very different fashion. Yet there is another element. Both poets mention some form of distraction. Bernard calls it "folia," Heinrich "wan." It is doubtful, however, whether the two poets are referring to the same thing. The poet-persona in the third stanza of Bernard's poem is referring to the stupidity of serving without reward, to service which is rejected and to folly which will be doubled if the service is not ended. This folly is far from being madness. The poet-persona is quite clear about his position and is merely stating the fact that his behavior in doing service is, by normal standards, mad. His continuation of it is a calculated risk, a hope that he can find the right way to play the game. In Heinrich's poem the concept of "wan" dominates the whole. It appears in the first line. In the two forms "wane" and "wan" it provides two of the six rhyming sounds used in the whole poem and there can be little doubt that Heinrich intends us to see the poem as an expression of the idea which has seized the lover. What kind of idea is this?

The lover-persona himself describes it as "tumb," naive, well-intentioned perhaps, but unsophisticated and likely to lead to trouble. This description cannot be applied to the service which the poet-persona provides for the lady but to the lover-persona's delusion that the lady can never love him. He thinks of her in the right way, his recollections of her are in the correct form, his constancy is impeccable, but she does not love him or recognize his existence. As we have already pointed out, the fault lies with the poet-persona, who is unable to convey the lover-persona's mental service. Surely, then, the "wan" must be the delusion that love is sufficient even though unexpressed. The lady cannot respond to a love of which she is unaware. In the mind of the lover-persona there arises another question about his "wan." Is the whole matter merely a product of his imagination?

This question needs serious discussion for, as we have seen, there is no actual audience for Heinrich's poem. He is presenting the matter to himself, arguing over his course of action. And his argument leads him to the conclusion that his love can get him nowhere with the lady, although it would with God, who can see into all hearts. Since there is no evidence that the lady knows of his love or that an audience can give him an opinion on it, it appears that his love exists only in his own mind. The fact is that there can be no love unless that love can be communicated and to communicate there is need of a poet-persona. To love is not enough. Love is not reciprocal in Bernard's poem either, but in that poem the stress is on communication. The love of the lover-persona may well become reciprocal if the effective means of communication can be found. Or, in other words, if the service is accepted. In Heinrich's poem, as in many poems of the German *Minnesang,* the lover-persona creates for himself a lady in the *canzon* image and pursues her in an endless internal monologue, while the Provençal poet pursues with equal tenacity the form of service, that is, of poetic communication, which will finally overcome her resistance.

The difference in intention of the two poets is well illustrated by their use of verbs. Bernard's verbs set forth a wide variety of situations: *vai, ven, vire, sai, pert, faih assire, es mantenguda, deuri' esser [blasmaire], nasquet, chastia, doblara, tem, pren, prec, vensa, partrai, es issida, balaya, es cochada, s'emen, formet, ai dezirada, agrada, formada, aten.* Forms of the verb "to be" (not used as compounds with other verbs) occur only nine times in fifty-nine lines. In the poem of Heinrich von Morungen there is no such variety. His verbs are of a neutral quality, passive in meaning if not in voice: *schiet, bin, mich underwinde, stan, betwungen, trage.* Such ideas are passive, even negative. The only positive action is indicated by the words *gesprochen und gesungen, sage, minne, 'ioldez herze] trage, leitet, gebot, gan, vinde, geloubet, gelungen, neme.* Yet every one of these active verbs is either negative directly *(nie gebot, niht geloubet, niht gelungen)* or by their context—"leitet" is opposed to "volge," "gan" is coupled with "ungesprochen," "vinde" with the fact that the thing found is useless, "neme" is an unfulfilled possibility. There is no action by the poet-persona, no action by the lady and even God's action remains potential. The verbs in Bernard's poem, on the other hand, whether they refer to the poet-persona, the lover-persona, to the lady, or even to time usually express positive action. The verbs reinforce the opinion that the Provençal lover-persona hopes and expects that the poet-persona will ultimately persuade the lady to yield, while in the German poem the lover-persona broods over why the poet-persona does not succeed.

An examination of the noun-adjective groups is equally revealing. Bernard uses such groups from a wide variety of fields. In the first three stanzas the noun groups are few and, except for four in the first two lines which place the poem in time, they belong to the standard emotional language of the *canzon*. But there is one important exception. *Joc,* as we have seen, sets the tone for the poet-persona's treatment of his theme. It is not a common way of describing the relations between lover and lady. Not one of these nouns is qualified by an adjective. In the following stanzas the nouns fall into fairly clearly defined word groups. In the first of these stanzas all nouns refer to singing, except one, *melhuramen.* In the second stanza the noun-group is emotion and particularly opposed emotions closely associated with the idea of sin and penance. The word *melhura* links the stanza with the preceding one by referring to a possible improvement in the lady's attitude, while *melhuramen* was used in connection with the unlikelihood of any such improvement in his own. The word *partimen* signals the event which will take place unless the conditions are met which are laid down in the following stanza and which constitute the improved situation. These conditions are the abandonment of the misuse of power and submission to pity, Christian behavior in fact, as the word *escritura* reminds us. Again there are no adjectives in all this description, except the colorless *breu [tems]* and *bona [aventura].* Christian images persist into the next stanza where the noun-group is composed of words contrasting soul and body, spirit and flesh, again scarcely modified by adjectives. In the last full stanza the noun-group becomes entirely sensuous, even tactile—*amors, cors, chara, mas*—and for the first time adjectives add force and color to the nouns—*bon'amors, cors be faitz, delgatz e plas, frescha car colorida.* These groups and the words with which they are associated present for the first time the vision of the beloved as seen through the eyes of the poet-persona. They are the words of the lover celebrating his mistress and her beauty, the words of formal panegyric, the language of the *canzon.*

The poet, by carefully selecting groups of nouns and by his non-use, or, in the last stanza, his use of adjectives has moved from an essentially pessimistic view of his hopes, expressed by the conventional phraseology of the *canzon,* through contrasting emotions and hopes for improvement to a glorification of his love. In doing so he has made skillful use of the imagery of the *canzon* genre, the Christian view of penitence overcoming turbulent emotions, the eternal spirit surviving the flesh to triumph over time and returning—to praise the lady's earthly beauty.

Heinrich's poem also begins with a stanza whose noun/adjective groups are those conventionalized by their use in the *Minnesang—trost, not, fraide, helfe, wünne, tot*—and images associated with such a context—*liljen, rosen, voller mane,* etc. The few adjectives which appear are those conventionally associated with such nouns. Heinrich seems to begin as Bernard does but there is one important difference. Whereas it is the lover-persona who uses these words directly in Bernard's poem, Heinrich obscures the issue by making his lover-persona first mention that all this is the result of "tumbem wane." The *Minnesang* images exist only within the fancy. They have been placed at one further remove from actuality than those of Bernard.

The second stanza abandons the noun/adjective groupings of the *Minnesang*. Only *steter muot* remains and this is contrasted with a large number of adjective/noun groups which convey instability—*wind, kleinem kinde, verholnen wan, torheit, wunder.* Nouns and adjectives almost disappear from the last stanza, which is summed up in the one word *müede. Wint* appears again, this time as a symbol of nothingness, *holdez herze* is associated with *trage,* meaning simply "love" and "e miner tage" means simply "before my time." The only two nouns remaining are *got,* forcibly contrasted with the object of the lover-persona's devotion, and *werde,* the poet's deserts, according to his own view, his *wan.* The scope of the noun/adjective groups is narrow and their use fades from *Minnesang* to instability to failure.

These two poems are separated by perhaps fifty years. Bernard's represents the full flower of the *canzon* before the genre had become the plaything of experimenters in esoteric expression. Heinrich's poem is typical of a great many of the "Lieder der höheren Minne." The two poems belong to the same genre and, as we have seen, the poets who wrote them were conscious of working in a particular poetic form, of the langue in which that form must be expressed and of the relationship between the lover-persona and the poet-persona. Yet they use the conventions of their genre in completely different ways. Bernard invites the audience for the poem to listen to the two personae debating on method. The audience of these two personae is the lady and at intervals she sits down to hear the poet-persona present the case for the lover-persona. This is the game, the *joc* (which poetically is a kind of *joc-parti*). Up to now the poet-persona has failed in his mission but whilever time lasts he can still try and the lover-persona's constancy ensures that the attempt will never end entirely. There are thus two audiences, that for Bernard's song, which appreciates the skill of the poet-persona and the flattery of the approach and is by inference invited to judge whether such a poet deserves to succeed, and the internal audience, the lady, upon whose approval of the poet-persona's skill depends the happiness of the lover-persona. The service to the lady is entirely the responsibility of the poet-persona and for the lover-persona to succeed the concept of service, and continuing service, must triumph over the lover-persona's despair. The poem is as much a hymn to the never-dying power of poetry as it is to the lady, and it stresses the unending struggle of the poet to convey his message. Heinrich's poem accepts the conception of winning a lady by poetic service. The poet is aware of the correct vocabulary and of the conventions of the situation, and he uses them; but the poet's audience is not expected to judge the power of his poetry to persuade the lady, only to accept his song as a complaint. As he himself says, his song is a "klage," an essentially negative statement of failure. The internal audience of the poet-persona is not the lady—we are told she does not listen—but the poet himself. He exists not in the objective world of Bernard's poem, where poetry is a form of communication, but in the subjective world of *wan,* where the qualities which would be ascribed to the lady by the poet-persona are imagined by the lover-persona but can never be expressed. Heinrich is thus using descriptions of the ideal lady developed by the *canzon* as service to the lady who constituted its "audience" to form in the mind of the lover-persona an image which he can love but which the poet-persona cannot address. Thus, from the lack of an internal audience, the German poem becomes a true "genre subjectif," an inward-turning contemplation of the lover-persona's emotions rather than an outward-turning, audience-directed form such as we find in the Provençal *canzon.* The idea of service exists in the German poem only as a theoretical possibility; in the Provençal poem it is still the heart of the matter. No one would pretend that these two poems sum up the relationship between the *canzon* and the *Minnelied,* but they do illustrate an important feature of that relationship. The *canzon* is an audience-directed genre where the persuasion of the lady is the end both proclaimed and actual. The *Minnelied* takes over the idea of service but stretches the concept to subjection and finally to the elimination of the recipient of that service. What was in the *canzon* a complaint of the poet-persona about the temporary wretchedness of the lover-persona becomes a permanent condition of the lover-persona in the *Minnelied.* The object of his service vanishes and he is left with the contemplation of an image which the genre itself had created and which he is afraid to destroy.

NOTE

1. The line "sit si mir niht geloubet daz ich sage" is usually interpreted as meaning "since she does not believe what I say of her." There is no reason why it should not mean "since she does not believe *that* I say. . . . . " There are numerous examples in Heinrich's own work (e.g., *Minnesangsfrühling* 122.10; 132.11 ff.) and elsewhere in Middle High German literature where "daz" simply introduces a noun clause. The meaning of "geloubet" is ambiguous. It may mean "believe" or "allow." I prefer the second meaning but, as so often in *Minnesang,* an interpretation should take account of both meanings and of the ambiguity itself.

5

The Medieval Pastourelle
As a Satirical Genre

THE INEVITABLE ASSOCIATION of the word "pastourelle" with scenes of country life and the innocent pleasures of the dance has not been without its effect on the criticism of the pastourelle as a literary genre. Even a critic such as Jeanroy,[1] who clearly recognizes the essentially aristocratic nature of the genre, is reluctant to give up altogether the idea of an origin in folk-poetry and the rustic dance. The present study proposes to deal only incidentally with the question of the origin of the pastourelle. Much more interesting for the study of the courtly lyric in general is the development of the pastourelle type as a poem stressing the social inequalities of contemporary society and making use of these inequalities to produce a type of realistic love poem which should act as a counterblast to the more idealistic poetry of the troubadours and Minnesinger. The satirical element develops gradually but its method is basically simple. It held up to ridicule the knight who was prepared to consort with the members of a despised class to gratify sensual desires and whose love passages are therefore as far from the spiritual ecstasies of the writers of the courtly lyric as it is possible to imagine. The study of the extant examples of the pastourelle which follows lays stress on those aspects which may be regarded as satirical. That there were other elements cannot be doubted but, as the following analysis will show, there can be little doubt of the satirical intent of the vast majority of the poems.

The development of the genre has been studied in some detail in several works, of which the most recent is that by Piguet.[2] Brinkmann, both in *Entstehungsgeschichte des Minnesangs* and in *Lateinische Liebesdichtung des*

Mittelalters, devotes some attention to the question of the origins of the pastourelle.[3] Neither of these two authors, however, attempts to study the social implications of the type nor makes any effort to reconcile it with the other types of courtly lyric by making a careful analysis of its essential, as opposed to its incidental, elements. Piguet classifies the variants of the genre, Brinkmann devotes himself largely to the literary form, with the result that his description of the pastourelle as essentially a dialogue between lovers, with origins which may be traced back to the "Invitatio Amicae,"[4] gives little clue to the nature of the pastourelle as we have it or of the reasons for the rise and cultivation of the type.

In the *vida* of Cercamon there is a statement that he composed pastourelles "in the ancient manner." Whatever this ancient manner may have been, it is certain that the majority of the pastourelles now extant had left it far behind. In Provençal the works of Giraut de Bornelh, Gavaudan, Gui d'Ussel, and especially Riquier are essentially formal pastoral poetry in which the characters, though designated as knight and peasant girl, are, in the best of the poems, the witty participants in a game of banter and verbal jousting which derives from classical models.[5] It is clear from the use of stylized phraseology and the well-developed convention of scene-setting, timing, and characterization that the genre had been developing along clearly defined lines for a considerable time before any of the extant Provençal pastourelles were written, and that the development had been conditioned by writers who had some knowledge of classical pastoral poetry, either first hand or from the anthologies used in the teaching of the *dictamen.*

In the literature of Northern France the genre is well represented and there is more variety than in the Provençal pastourelles. The writers of *langue d'oïl* are coarser and more direct and show the pastourelle at an earlier stage of its development.

In Germany, the pastourelle was either unknown to the predecessors of Walther von der Vogelweide or it was studiously ignored by them. The latter event is the more probable and is significant. The natural description in some of the poems of von Morungen cannot be regarded with certainty as showing the influence of the pastourelle but it is clear that Albrecht von Johannsdorf, in one poem, Walther, and Neidhart von Reuenthal knew of the genre and were influenced by it. Such poems as Walther's "Unter der Linden" reflect the attitudes of the pastourelle even though there is no male present, and the poem is one of recollection rather

than of narrative. It is not surprising that the pastourelle should be ignored by the exponents of the *höhere Minne* in its more serious German
manifestations when the question of its origin is considered.

The extant examples of the vernacular pastourelle are therefore of relatively late date and of a conventional type. Do they contain any evidence
as to their origin? Their conventional nature itself makes it possible to
give an affirmative answer.

It is first necessary to determine what the essential features of the pastourelle are. Dialogue, though common, is not essential.[6] The setting of
the country scene, often in spring, is normal, though it later becomes a
mere formula, expressed in the briefest possible way. The whole action
derives from the meeting between a man and a woman of lower birth,
and all the conventions spring from the relationship, social and personal,
between them. The man is often a knight, though the fact is rather implied than stated. The stress on the difference in rank and the significance
of this difference for the contemporary reader have often been ignored
by critics. The knight was, by all social canons, in a superior position in
any bargaining with the girl. The shadings where the knight is outwitted,
mocked, or even consoled for the loss of a courtly lover by the love of a
peasant are later refinements due to a change in attitude to courtly poetry
and to the growing influence of the classical conventions of pastoral poetry. There can be little doubt that the earlier form was more simple and
more brutal. It described the chance discovery of a peasant girl by a knight,
his immediate physical attraction to her and his attempts, often by no
means subtle, to win her over, either by presents or fair words, his success, sometimes achieved by the use of the most brutal measures, and his
final mocking departure. There are many variations on the theme, but
this is the essential core of the pastourelle and some examples of the simplest form are extant.[7] These examples are not to be taken as aberrations
from a type normally cultured and literary. It is rather from this type that
the later polished works of the Provençal troubadours developed. The neat
use of the situation by Marcabru, where the tables are turned on the knight,
is a far more sophisticated development, of which much of the force would
be lost if there were no comparison with the usual type of pastourelle.

What may be called the basic type of pastourelle is, therefore, a reflection of the true relationship between the classes during the period of the
courtly lyric, a relationship in which the peasant girl was regarded as fair
game by any wandering knight and one far removed from the spiritual

ecstacy and torment of the *Minnesang*. The pastourelle in its original form expressed the crude ideas of love so clearly set forth by Andreas Capellanus: [8] the true end of love was sensual enjoyment and there was no point about being too delicate in the obtaining of it if a peasant girl was the object of one's desires. We may be sure that it was these ideas, rather than those of the courts of love, which governed the conduct of the majority of the members of the knightly class and that the German poems of the *niedere Minne* are a reflection of the ideas of this majority.

The morality and conventions of the pastourelle may, therefore, be said to run counter in many ways to the ideals of courtly poetry, and the questions of its purpose and of its origin are closely related. Once its nature as a genre which mocked at or criticized sublimations of the troubadours was established, it was hardly likely to be cultivated in the circles devoted to courtly poetry. We have already seen how it was ignored by the earlier German Minnesingers. The Provençal poets show less disinclination, but it has already been pointed out that most of our extant examples in Provençal are of late date, when the attack on courtly poetry would be less sharply felt. Marcabru's satirical use of the genre would indicate that the pastourelle stood in his day outside the number of accepted types of courtly poetry. If the educated court circles did not cultivate the pastourelle, we are obliged to turn to the one other class capable of writing poetry, the clerics and those professional or amateur singers who were educated under their influence.

Here we are on surer ground. The rivalry between the knights and the clerics for the favors of noble ladies is well attested.[9] One of the principal counts urged against the knight was his unlettered crudity, his inability to make love in smooth and polished fashion. The subject is mentioned several times in the *Carmina Burana* and always with the implication that knights and laymen in general did not know how to make love in any but the crudest manner.[10] They are described as "pecus bestiale" and *Carmina Burana* 166 seems to be a satire on their ways. On the other hand, the skill of the priest in love-making, his use and often abuse of his privileged position as private chaplain to women of good family are commonplaces of medieval literature. Whatever one's views on Brinkmann's theory of the clerical origin of the courtly love lyric may be,[11] it is highly probable that the development of the lyric was largely conditiond by contributions from clerical writers. Only through them could the classical influences, which are so marked in the form of the developed lyric, and

the Ovidian attitude to love which is an essential feature of courtly poetry, have penetrated into the vernacular literatures.

Numerous poems are found in medieval Latin literature which have
one or more features in common with the pastourelle. The problem is to
determine when, if at all, these poems were written consciously as examples of a type, as they were in the Romance vernaculars and in German. The earliest examples of poems of a type which might develop into
the pastourelle are simple invitations to love. A well-known example is
the "Invitatio Amicae" already cited. In this poem many of the elements
mentioned as essential to the pastourelle are lacking: there is no mascu-
line triumph, the invitation is couched in general terms, and the scene is
not laid in the open air. Though such a poem may have developed into
a pastourelle, the connection is too vague to permit conclusions to be
drawn. It is equally difficult to see in the poems from Ivrea any direct
evidence of the rise of a genre identifiable with the pastourelle.[12] The influence of Ovid upon the style is clear, but this in itself proves nothing.
Almost all the essential features of the pastourelle are absent, for there is
little dialogue and the narrative and descriptive passages are of a length
altogether out of proportion to the limits of the pastourelle.

In the well-known dialogue in the *Cambridge Songs*,[13] we find a poem
whose resemblances to the pastourelle are very clear. Though the scene
is laid in a town, in or near the lodgings of a student or cleric, the girl's
first speech indicates that she is from the country and she lays great stress
on her preference for country life, mentioning the very features which
were to become the stock opening of the genre—the birds, especially the
nightingale, the joys of spring, and the beauty of the woods. The man's
method of procedure was also to become standardized in later poetry; he
offers presents, promises a gay and easy life, and flatters excessively. The
use of the word "soror" seems to imply that the woman may have been
a nun and that this poem is a descendant of the numerous cleric-nun epistles
and dialogues. It is certainly only a remote ancestor of the pastourelle.
The scene has not yet been fixed definitely in a rural setting, the character
of the girl has not been firmly established. The attempt to seduce the girl
and the appeal to purely sensual blandishments foreshadows the pastourelle, but there is no element of triumph, nor indeed, in the poem as we
have it, is there any statement that the man in fact does succeed in his
attempts at all. We may say with some certainty that the pastourelle as it
exists in the later vernacular literature developed from poems of this kind.

In the poems of Walther von Châtillon there are two poems which are much closer to the pastourelle form than anything so far mentioned.[14] The one numbered 17 in Strecker's edition shows great care in the setting of the conventional country scene—much more space is devoted to it than is the case in the later pastourelle—and to the way in which the girl is dressed. Both these characteristics are very marked in the first examples of the pastourelle which we possess in Provençal. In the Latin poem the girl is dressed in a fashion which can only be regarded as absurd in the country setting:

> Vestis erat Tyrio
> colorata murice
> opere plumario.

Such a description can be regarded only as ironical when the girl's probable social status is considered, for the rest of the poem surely precludes any idea of regarding her as a noblewoman or a nun. The development of this description of the dress of the *vilana* will be seen in the Provençal version of the genre. The character of the girl throughout Walther's poem remains in keeping with this description of her dress. She is very easily prevailed upon by the author of the poem to part with her virtue. The superiority of the man, both socially and intellectually, is stressed throughout the poem, which is clearly a mild satire on the naiveté of country girls and the amatory skill of the clerics.

In the poems of the *Carmina Burana* the satirical element is much more obvious.[15] In all the poems, the girl is very clearly a country wench very much at the mercy of the suave skill or the force of the man. She shows none of the wit and spirit of the *vilana* of the Provençal pastourelle. The status of the man is more doubtful. Since he is usually the narrator, only a few hints are given as to his social condition. It is usually made clear that he is visiting the country scene and does not live there. He may therefore be a knight or a cleric. Such expressions as "denudato gladio" in *Carmina Burana* 157 seem to indicate the knight rather than the cleric, but too much significance should not be attributed to what are after all little more than clichés.

In all the pastourelles in the *Carmina Burana* the winning of the girl by persuasion or force is the principal theme. Little interest attaches to the characters or to the dialogue form. The act of seduction is treated very lightly and with no scruples as to the ultimate fate of the girl. The lamentation of a betrayed girl over her fate is left to a completely different genre. In 72 the use of force to achieve the man's object is described in considerable detail, but the poem still succeeds in leaving the impression that the girl put up merely token resistance and that there is no necessity to grieve over her fate. In 158 the main concern of the girl is to conceal what has happened from her parents, not because of any sense of shame, but because she wishes to escape the punishment which will follow. We shall have occasion to refer to this theme again in connection with the Romance and German pastourelle. In all the pastourelles in the *Carmina Burana* it is impossible to escape the conclusion that the girl's feelings were regarded as of little account and that the scenes portrayed were to be regarded as the normal kind of love-making for the wandering knight. This impression is heightened by the satirical, even cynical, nature of 157. The references to the wolf and the lost sheep

> Forte lupus aderat
> quem fames expulerat
> > gutturis avari.
> ove rapta properat
> > cupiens saturari.

must inevitably have recalled the biblical imagery of the lost sheep for whom the shepherd deserts the rest of the flock. His reward here is hardly the reward of virtue. In the macaronic poem 185 there is little pretense at anything but a description of a brutal rape, again with a cynical double meaning:

> da hab ih mine herphe lan
> tympanum cum lyra.

It is clear that the poems of the *Carmina Burana* represent a more developed form of the poems which were found in the *Cambridge Songs* and in the works of Walther von Châtillon. The opening and the scene setting have become conventionalized, and the attitude of the author to the peasant girls of whom he is writing becomes increasingly scornful, and often, though not always, this scorn is extended by implication to the male participant. Instead of the unattainable lady, we see the eminently accessible peasant girl, who could not resist even if she would; instead of years of patience and unfulfilled longing, we have instant gratification and quick satiety. It is clear that any author who did not believe in the professions of the courtly lovers would find here a suitable vehicle to chastise them. It is equally clear that such a genre would hardly be acceptable to those who belonged to the circle of courtly poets. The methods of satirization could be varied. The obvious way, and the one most used at first, was to make the knight a brutal sensualist with no regard for the feelings of the peasant girl and, what is more important, with insufficient taste or delicacy to realize that this kind of love-making was as boorish as the persons with whom it was shared. As the satirical nature of the genre develops, it becomes possible to use other means. The knight can be mocked by a girl who has more sense than to yield to him; he can be beaten by enraged peasants, or retire before the threat of such a beating; he can be beaten in a game of wits with a girl who may be of inferior social status but who is infinitely more intelligent than her seducer. Finally, the social distinction is ignored and the pastourelle becomes a game of wits between two virtual equals.

These variants do not appear in any Latin poems with which I am acquainted. It was left to the poets in the vernacular languages to develop the pastourelle beyond the stage of mere mockery of general characteristics of a class. This development varied very considerably from one country to another. The writers of Northern France show the greatest variety in their treatment of the theme.[16] It is significant that of the approximately one hundred and fifty pastourelles which are extant, some fifty show the pastourelle in its crudest form, namely the seduction of the peasant girl by the knight, often with the use of force. It is in these poems that the circumstances correspond most closely to the actual social conditions of the time. They differ from the poems in the *Carmina Burana* mainly in the fact that they make perfectly clear that the man is a knight and that he is fully conscious that he is carrying out a piece of trickery of a simple peasant girl and is proud of the fact. The contrast between this behavior and that ascribed to the knight in the courtly lyric is so obvious that it must have been regarded at best as satirical, at worst as insulting. About a third of the poems show the girl rescued by the intervention of other peasants, although it is not always clear that the girl was willing to be rescued. The knight in many of these poems plays a role little better than that of a buffoon, and the satirical implications cannot be avoided. Of the rest, some are poems in the tradition of classical pastoral poetry, a type which will be discussed under the Provençal examples, some show the knight merely as a spectator of a rural love scene, where he may act as a peacemaker or may even take advantage of a lovers' quarrel to further his own interests with a country girl. One element deserves mention, the introduction of the mother to the pastourelle. At first she is merely mentioned, as in *Carmina Burana* 158, but in some of the French examples she plays a leading role in reproaching her daughter and being in her turn deceived.[17] This anticipation of the role of the old woman in the poems of Neidhardt von Reuental needs no explanation other than the perfectly natural one that the remark in dialogue that the girl was afraid of what her parent would say was expanded into the action in later examples.

The pastourelle of Northern France is less developed than that of Provence. The large proportion of the "basic" type has already been noted. The tendency to stress the rural, clownish element is strong and the influence of the classical pastoral is relatively small. This situation is reversed in the Provençal examples.[18] Here the rural setting has been reduced to a conventional formula and the status of the *vilana* has been immeasurably raised. In none of the poems is she a mere silly peasant girl and in most she is the equal or superior in wit of the knight who courts her. The earliest extant example, the poem of Marcabru "L'autrier, jost'una sebissa" is very obviously satirical in general conception and in detail. It is typical of the author that he should be one of the first of the Provençal poets to use the pastourelle as satire. The method he established was copied extensively by his successors. It consisted in making the knight talk to the peasant girl in the same words that he might have been expected to use to a lady of noble birth and to receive replies which are based on hard common sense, a full realization of the difference in rank between knight and peasant and the fact that these differences made any advantage for the girl out of the question.

> Dom, dis ela, qui que m sia,
> Ben conosc sen o folia
> La vostra parelharia,
> Senher, so dis la vilana,
> Lai on se tanh si s'estia
> Que tals la cuj'en bailia
> Tener, non'a mas l'ufana.

The technique of persuasion used by the knight follows very closely that recommended by Andreas Capellanus in addressing girls of inferior birth,[19] and it ends in ignominious failure. The peasant girl has developed into a woman of the world and the knight and his fine phrases are proved equally ineffective. It should be noted that the peasant girl here proves to be a much superior figure to the noble lady of the troubadours. She is honest and her feet are on the ground.

Not all the Provençal troubadours follow the example of Marcabru in using the pastourelle as satire. With the general decline of the courtly ideal of love poetry in the thirteenth century, the satire came to have less point. Its technique was, therefore, adapted to a different class of poetry. The *vilana* remains in the superior status in which she had been placed by Marcabru but not for the same purpose. She takes up her position in a type of pastoral poetry which has strong affinities with the classical pastoral poetry of Vergil and Theocritus.[20] The stock situations arise—the upbraiding of the dejected lover, the jealous rival, consolation from another source.[21] These pastourelles have developed an element originally satirical, namely the raising of the status of the *vilana,* and have made from it a nonsatirical pastoral genre.

It is instructive to follow the fortunes of the pastourelle in Germany. That the Latin forms already mentioned were known there can hardly be doubted, and yet there is little trace of such influence in the earlier Minnesingers. Even its most conventional element, the *Natureingang,* is found only in the most sketchy form in these writers. There are two important exceptions. Heinrich von Morungen has an adaptation of a pastourelle, which obviously recalls the natural setting but otherwise has little resemblance.[22] One poem of Albrecht von Johannsdorf on the other hand has the genuine flavor of the pastourelle.[23] The place of meeting is not stated, but we are told that the lady is "ane huote" and the direct plea for love is answered by the lady with much the same arguments as are used by her more lowly sisters in the pastourelles. She asks him whether he is mad in his clear-cut demand for her love but, as a result of his continued pleading, tells him that he shall not go unrewarded. The promise is ambiguous but the use of dialogue and the direct plea for love and its answer seem to reflect the influence of the pastourelle. Albrecht von Johannsdorf was an unusual writer, and his style is often more direct and more daring than that of the majority of his contemporaries. It is highly probable that he was here using the conventions of a genre which was regarded with disfavor by the writers of courtly lyric in order to emphasize his plea. The whole of his poetry is of a more deeply personal kind than that of the conventional *Minnesang,* and the use of a genre normally regarded as satirical, or at least unconventional, would be highly characteristic.

It is a commonplace of the criticism of the German *Minnesang* that its horizon was widened by Walther von der Vogelweide by the inclusion of elements of natural description and of social life outside the strata normally covered by the writers of the courtly lyric. It is no part of the object of this paper to attempt to trace the influence of the pastourelle in effecting this change except in so far as elements which we have regarded as basic in the pastourelle reappear in Walther's poems. The satirical elements remain strongly marked in the poem which shows most influence of the pastourelle, the well-known "Unter der linden."[24] This poem, so often spoken of as a gem of pure lyric verse, is, as more discerning critics have pointed out, a *tour de force* in which the highly skilled verbal treatment gives the impression of real emotion. The skill is in fact so great that it made respectable a genre hitherto regarded as beneath notice. By removing the coarser aspects of the pastourelle and concentrating attention on the more idyllic aspects, Walther was able to gain acceptance for the *niedere Minne,* which is in fact little more than another name for the pastourelle and its developments. It is important to notice that there is no folk element in this poetry. Its conventions are derived directly from the Latin forms of the pastourelle which had hitherto been ignored by the writers of the *Minnesang.* Sacrilegious as it may seem, the satirical element is still very clear in Walther's poem. The peasant girl is still the same foolish, empty-headed goose that she was in the poems of Walther von Châtillon. Her awareness of the social gulf between her and her lover is pitifully obvious and she goes out of her way to emphasize his condescension in stooping to a person of her type:

> Ich kam gegangen
> zuo der ouwe;
> do was min friedel komen e.
> da wart ich enfangen
> here frouwe
> das ich bin saelic iemer me.

The attitude toward love between the peasant and the noble is exactly as it was in the Latin and French examples of the pastourelle. The whole episode is a game, and we can be sure that the knight in Walther's poem will take himself off just as rapidly as his French counterparts when the amusement palls. The charm of this poem for the modern reader lies in its verbal skill and in changed conceptions of love. Basically, the poem is a pastourelle and preserves the satirical aspects of the genre so far as the peasant is concerned.

It is when we turn to the poems of Neidhardt von Reuenthal that that we observe the full effect of the satirical elements in the pastourelle on German poetry. Both satirical elements, the satire of the knight and the satire of the peasant, are fully developed. Not only is the subject of the encounter between the peasant girl and the knight treated but also those events which may be assumed to have occurred immediately before and after. In this regard, the introduction of the mother into the story, which we have already noted in a poem of Jocelin de Bruges, takes on a greater significance. Not only is she shown after the encounter but also appears in scenes where her daughter tries to gain her consent to visit the knight of her own free will. Finally the mother herself is shown as wishing to take part in the revelry. The introduction of rural scenes of festivity cannot obscure the fact that we have in the poems of Neidhardt the same basic situation that we had in the pastourelle, namely, the seduction of a country girl by a knight, and the same attitude of scorn for the peasants, this time made more vivid by the poet's descriptive ability and his willingness to introduce details of rustic life which would have been regarded as outside the pale of cultured writing by his predecessors. What Neidhardt did was to expand those elements in the pastourelle which had hitherto been regarded as incidental, and use them to reinforce his satire. Neither the knightly nor the peasant class comes out very well in his work, for if the peasant is a crude bumpkin without manners or breeding, the knight is a mere sensualist who roams the countryside in search of cheap conquests. The whole fabric of the *Minnesang* convention collapses under this attack which reflects contemporary society with deadly accuracy.

What may be called Neidhardt's development of the pastourelle appealed so exactly to the taste of subsequent writers that examples of the more regular type are hard to find. The most interesting example is the poem by Gottfried von Neifen, which might be called the pastourelle at the fountain. The theme approaches closely that of the "bergère et le loup" in as much as the knight is promised his reward by the servant girl for extricating her from an awkward situation. The element of social superiority is emphasized and the use made of the pastourelle convention in this poem is typical of a writer who wars perpetually with the sillier conventions of the *Minnesang*.

From this brief account of the pastourelle in Latin and in the three chief vernaculars in which it appears, it is possible to draw certain conclusions as to its development and influence. There is little point in speculating as to its ultimate origins or even on the extent of its classical heritage. What is important is that a poem originally a simple account of a man's attempt to win over a girl to his wishes develops in a definite direction in accordance with social ideas of the time which possibly reflect more accurately than those of courtly poetry the true state of mind of the knightly classes and their views on love. The earliest significant feature is the emphasis on the social superiority of the man and a corresponding tendency to represent the girl as a naive rustic who is to be regarded as legitimate prey for any wandering knight. It is at this point in the development of the genre that the satirical element may be said to appear. The obvious opportunity to represent the knight as insensitive, brutal, and lacking in any of the finesse which courtly circles associated with lovemaking in the higher sense was not ignored by those to whom the pretensions of the knights were offensive. It is thus that the male participants appear in the later Latin examples of the genre and in a large part of the poems from Northern France. These poems reveal the knightly class in a light very different from that in which its more cultured members loved to represent themselves, and it is highly likely that these earlier examples of what we may call the basic pastourelle form were written by clerics or under their influence. They are a definite counterblast to courtly poetry and are consequently ignored by its writers until it had ceased to be self-conscious and could afford to be amused at its own more extreme manifestations. The pastourelle remains a "fringe" genre until the later period of courtly poetry, when it is adopted and modified by writers who were seeking some relief from the more conventional types. In Provence the satirical element gradually disappears as the pastoral element becomes more dominant. It may be noted that even in the later examples the knight is never a noble or even very successful character. German *Minnesang* shows the position of the pastourelle most clearly. In the earlier period, two authors only show any influence of the pastourelle, but after it has been used by such a commanding figure as Walther von der Vogelweide, it develops rapidly in several directions in the hands of Neidhardt von Reuenthal and his successors. Its incidental features are exploited and give rise to new types. Wherever the influence of the pastourelle can be noted, it is possible to trace its original satirical undertone. The peasant girl is mocked for her naiveté, her mother for her shrewishness and cupidity, the knight for his sensuality, his materialism, and his crudity in love-making. The pastourelles are essentially the poems of the mocking bystander, the worldly cynic—in other words, the poems of the wandering cleric or his disciples. Later modification may blunt the barb of the satire but the essentially sophisticated, cynical nature of the genre remains.

NOTES

1. A. Jeanroy, *Les origines de la poésie lyrique en France au moyen âge* (Paris: Champion, 1925), p. 19.

2. E. Piguet, *L'évolution de la pastourelle du XIIe siècle à nos jours* (Basel: Heibing und Lichterhahn, 1927).

3. H. Brinkmann, *Die Entstehungsgeschichte des Minnesangs* (Halle: Niemeyer, 1925), p. 65; Brinkmann, *Geschichte der lateinischen Liebesdichtung im Mittelalter* (Halle: Niemeyer, 1925), pp. 77ff.

4. Brinkmann, *Liebesdichtung*, pp. 79ff.

5. The Provençal pastourelles are collected in J. Audiau, *La pastourelle dans la poèsie occitane* (Paris: Boccard, 1923).

6. It is invariably found in the Provençal examples, but in the Latin poems the girl often does not speak.

7. In French they are listed by E. Faral, "La pastourelle," *Romania* (1923), 49:204ff.

8. Andreas Capellanus, *De amore libri tres,* Trojel ed. (Copenhagen, 1892), p. 236.

9. Brinkmann, *Entstehungsgeschichte,* gives several examples on pp. 6ff.

10. The best-known example is the poem "Phyllis and Flora" (*Carmina Burana* 92), but the subject is also mentioned in 138, 142, 168.

11. As set forth in the two works already mentioned.

12. Published in *ZfdA* (1869), 14:245ff.

13. *The Cambridge Songs*, Karl Breul, ed. (Cambridge: University Press, 1915), no. 35.

14. *Die Gedichte Walthers von Châtillon,* Karl Strecker, ed. (Berlin: Weidmannsche Buchhandlung, 1925).

15. *Carmina Burana,* Hilka and Schumann, eds. (Heidelberg: Carl Winter, 1931–1970), nos. 72, 157, 158, 184, 185.

16. E. Faral, "La pastourelle," lists the various types. They may also be found in Piguet, *L'évolution de la pastourelle.*

17. For example, Jocelin de Bruges. A. Scheler, *Trouvères belges du XIIe au XIVe siècle* (Brussels: Mathieu Closson, 1876), pp. 154ff.

18. Audiau, *La pastourelle dans la poésie occitane*, pp. 3ff.

19. Particularly in the French verse adaptation by Drouart La Vache (Paris: Champion, 1926), pp. 67ff.

20. It has already been pointed out by several critics that the twenty-seventh idyll of Theocritus bears a very strong resemblance to the pastourelle. The elements of brutality and of social inequality are lacking, but the dialogue form and the narrative are virtually identical.

21. Audiau, pp. 29ff. (Gui d'Ussel); Audiau, pp. 39ff. (Gui d'Ussel); Audiau, pp. 10ff. (Giraut de Bornelh).

22. *Des Minnesangs Frühling*, Lachmann, Haupt, and Vogt, eds. (Leipzig: Hirzel, 1911), 139, 14–140, 9.

23. *Minnesangs Frühling*, 93, 12–94, 114.

24. Walther von der Vogelweide, Wilmanns, ed. (Halle: Verlag des Waisenhauses, 1883), p. 202.

6

The Politics of a Poet:
The Archipoeta As Revealed
by His Imagery

MOST OF THE POETS of the High Middle Ages are anonymous in the sense that of their lives we know nothing. But of the Archipoeta we know less than nothing, for even his name is a mocking travesty of a title, probably a play on that of his patron, the Archicancellarius, Reinald von Dassel, Archbishop of Cologne. Only ten poems can be ascribed with any certainty to a poet whose sense of form and whose verbal agility equal or exceed those of any medieval poet. These ten short poems appear to be intensely personal and to reflect the idiosyncrasies of their author and his reactions to the events and personages of his time. There is no independent evidence about this remarkable man, no documents exist to which he was a witness; there are no records of his relations with other poets or with his patrons. He is thus to an even greater degree than most contemporary writers in Latin or the vernacular a *persona*, a poet who appears only in his works. Since many of these works present the poet in the first person, it is a natural assumption that the statements made there are those of the poet himself, that he is telling of his own feelings and views and using the vehicle of his verse to make known to the world his personal reactions to patrons, to emperors, to courtiers, and to bishops.

Such a view might be described as a pathetic fallacy, although not in the way in which the expression is usually used. The ideas he expresses are, of course, his own but they are conditioned by the genre in which he writes and the effects which he wishes to produce. When a poet undertakes to write an epic, he knows that he must take an elevated subject and treat it in a noble style, that he must assume the *persona* of an objective narrator who nevertheless is aware of the deep significance of the events he records and who therefore tells them with the gravity and dignity they deserve. He sets himself to deal with the subject in a form which his readers will recognize as suitable for the subject. If he does not do this, he runs a grave risk of being misunderstood. His epic may be regarded as a mock epic, as a parody, as a satire, even as a piece of light verse. In other words, the poet must subordinate his personality to the demands of the genre in which he writes and he may assume only the *persona* which is appropriate to that genre.

The Archipoeta wrote only short poems. At first sight they may appear to suffer from a certain monotony of subject, for all contain an element of complaint. Usually it is a lament on the poet's poverty which leads to a plea for more aid and more frequent aid from his patron, Reinald von Dassel. There is no need to imagine that the poet did not need the support he asked for. He says himself that he was of a knightly family and that he was not prepared to perform any of the more menial jobs that might support him. But no poet was likely to secure the support of a prince of the church merely by writing versified complaint, and we must look for other explanations of the poet's apparent ability to move in the highest circles of the empire and address with freedom, almost with impertinence, the most important subject in the land.

The *persona* of the poverty-stricken artist is only one of several which the poet assumes. Its frequency is due to the fact that the great majority of his poems are written from the point of view of the humble commentator—or, more accurately, from the pose of the humble commentator. Since they are short poems of social comment, the author cannot assume the stance of the epic narrator nor the personal involvement of the elegist. He has chosen the "I" form to comment on contemporary events and must therefore assume one of two stances. He can present himself as superior to the events he describes and on which he comments, or he can speak as a seer, as one whose judgment of events was to be valued because of superior knowledge or even divine inspiration. There was plenty of precedent for such a stance—the political odes of Horace and the satires of Juvenal come to mind—but such an attitude would have committed the Archipoeta to a position which would have deprived him of all possibility of the use of irony, and it would have been inconsistent with his constant reiteration of his utter dependence on his patron. He prefers rather to portray himself as *poeta humilis*. Such an attitude offered several advantages. The poet could ask in the most brazen fashion for material assistance, since he was "poeta humilis et pauper." But, perhaps more important, it deprived his often waspish comments of any sting. Since he proclaimed himself as a poor poet who was singing for his supper, there was no need for his betters to take seriously the almost insolent comments which he made about them, particularly since such comments were often veiled by the stylistic methods which he employed.

In adopting his pose of "poeta humilis," the Archipoeta was careful to use the appropriate imagery. He describes himself in terms such as:

> sic et ego dignus morte
> prave vivens et distorte[1]
> (II.39f.)

or

> asperitas brume necat horriferumque gelu me
> continuam tussim pacior, tamquam tisicus sim.
> (III.17)

or

> Iam febre vexatus nimioque dolore gravatus
> (VI.8)

or

> Nudus et incultus cunctis appareo stultus;
> pro vili panno sum vilis parque trutanno.
> nec me nudavit ludus neque fur spoliavit:
> pro solo victu sic sum spoliatus amictu,
> pro victu vestes consumpsi, dii mihi testes.
> (VI.18ff.)

The poet is sick, poor, hungry, and ill-clothed. He is the very prototype of the neglected artist, but still he struggles on to write poetry. The stance of sickness, weakness, and humility gives him the opportunity to poke fun at the great ones of the earth by comparing his own sad state to that of wealth and power. The apostrophe of his audience is often made through images and descriptive epithets which contrast forcibly with the poet's description of himself:

> Lingua balbus, hebes ingenio
> viris doctis sermonem facio.
>
> (I.1f.)

or

> stultus ego qui penes te
> nummis equis victu veste
> dies omnes duxi feste
> nunc insanus plus Oreste,
> male vivens et moleste . . .

compared with

> Pacis auctor, ultor litis
> esto vati tuo mitis . . .
>
> (II.78ff.)

The Archipoeta spends a whole poem in extravagant praise of Reinald von Dassel, showering upon him every figure from the rhetorical text-books—"Ulixe facundior Tulliane loqueris/columba simplicior . . . serpente callidior . . . Alexandro forcior . . . David mansuetior . . . Martinoque largior"—only to conclude with a sharp contrast with his own position:

> Dum sanctorum omnium   colitur celebritas
> singuli colentium   gerunt vestes inclitas,
> archicancellarium   vatis pulsat nuditas.
> Poeta composuit   racionem rithmicam
> satyrus imposuit   melodiam musicam
> unde bene meruit   mantellum et tunicam.
>
> (II.x,xi)

The great/small topos was never better illustrated—the Archbishop and his companions in glittering robes, the poet in rags. But it is this tattered poet who is telling us of these great ones, and without him their fame would be nothing. It is he who provides them with the appropriate descriptive epithets and with their one claim to fame among posterity. The question of who is in fact *humilis* and who is *magnus* is thus left to the audience.

The poet helps the audience by the assumption of other stances. For, as a poet, he is also a seer. The appropriate imagery for the poet as prophet and seer is well enough illustrated by Horace:

> Quem virum aut heroa lyra vel acri
> tibia sumis celebrare, Clio?

or in the great political odes such as III.2, III.3, IV.4, and IV.5. Even more appropriate for the Archipoeta is the calm statement of superiority made by Horace in Odes III.1 "Odi profanum vulgus et arceo," which sets him above the common herd and makes his pronouncements infinitely more significant to those of a mere mortal. When the Archipoeta adopts the stance of a poet-seer, he does not use this kind of imagery. He refuses to set himself apart from the herd but rather claims that his powers, such as they are, are mere accidentals of his personality, traits which will be intensified by the liberal provision of good wine. The result is an ironical opposition of the statements of the Archipoeta on matters of grave concern—public policy, charity, the prowess of the emperor, and even the ultimate destiny of a man's soul—which are delivered in all seriousness and often with an air of authority, and the *persona* of the poet who is allegedly making these pronouncements: a man beset by poverty, ragged, sick, hungry, and apparently unable to write unless reinforced by wine and the generosity of his patron. The only justification for the Archipoeta's existence is his ability to exercise the poet's craft in the service of Reinald von Dassel, and over and over again he emphasizes that without him the world would little note nor long remember what the Archbishop of Cologne did or even who he was. Here lies his ultimate strength, the reason why he is able to talk to his patron as he does, to beg without shame, and even to be insolent if the spirit moves him, for without his poetic gift and the fame he spreads, Reinald would be a cypher.

The opposition between the various *personae* assumed by the Archipoeta and the ironic interplay between them is best seen in the two poems most intimately connected with political matters, numbers IV and IX in

Krefeld's edition.[2] Both are concerned with the successes enjoyed by Friedrich Barbarossa in his campaigns in Italy and each, from a different point of view, examines the problems of a man who, whether he likes it or not, finds himself in the position of a poet-laureate. There can be no doubt that in each of these two poems an actual historical situation is being described—Reinald von Dessel did ask his court poet to celebrate the deeds of Friedrich Barbarossa in epic fashion, and the Archipoeta was talking about actual achievements of the Emperor in his later poem. The poem which disclaims any ability to write an epic on the imperial achievement has thirty-three strophes (if the gap at strophe xxi is only two lines long), the poem on the *gesta Friderici* has thirty-four. The similarity—perhaps even identity—of length is surely not accidental. For what he had refused to do when requested by the Archbishop, he performs spontaneously—in his own fashion. Thus both poems are a testimony to his personal attitudes. One demonstrates his independence, his determination to write only when he wants and what he wants; the second demonstrates that if he wishes to do so he can celebrate the Emperor's achievements at least as well as an epic poet-laureate, even if not in a formal epic poem.

The two poems are a personal declaration of independence but they are not necessarily conveyed in a true first person. In reading them we must distinguish between various types of utterance. The poet may actually speak as himself. This kind of declaration is much rarer than might appear at first sight. He may adopt various *personae*, all of them variations on *poeta*, through whom he expresses views which may coincide with his own, which purport to be his own, but which may be and frequently are poses to make a point with which, as a person, he does not agree. To all this should be added another and far more subtle method of indicating the views of the poet, not of the *persona*. The imagery and rhetorical techniques employed by the poet may be in obvious opposition to those demanded by the theme he is pursuing and thus may show more clearly than a personal statement could reveal what the poet really thought. A detailed examination of the poems will demonstrate the interaction of the two methods.

What we may call the "epic disclaimer" presents an opposition between the Archbishop, apostrophized in each of the first seven strophes of poem IV, and a poetical statement by a person who claims to be his humble, indeed abject slave, who yet happens to write poetry. Reinald is carefully described as a man of a clear judgment ("discrete mentis") but also as a person who would never go beyond the bounds of a wise man. Such a description means that he is capable of being convinced by logical argument ("probare potero multis argumentis"). In fact, however, no such logical arguments are produced. The Archipoeta prefers to pervert the whole situation and make it farcical. He quickly adopts the stance of the "poeta servus," ready for anything and prepared to go through fire and water ("ibo, si preceperis, eciam trans freta") for his master—but not prepared to do what he is asked. His excuse is that he is expected to do in a week what Virgil or Homer could not have done in five years. The implications are that the deeds of Friedrich would take these poets five years or more to write—if they undertook them. Is Friedrich then the equivalent of Aeneas and Achilles? The Archbishop must think that he is, if he wants his tame poet to write an epic about his achievements.

The Archipoeta does not linger on this thought, for he has something else in mind. If a wretched poet is to write on such a magnificent subject, he must surely be inspired—and how is he to come by the inspiration which will make him the equivalent of Vergil and Lucan? Even the little poetic fire and power of prophecy he possesses deserts him on occasion:

> prophecie spiritus fugit ab Helya,
> Helyseum deserit saepe prophecia,
> nec me semper sequitur mea poetria.
> (IV.vii)

The words are a sharp rebuke to the Archbishop—poetical inspiration cannot be turned on to order—made by the poet in his own person, a defense, one may say, of the poet against the Philistine, but made in the *persona* of the poet-slave which he has adopted. This assertion of independence is not allowed to become offensive. The Archipoeta quickly reverts to his favorite protective covering, that of the poet who cannot work in solitude or in a state of abstinence from food and wine. By adopting this stance he can evade the request to write a Barbarossa epic by demonstrating his unsuitability rather than his inability. Epic poetry belongs to the elevated style. It is a lofty genre, not to be attempted by flighty poets but by those who take their craft seriously. Such are the poets who are described in strophes x and xi. But the Archipoeta does not belong to this group. He does not abstain. His poetry is directly dependent on the quality and quantity of the wine he consumes:

> Tales versus facio quale vinum bibo
> (IV.xiv)

and on the provision of food:

> nihil possum facere nisi sumpto cibo . . .
> (IV.xiv)

The situation is summed up in these lines:

> scribere non valeo pauper et mendicus
> que gessit in Latio Cesar Friedericus. . .
> (IV.xvi)

This is not a mere request for financial support. It is a statement that great themes cannot be attempted by poor poets, a contrast made perfectly clear:

> unde sepe lugeo quando vos ridetis
> (IV.xvii)

The poet then explains at considerable length why action should be taken to bring the poet of Barbarossa up to the standard required for an epic poet. He is too noble to beg—or to dig—and it would not be consistent with the dignity of Reinald to do other than support him, still less would it be right for a German as opposed to an Italian prelate. Suddenly the poem ceases to be a matter of whether the Archipoeta should write about the deeds of Barbarossa. The question to be discussed is the relation between poet and patron. After demonstrating that the poet whom Reinald von Dassel has been supporting, or failing to support, is incapable of handling an epic theme, because such a theme demands a man not dependent on occasional gifts of food and wine, the Archipoeta assumes the mantle of the seer (which he had previously discarded) and talks of the need for true patronage. Not only is generosity characteristic of any true Christian, it is also politically wise:

> In regni negociis potens et peritus
> a regni negocio nomen est sortitus;
> precepti dominici memor, non oblitus
> tribuit hilariter, non velud invitus.
>
> (IV.xxvii)

A clear connection is made between Reinald's position as chief minister and the necessity to give generously. The Archbishop owes his high position to political skill, but it is only the poet who can advertise his worthiness for that position.

To view this poem as a somewhat crude effort by the Archipoeta to obtain material benefits by saying that he cannot write an epic poem about the deeds of Barbarossa unless he is well paid for it is an oversimplification. The poet rarely speaks in his own person. He is stating that a "poeta humilis" cannot be expected to write the "sermo sublimior." If Reinald wishes his poet to speak of grave matters of state, then he must behave like a generous lord. His style must be appropriate to the epic style. The poet, while adopting for most of the poem the *persona* of the "poeta servus," speaks in the tone of the "poeta vates" and at times comes very close to lecturing his patron on his duties. Thus there is throughout the ironical contrast between the *persona* of the poverty-stricken, dependent, almost servile poet-laureate and the independent, superior, and quite unrepentant poet who is well aware of his value to his patron.

It is the second *persona* who is in evidence in the poem on the deeds of Friedrich Barbarossa, number IX in Krefeld's edition. Although he does not fail to mention his patron, the Archbishop, the poem is not written from the stance of the "poeta humilis." Here the poet assumes the stance of *vates* and goes even further. He purports to be able to determine what is good for the world and to see the course of history. From the very beginning there is assumed identification between the panegyrist of Barbarossa and the poet-prophet who surveys the world and lays down the principles of imperial rule.

The poem is dominated by one image derived from a statement of Jesus himself: Render unto Caesar the things which are Caesar's. Cities and magnates who do so are praised, those who fail to do so are damned. But to this statement there is a corollary: Render to God the things which are God's. There is no explicit opposition between these two commandments, but the tension between them is implicit throughout the poem, as it was in contemporary politics, and it is indicated by a different and perhaps more subtle variation of the poetical stance.

The poem opens with what is apparently the standard apostrophe of the ruler. The poet does not appear as an individual *persona* but (in the second strophe) as a spokesman for Barbarossa's loyal subjects. It is not until strophe vii that a verb appears in the first person singular, unless we count "me pudet" in strophe iv. The poet has deliberately avoided the impression of offering a personal opinion. He is creating the illusion of being the spokesman of many and of setting down in verse what everyone in the empire believes. If he had actually done this, the poem would hardly be worth a comment. The imagery appropriate to imperial panegyric had developed, so far as the Christian West was concerned, at the court of Charlemagne, and subsequent poets had improved on it. There is ample evidence that Barbarossa himself was well aware of the importance of such poetic propaganda.[3] It would therefore seem reasonable that a poem in praise of the Emperor's deeds in Italy, whether written in response to a direct request or not, would employ the imagery appropriate to such an occasion, which would be familiar to the Emperor and to his chief advisor, Reinald von Dassel. But in fact the appropriate imagery is not used. Quite the contrary. In the first three strophes the poet uses only those images which would be appropriate to God, not to his secular regent. For convenience we may set side by side the attributes of Barbarossa, as the poem gives them, and the biblical passages with which they are connected.

mundi domine	Verbo Domini caeli firmati sunt; et spiritu oris eius omnis virtus eorum
	(Ps. 36.6)
Cesar noster	Pater noster qui est in celis, sanctificetur nomen tuum
	(Matt. 6.9)
ave	Ave, Rabbi, et osculatus est eum. [The reference is to Judas]
	(Matt. 26.49)
	Ave Maria, gratia plena; Dominus tecum benedicta tu in mulieribus
	(Luke 1.28)

cuius iugum est suave	Tollite iugum meum super vos, et discite a me quia mitis sum et humilis corde; et invenietis quietum animabus vestris. Iugum enim meum suave est et onus meum leve.
	(Matt. 11.29, 30)
Quisquis contra calcitrat	Saule, Saule quid me persequeris? Qui dixit: Quis es, Domine? Et ille: Ego sum Jesus quem tu persequeris; durum est tibi contra stimulum calcitrare.
	(Acts 9.4, 5)
obstinati cordis est et cervicis prave	Caelum mihi sedes est, terra autem scabellum pedum meorum; quam domum aedificabitis mihi? dicit Dominus; aut quis locus requietionis meae est? Nonne manus mea fecit haec omnia? Dura cervice et incircumcisis cordibus et auribus vos semper Spiritui Sancto resistitis; sicut patres vestri, ita et vos.
	(Acts 7.49–51)
Princeps terrae principum	Et post regnum eorum, cum creverint iniquitates, consurget rex impudens facie, intelligens propositiones. Et roborabitur fortitudo eius; et non in viribus suis; et supra quam credi potest, universa vastabit, et prosperabitur, et faciet. Et interficiet robustos et populum sanctorum. Secundum voluntatem suam et dirigetur dolus in manu eius; et cor suum magnificabit et in copia rerum omnium occidet plurimos; et contra principem principum consurget, et sine manu conteretur.
	(Dan. 8.23–25)
	Haec dicit Dominus Deus: Ecco ego suscitabo omnes amatores tuos contra te, de quibus satiata est anima tua, et congregabo eos adversum te in circuitu: Filios Babylonis et universos Chaldaeos, nobiles, tyrannosque et principes, omnes filios Assyriorum, iuvenes

forma egregia duces et magistratus universos,
principes principum . . .

(Ezech. 23.22, 23)

cuius tuba titu-   Et septem angeli qui habebant septem tubas,
bant arces inimice   praeparaverunt se ut tuba canerent
tibi

(Rev. 8.6)

colla subdimus   Porro gens quae subiecerit cervicem suam sub
iugo regis Babylonis et servierit ei, dimittam
eam in terra sua, dicit Dominus, et colet eam
et habitabit in ea. Et ad Sedeciam, regem Juda,
locutus sum secundum omnia verba haec, di-
cens: Subiicite colla vestra sub iugo regis Babylonis, et servite ei, et populo eius et vivetis.

(Jer. 27.11, 12)

tibi colla subdi-   Domine, Dominus noster, quam admirabile est
mus tygres et   nomen tuum in universa terra!
formice et cum   Omnia subiecisti sub pedibus eius oves et
cedris Libani   boves universas insuper et pecora campi, Volu-
vepres et mirice   cres caeli et pisces maris qui perambulant semitas maris.

(Ps. 8.2, 8, 9)

Nemo prudens   Quare fremuerunt gentes, et populi meditati
ambigit te per dei   sunt inania? Astiterunt reges terrae, et prin-
nutum super   cipes convenerunt in unum adversus Dom-
reges alios regem   inum, et adversus Christum eius.
constitutum   Dirumpamus vincula eorum et proiciamus a
nobis iugum ipsorum. Qui habitat in caelis ir-
ridebit eos et Dominus subsannabit eos. Tunc
loquetur ad eos in ira sua, et in furore suo
conturbabit eos. Ego autem constitutus sum
rex ab eo super Sion, montem sanctum eius
praedicans praeceptum eius. Dominus dixit ad
me: Filius meus es tu; ego hodie genui te.

(Ps. 2.1–7)

Ego constitui te hodie super gentes et super
regna ut evellas et destruas et disperdas et dis-
sipes et aedifices et plantes.

(Jer. 1.10)

> Subiecti igitur estote omni humanae creaturae
> propter Deum, sive regi quasi praecellenti, sive
> ducibus, tamquam ab eo missis ad vindictam
> malefactorum, laudem vero bonorum; quia sic
> est voluntas Dei ut benefacientes obmutescere
> faciatis imprudentium hominum ignoran-
> tiam . . .
>
> (1 Pet. 2.13–15)

The first general point to be noted about all the images used of Barbarossa in the first three strophes is that they are directly connected with
God in their biblical context. The biblical passages show God as the ruler
of the universe, and in a few cases there is clear reference to what happens to those who try to usurp his power, as may be seen in the quoted
passages from Daniel and Ezechiel. Here, as frequently in the "Confession,"[4] the context surrounding a biblical reference often gives more of
the poet's true opinion than the actual words which appear in the poem.
The use of images and attributes which are used in Holy Writ of God
himself must inevitably have caused the audience to think that the Archipoeta was concerned to show his Emperor as the only power on earth,
a union of spiritual and temporal function. There is good evidence that
Barbarossa himself was much of that opinion. He created two antipopes,
Victor IV and Pascal III, and caused the latter to canonize his predecessor, Charlemagne, the earliest of those who had sought the union of spiritual and temporal powers. There can be little doubt that Barbarossa would
be gratified to be described in divine imagery. But on closer examination
the use of such imagery is not quite so flattering as might appear.

We have already noted that in the passages in which several of the images appear, there are references to upstart kings whose aspirations were
crushed. Other modifications are less obvious. The Archipoeta says: "cuius
bonis omnibus iugum est suave." The passage from Matthew already
quoted occurs in the following context: "Venite ad me omnes qui labor-
atis et onerati estis et ego reficiam vos." The whole point of the biblical
passages is the relief given by Jesus to all those who come to Him, particularly the weak and oppressed, whereas Barbarossa's yoke is light "for
all good men." Presumably the Emperor is the judge of who is good and
who is not and the greater part of the poem seems to indicate that the

imperial yoke was by no means light on those who did not conform to his plans. Nor is the allusion to Acts 9.5 more encouraging. Anyone who thinks that the yoke is too hard is warned that it is difficult to kick against the pricks. The text shows that Paul is resisting the commands of God and that he cannot be allowed to do so for very long. Does Barbarossa think that resistance to him is tantamount to resistance to God? Apparently so, for in the very next strophe we are reminded of the fate of those who resist, and the biblical passages are concerned with the ruthless suppression of disobedience to the supreme ruler. The selection of images in these strophes presents Barbarossa as the supreme arbiter of all matters both temporal and spiritual, as something very close to God himself. It is clearly the duty of each member of the audience to decide for himself whether the images presented here are to be taken seriously. There can be little doubt that Barbarossa himself was prepared to accept them at face value because he believed he merited such attributes. We must examine the rest of the poem to find out whether he was right.

The third strophe gives a hint about the method of intrepretation we should follow. (The poet is still speaking in the *persona* of the all-wise seer.)

> Nemo prudens ambigit te per dei nutum
> super reges alios regem constitutum
> et in dei populo digne consecutum
> tam vindicte gladium quam tutele scutum.
>   (IX.iii)

The important word here is "prudens." Does it mean "wise" in the sense of "sensible," "aware of the arguments," wise in the sense of the man who builds his foundation on a rock[5]—such an interpretation would be complimentary to Barbarossa—or does it perhaps mean "anyone who knows what is good for him." Certainly the latter interpretation would be true for the Archipoeta, for he is in many respects a court poet, but it would also be true of the generality of the empire, if they wish to avoid the fate of Milan. Both power and protection are in the hands of the Emperor. Indeed it would appear that the spiritual arm, the papacy, is totally without influence.

Another hint is given in the next strophe:

> Unde diu cogitans quod non esset tutum
> Cesari non reddere censum vel tributum.
>
> (IX.iv)

The reference is clear: "Licet censum dare Caesari an non? Cognita autem Jesus enquitia eorum ait: Quid me tentatis, hypocritae? Ostendite mihi numisma census. At obtulerunt ei denarium. Et ait illis Jesus: Cuius est imago haec et superscriptio? Dicunt ei: Caesaris. Tunc ait illis: Reddite ergo quae sunt Caesaris Caesari et quae sunt Dei, Deo." But the poem seems to call for more than the biblical reference. The distinction between what is due to God and what is due to Caesar has been deliberately blurred by the imagery. And furthermore, a person who does not recognize the elevation of the Emperor's status is not only not "prudens"—he is not safe. What contribution is the Archipoeta to make? Since it is apparently dangerous not to pay "censum et tributum" to Caesar, he, poorer than the widow in the biblical story, will give his mite. And what is this mite? It is the use of his talent to praise Barbarossa. The poem written in praise of Barbarossa thus proves to be something which is performed because it is not safe to do anything else. Yet if we read the passage in the Bible, his contribution is greater than that of anyone else: "Et sedens Jesus contra gazophylacium, aspiciebat quomodo turba iactaret aes in gazophylacium et multi divites iactabant multa. Cum venisset autem vidua una, misit duo minuta, quod est quadrans. Et convocans discipulos suos ait illis: Amen dico vobis quoniam vidua haec pauper plus omnibus misit, qui miserunt in gazophylacium."[6] Thus in the first three strophes we have imagery which implies that the Emperor is laying claim to the divine as well as the secular role, and a statement by his panegyrist that he is functioning as an official poet because he must pay his tribute to Caesar.

What follows is an *amplificatio* of the theme of the poet rendering service to his master—the picture of *potestas larga*, of the Emperor using his power for the benefit of his people. It is the function of a professional poet and of a formal panegyrist to call attention to these virtues—especially if he needs the money ("nos poetae pauperes"). The poet affirms strongly that he is writing from the Christian, not the classical point of view, as a son of the church, not a follower of Cicero or the Muses. It is from the Christian point of view that he will write of a man who has restored the image of Rome by undertaking its secular burdens. But the poet's statement actually goes further, for it plays on several possible meanings:

> Christi sensus imbuat mentem Christianam
> ut de christo domini digna laude canam,
> qui potenter sustinens sarcinam mundanam
> relevat in pristinum gradum rem Romanam.
>
> (IX.viii)

The poet's task is to sing the praises of the Lord's anointed—anything from Saul to Barbarossa—but the presence of the word "christo" inevitably recalls "Christ," particularly since it is associated with "Christi" in the first line. The implication that Christ has inspired the poet to sing of things worthy of HIM is inescapable, as is the confusion between Christ and the Lord's anointed. The confusion between the secular and the spiritual is continued in the next strophe, where the decline of Rome and the consequent impudence of the barbaric tribes are described in language reminiscent of the spiritual life—"ortas in imperio spinas impiorum."

Yet the following strophes are clearly secular in intent. The Lombards are compared with the rebels against Jupiter, not those who rebelled against God. It is the tribute due to Caesar that they have refused to give; and the city of Ambrose, one of the greatest of the Christian fathers, is compared to Troy, which had resisted the will of the pagan gods. Yet the bibical imagery is always present:

> omnes erant caesares, nemo censum dabat
> . . . .
> ut quod erat Caesaris daret ei gratis
>
> (IX.xiii)

The citizens of Milan should obey Barbarossa because of the biblical injunction to render to Caesar the things which are Caesar's. The reputation of the emperor needs no further clarification—according to the poet, who has been building it for fifteen strophes—but it is a combination of the religious and the secular. The first half of the poem concludes with his reference:

> qui rebelles lancea fodiens ultrici
> representat Karolum dextera victrici.
>> (IX.xvi)

Barbarossa is the heir of Charlemagne, whom he had canonized, at once the Emperor and the saint. It is clear that the imperial mandate to the Archipoeta, conveyed through Reinald von Dassel, had been to the effect that Barbarossa was to be celebrated as the combination of the secular and the spiritual powers of the empire. Yet the imagery which the poet, the independent seer, uses makes only too clear the incongruity between the Emperor's desires and what was really due to him as the tribute due to Caesar. In asking for more than this tribute from the poet, he has to suffer the consequences in veiled but nevertheless sharp sarcasm.

The second half of the poem moves to epic recital, but epic recital with a difference. It is clearly impossible in a short poem like this to use the full epic style, but there are ways of imitating it. The poet himself gives a hint of what he is going to do:

> Primo suo domino paruit Papia
> urbs bona, flos urbium, clara, potens, pia;
> digna foret laudibus et topographia,
> nisi quod nunc utimur brevitatis via.
>> (IX.xviii)

In other words, rhetoric would call for a full treatment of Barbarossa's first triumph, Pavia—if this were not a short poem. Nevertheless, the roll-call of victories continues, complete with figures—hyperbole: "donec desunt Alpibus frigora vel nives"; apostrophe: "letare, Novaria, numquam vetus fies"; and many others. There are the appropriate references to Constantine and the denigration of the Byzantine empire, the almost inevitable comparison with the deeds of the Greeks, the assertion that an account of his exploits would be another *Aeneid*. All this is narrative, flattering, factual, inflated. Neither Barbarossa nor Reinald can object, even if they perceive the irony and even if they perceive that the high-sounding conflicts promised in strophe xxvii in words reminiscent of "arma virumque cano" prove to be punitive expeditions against highwaymen. To have removed these malefactors is one of the great "gesta Friderici," and there is no doubt that he has brought peace to Italy, but it is peace at the price of great cruelty and destruction. This certainly is not the peace which is brought to mind by the words "Iterum describitur orbis ab Augusto."[7] This is not the coming of the Prince of Peace. The whole strophe is a nicely ambiguous play on Christian and classical figures.

> Iterum describitur orbis ab Augusto
> redditur respublica statui vetusto
> pax terras ingreditur habitu venusto
> et iam non opprimitur iustus ab iniusto.
>
> (IX.xxx)

There is no harm in describing Barbarossa as Augustus—indeed that was one of his titles—but the first Augustus was parceling out the world for taxation purposes, as an absolute ruler with no regard for the babe who was born in Bethlehem of Judaea. Order is being restored but what is the "statui vetusto" to which it is returning? Is it that of Italy before the revolt or that of Augustus Caesar, Emperor of pagan Rome? The use of "respublica" and "vetusto" seems to imply the latter. The return of peace to the earth is a theme pursued by Ovid and particularly by Vergil in the Messianic eclogue (even though the actual word "pax" does not appear there), and it should not be forgotten that *pax Romana* implied the absolute control of the Emperor. It is naturally desirable that the just should not be persecuted by the unjust, provided we know which are which. Watenpuhl is no doubt correct in saying that the "hominibus bonae voluntatis" of Luke 2.14 are the same as the "iusti," but this does not solve the problem. They may very well correspond also to the "prudens" of strophe iii. In the end it is the friends of the new Augustus who will triumph.

It is the same conception of Barbarossa as the heir to the secular principate which motivates the anti-Byzantine feeling of the next strophe. The "volat fama" is reminiscent of Vergil, while the scorn for the Greek emperor is more in accord with Roman scorn for the Greeks than with the official attitude towards the successors of Constantine, although it must be remembered that there was a long tradition of anti-Byzantine feeling in the West. The obvious intention of the poet is to show Barbarossa as a Western, legitimate successor of Augustus. The Christian element is deliberately played down. These are matters of general principle but, as the next strophe shows, there were actual historical events of great importance which colored the attitude of the poet. Barbarossa was at this time supporting an antipope against Alexander who, after a struggle with William I of Sicily, had endorsed his rule. This same Alexander had even cooperated with the Byzantines in his opposition to Barbarossa. It is thus incumbent upon the Archipoeta to describe William of Sicily as "tyrannus" or "rex iniustus" and to condemn the Byzantines who had dared to oppose Friedrich. The Emperor, in this poem, has restored peace in Italy but, as everyone knew, it was a peace of devastation, imposed in defiance of a duly elected pope by an emperor who abrogated to himself both secular and divine powers. Thus the poet's statement in strophe vii becomes the grimmest of irony:

> Filius ecclesie fidem sequor sanam
> contempno gentilium falsitatem vanam.
> (IX.vii)

In fact he is celebrating Barbarossa for the rest of the poem not as a Christian Emperor but rather as the restorer of the old Roman principate of Augustus, the pre-Christian, pagan rule in which the church could have no part. The images and the allusions make this clear. It is the *pax Romana*, not the *pax Christiana*, which is being restored.

The last two strophes thus become of great importance, strophes xxxiii and xxxiv, the years of the life of Christ and a final prayer. Reinald von Dassel, the Archbishop who alone supported the uncanonical election of the new antipope, Paschal III, the Archbishop who was chancellor first and bishop very much second, is described in language drawn from the Gospels. He is John the Baptist making straight the way of the Lord,[8] but the verbs used of his activities convey not peace but a sword—*preparavit, extirpavit, subiugavit.* Only the last verb is one of peace, *liberavit,* but this applies only to the poet himself. The poem he has just written has freed him from the constant pressure of the Archbishop to write about the deeds of Barbarossa and had perhaps brought in a little money as an incidental. The poet has celebrated the new *princeps principum* and his John the Baptist and has thus earned his pay. Nor does he spare the Emperor a highly ambiguous final strophe. Barbarossa is described as "nobilis," surely a reference more to his deeds than to his brith, and there is therefore an assumption that the ruthless deeds just described are noble. "Age sicut agis," "Go on acting in the way you are," continues the same idea.[9] Possibly such a statement constitutes poetic approval but it could equally well mean "This is the way to continue your policy of secular imperialism." Certainly the next line implies that this is the way to gain fame: "sicut exaltatus es, exaltare magis." Again the words are biblical and are almost always used in connection with God, not a secular ruler. The impression of Godlike power is continued in the last two lines, which have a deliberately Old Testament quality,[10] the Lord of Hosts striking down His enemies:

> fove tuos subditos hostes cede plagis
> super eos irruens ultione stragis!

Vengeance is mine, saith the Lord, but Barbarossa is taking his own revenge, as if he were God himself.

The poem closes as it opened, with images reserved for God used of a secular ruler. The poet has fulfilled the command of his patron, Reinald von Dassel, and has glorified the Italian policies of his Emperor in words which could without difficulty be interpreted as a sincere endorsement of those policies. But this endorsement is made by the *persona* of the poet, the one who has been commanded to perform, the "prudens" of strophe iii, the "vidua pauperior" of strophe iv, the "filius ecclesie" of strophe vii. All these are masks and furthermore they are poses which carry ironical possibilities. The real views of the poet are to be sought not in the statements made by the various *personae* but in the imagery used by the poet himself. In applying to a secular ruler images which were, in the mind of the audience, associated exclusively with God, the poet strongly criticizes Barbarossa's usurpation of spiritual functions; by using the classical, imperial image and the epic form, albeit in mocking fashion, he associates Barbarossa not with the Holy Roman Empire but with secular Roman rule. His patron Reinald von Dassel becomes a secularized John the Baptist proclaiming the legitimacy of the new imperialism. The distinction so clearly proclaimed by the *persona* between the things which are Caesar's and the things which are God's is utterly denied by the poet's use or abuse of the imagery conventions of the two genres, the panegyric and the epic.

It is hard to escape the feeling that the two poems of the Archipoeta concerned with the deeds of Barbarossa are closely connected. His refusal to write an epic because he was not the man for such a task is nullified by his poem praising the very deeds which would have been the stuff of the epic and ostensibly showing his Emperor as the personification of imperial justice. Yet the imagery shows that he regards these deeds as the subject for a mock-epic, not an epic, and his biblical imagery makes it clear that the tribute due to Caesar has been vastly exceeded by the powers which Barbarossa has abrogated to himself. The Archipoeta demonstrates that it is not the *persona* of the poet who tells the truth but the poet who juggles the imagery and conventions of a genre to produce effects which are often totally different from the apparent intention of the poem.

NOTES

1. All quotations are taken from Heinrich Krefeld, *Die Gedichte des Archipoeta,* Heinrich Watenphul, ed. (Heidelberg, 1958). I have followed the numbering of the poems in this edition.

2. The exact dates of the two poems are difficult to determine. Milan was captured on March 1, 1162, so that IX must have been written after that date. It seems probable, as Krefeld suggests, that the poem would be particularly suited for presentation in Novara, and that the most likely date would therefore be September/October 1163. A date very close to this seems indicated for IV, although the evidence is much less clear. See Krefeld, pp. 104 ff. and 131.

3. The subject is treated in the following works: Paul Lehmann, *Das literarische Bild Karls des Grossen* (Munich, 1934, repr. 1959); N. Rubinstein, "Political Rhetoric in the Imperial Chancery During the Twelfth and Thirteenth Centuries," *Medium Aevum* (1945), 14:22 ff.; Anette Georgi, *Das lateinische und deutsche Preisgedicht des Mittelalters,* Philologische Studien und Quellen, no. 48 (Berlin, 1969).

4. No. X in Krefeld's edition. The frequent biblical allusions, when read in context, provide a brilliant satirical commentary on the relations between the poet and Reinald von Dassel.

5. "Omnis ergo qui audit verba mea haec et facit ea assimilabitur viro sapienti qui aedificavit domum supra petram" (Matt. 7.24).

6. Mark 12.41 ff.

7. "Factum est autem in diebus illis exiit edictum Caesaris Augusti, ut describeretur universus orbis" (Luke 2.1).

8. "Vox clamantis in deserto parate viam Domini; rectas facite semitas eius" (Luke 2.4).

9. "Interrogabant autem eum et milites dicentes 'Quid faciemus et nos?' Et ait illis: neminem concutiatis neque calumniam faciatis et contenti estote stipendiis vestris" (Luke 3.14).

10. "Iudica illos, Deus, decidant a cognitionibus suis; secundum multitudinem impietatum eorum expelle eos, quoniam irritaverunt te, Domine" (Ps. 5.11); "Exsurgat Deus et dissipentur inimici eius et fugiant qui oderunt eum a facie eius. Sicut deficit fumus, deficiant. Sicut fluit cera a facie ignis, sic pereant peccatores a facie Dei et iusti epulentur et exultent" (Ps. 67.1).

THREE
EPIC AND DRAMA

7

The Epic Center
As Structural Determinant
in Medieval Narrative Poetry

CRITICISM OF medieval narrative poetry has tended to emphasize the differences between the works which we so conveniently classify as national epics, *chansons de geste*, and romances. It is not difficult to point to distinguishing features—the difference in the role of women, the great importance of national pride in the first two and the lack of it in the third, the total involvement of person and country in the national epics, the concentration on leisure time in the romance. Such distinctions are convenient and make categorization and the writing of literary history easier. Yet any student of literary history knows that the categories are by no means clear-cut. The later *chansons de geste* are very close to becoming romances, the *Niebelungenlied* certainly gives the impression that its author was trying to convert his material into Romance form, and Wolfram von Eschenbach used French *chansons de geste* as sources for his romance *Willehalm*. The differences were apparent to contemporaries. Writers of romance did not, so far as we know, write national epics, and most critics would agree that the romance is the more sophisticated form. Yet these types did flourish during the same period, and it seems highly improbable that the early stages of the romance, wherever they were effected, could have escaped the influences of the other two types, which were already well established. It may therefore be worthwhile to explore the possibility of finding connecting links rather than points of difference between the various types of medieval poetic narrative.

Erich Auerbach's famous essay reminds us that one of the principal motifs of Arthurian romance is the departure of the knight from Arthur's court to seek adventure. The "quest motif" is one of the clichés of Arthurian criticism and the departure–return–new departure–final return structure is characteristic of a large number of romances, notably those of Chrétien de Troyes. Auerbach does not mention that the structure is equally characteristic of a large number of national epics and *chansons de geste*. The hero leaves a court, either voluntarily or under compulsion, seeks fame abroad, and returns. His triumphs are not gained among his own people, although recognition can come only from them. What cause can be assigned for the frequency of this motif? It is not due to the influence of classical antiquity, for there the hero always moves with his own kind. The wanderings of Odysseus are not those of a hero seeking glory but the "marvelous voyage" of a man desperately trying to return home.

The motif appears rather to have a historical basis. The *Völkerwanderungen* seem to have produced a large number of heroes who set out to seek their fortune in other lands. Pressure of population, greed, strife with kinsmen, and sheer love of adventure all prompted these moves, and in many instances the departure from the homeland was an act of official policy. A younger son or landless noble collected warriors and set out to seek new possessions. There was no thought of return, but ties with the homeland often remained close. The voyages of the Norsemen are often of this type. In other instances it was disagreement or oppression which caused a dissident group to leave, a group such as the one which originally colonized Iceland. If the emigrants struck roots in a new area, as the Norsemen did in Normandy and Sicily, we can hardly speak of a motif of departure and return. But there were many groups whose purpose was sheer plunder, and their return would be greeted with acclamation.

There was, however, a type of exile who certainly existed in history, though less frequently than the types just mentioned, but who was of much greater interest to the writers of literature. This was the lonely exile who appeared at a foreign court and who, by a combination of bravery and skill, so impressed his hosts that they entrusted him with higher and higher offices. In the works whose hero is of this sort, emphasis tends to be on the possession of unusual knowledge, particularly the use of exotic skills, rather than one mere physical proficiency. Such a hero rarely remains for life at the courts which receive him. Sometimes he returns home loaded with honors and gifts, as he does in the *Ruodlieb,* sometimes he flees back to his own country, as Waltharius does in the poem which bears his name, more often he provokes jealousy and is either killed or exiled, as Siegfried is in the *Nibelungenlied* and Tristan in the numerous poems which deal with his love for Isolde.

It is significant that it is the exiled *Recke* who is the prototype of so many literary heroes. The wanderers who left their homelands rarely returned, for the very object of their departure was the acquisition of land, but such men provided little of the stuff of tragic adventure. The writers knew that it was the true *Recke,* the man who left his homeland under compulsion and whose return, if it occurred at all, had to be a triumph, who provided the material of which epics were fashioned. Whether the hero returns or not, he carries which him the values of his homeland, and he regulates his conduct by these values, not by those of the court or individual to whom he is attached. It was the recognition by writers of literature of the importance of such values which led to the presence in virtually all narrative poetry of what we may call the epic center. Such a center is rarely the principal scene of action, important decisions are not made there, nor does the center determine the details of the hero's conduct. It is rather a center of civilization, representative of the ethic which the hero recognizes as binding upon his own behavior, and the hero recognizes that it is to this center that his loyalty is due. The conduct of those who live in the center permanently and of the sovereigns who control them is of much less importance than the values which the center represents. Perhaps the most important characteristic of the epic center is that the hero recognizes that here alone can he obtain the approbation which makes his conduct fitting. In the more important narratives, the conduct of the hero invariably transcends the demands of the standards of the epic center, and the tension between those standards and those of the hero constitute the principal interest of the work, but this does not alter the fact that for the hero himself the standards of the epic center remain those to which he must conform, for without them he has no background, no home, no reason for existing.

The existence of epic centers is undoubtedly one of the principal reasons for the development of cycles, for the feature which all poems of a cycle have in common is their epic center—the courts of Charlemagne, Louis the Pious, Arthur, Attila, and Gunther. The character of the rulers in these epic centers shows wide variation in the different poems of the various cycles, but the epic center itself is a constant, and the hero returns to it even when, as frequently happens, its ruler by character and conduct has forfeited all claim to his loyalty. The hero does indeed always return to the epic center, but it must be stated that he always leaves it and the reason for the inevitable departure is clear. The epic center is static. It represents a society whose values have become fixed and mechanical and whose conduct, determined as it is by these values, has often ceased to have any relevance to life. This lack of relevance may take various forms—the concentration on leisure pursuits and social graces in many of the Arthurian romances, the decline of military valor in many of the national epics. The conduct of the hero is judged by comparing it with that of the epic center, with which it is often markedly in contrast. Thus the hero must be of the society of the center, must depart from it to establish his individuality, must return to it, usually more than once, for its approbation, but must prove in the end that he has transcended it. Thus tension with the epic center, often expressed in physical terms as departure and return, becomes the basic structural principle of medieval narrative.

The earliest medieval narrative poem which illustrates this principle is, of course, *Beowulf.* The situation is an interesting one, for the epic center is undoubtedly Hygelac's court among the Geats. It is from this court that Beowulf sets out, to it he returns loaded with gifts, and the approbation of its ruler is his reward. Its standards are his standards and, as a young man, he seems to have no concern about the efficacy of its code of morals. Yet the last section of the poem casts serious doubts on the values which the court held. Hygelac dies in war, and Beowulf eventually takes over the kingdom. The problem which he has to face has already been foreshadowed by the parallel stories told of other courts. Beowulf finds that his personal values transcend those of the people of the epic center over which he rules, and he dies in an attempt to justify his personal ethos and to make it valid for his kingdom. Although he is successful in saving that kingdom from the immediate danger which threatens it, everything seems to point to eventual failure to restore the standards of the kingdom itself.

There is, however, another epic center in the poem which parallels in many but not all respects the kingdom which Beowulf has left behind. Heorot is the center of the kingdom of Hrothgar. It is not a warrior kingdom, but one which has reached the static position already described of stable comfort, a high standard of living, and a noble, courteous, civilized—and unenterprising—way of life. In giving gifts, in welcoming strangers, in telling stories at the mead benches Hrothgar's kingdom has no peer—but it cannot cope with Grendel. For this purpose the hero from across the sea, from a more virile culture is needed. Thus Heorot, unlike the normal epic center, becomes the scene of action for the hero who has departed from his own epic center. For the youthful Beowulf, however, it is an epic center. The author makes it clear that he is contrasting a center of light with a center of darkness, civilization with horror, good with evil. Both the attacker Grendel and the defender Beowulf converge on the center.

The first battle is defensive and indecisive, while in the second the situation is reversed. Beowulf leaves the center to attack Grendel's mother. The hero, having reestablished the center, follows the usual path in seeking evil outside its walls, in destroying that evil in spite of the failure of the representatives of the center to aid him, and in returning to the center to find complete approbation. Yet his conduct has transcended the static, even overblown civilization whose approval he seeks.

The courtly but feeble Hrothgar confers on him all the gifts which his hall affords, and Beowulf returns to his own epic center. The second epic center has fulfilled its function of providing the hero with a scene of action, of defensive-offensive battle in which he can gain the fame which can be conferred only by such a center. The whole action is a series of departures and returns, not only for Beowulf but also for his opponents, who have their own center of evil in the mere.

Beowulf's final struggle is centered around his own court. Again the attack of evil forces comes from outside and again the attack would be ineffective were it not for the moral weakness of the center itself. Beowulf's departure this time is contrasted strongly with the incidents of his youth. His principal driving force at that time had been fame; success for him meant approbation through gifts, and the center to be protected was not his own. This, his last departure, has no relevance to his personal reputation. It is forced on him by the necessity to protect his people from physical and moral degradation. The center, in other words, can no longer function as the arbiter of great deeds. Hence there is no return. Beowulf comes back dead. He has saved his people from the immediate threat but, as usual, the inhabitants of the center, with the exception of Wyglaf, are incapable of aiding him. Only Wyglaf gives us any reason to hope that the epic center may be restored.

The story of Beowulf is concerned with its hero, but that hero's conduct is determined by his relation to the epic centers which dominate the structure. It is their standards which decide his actions, their approbation which gives him fame. When he is identified with an epic center, as he is in the last episode, there is no possibility of further advance, only of defense and ultimately of destruction.

The use of the French court—that of Charlemagne and Louis the Pious—as an epic center presents some interesting problems. We may note at once that the historical situation of the court is of little significance, since literary tradition made both courts centers of French culture. As always, the courts offer the only way in which a man may gain fame, and loyalty to the sovereign, even the weak Louis, is essential. Yet the greatest of the poems centered on the court of Charlemagne, the *Chanson de Roland,* presents situations in which this loyalty, or rather the lack of it, is the mainspring of the action. Ganelon is obviously disloyal, and his defiance of the laws of the epic center brings tragedy, but Roland's own attitude is ambiguous. While purporting to be utterly loyal, he shows by his actions that he is more concerned with personal reputation at the expense of the court than with true loyalty. His conduct is affected by that of Charlemagne, who, as is typical of rulers within the epic center, fails to exert decisive influence on the course of events at a crucial period. Thus Roland, although he shows in abundance the values of bravery and leadership which are the means of gaining reputation at the court, misdirects those virtues because he believes that his own judgment is superior to that of the king and Oliver (who represents the values of the epic center more exactly). Instead of recognizing the validity of those values and transcending them, Roland attempts to set his individual judgment against them and is compelled by the force of events to recognize the futility of his efforts and to bring his conduct into agreement with that prescribed by the epic center. In the terms in which the extant version of the poem is written, his action can and should be expressed as *humilitas* succeeding *superbia,* but in terms of medieval narrative form it is a return to conformity with the values of the epic center, values from which he has temporarily departed. Even so, Roland is unusual inasmuch as he transcends the values of the center only in the manner of his death. Unlike the Cid, Beowulf, and many Arthurian heroes, he fails to demonstrate the validity of those values in his conduct during life. The interest of the author in Christian redemption is undoubtedly responsible for this stress on self-sacrifice in calling back the emperor to deal with the pagans. This interest is also responsible for the feeling most readers have of a sharp break be-

tween the "Roland" and the "Baligant" episodes, for in the second part
the idea of an epic center is absent. All interest is concentrated on a clash
between Christian and pagan forces, and the respective rulers become mere
figures representing their respective religions. Only at the trial of Ganelon do we revert to the normal relationship of the individual to the center, and here, of course, it is the traitor who has cut himself off completely from its rules of conduct.

The court of Louis the Pious in the Guillaume cycle and the "revolted
barons cycle" shows the epic center in a different literary form. Here it is
the theoretical values alone which are of significance. The ruler does not
himself embody those virtues, even though he pays lip-service to them,
nor do those who surround him see in him a true representative of the
virtues by which their own conduct should be determined. They quarrel
with him, even abuse him openly but nevertheless continue to regard his
court as the center of their activities. Guillaume d'Orange is placated by
a gift of land which is in the hands of the enemy and hence not the emperor's to give, but he accepts and conquers the land for himself. It is
noteworthy that here, as in the *Cid* and other works, there is a group of
evil advisers who seem to regard it as their function to destroy the values
of the epic center and corrupt it to their own use, again while paying lip
service to the very values they are corrupting. Hence a conflict arises in
which the person who has been, for one reason or other, exiled from the
center represents its values better than those who remain and purport to
represent them. In the *Couronnement de Louis,* Guillaume is virtually driven
away from the center whose values he best represents, as is the Cid by
the intrigues of the Garcia family. There is no question of the failure of
either of the two men to observe the values at the center, nor any question of their having to prove themselves in order to justify their return.
Each conducts a series of actions in which he exemplifies the virtues which
were those of the epic center before it became corrupted. In other words,
he transcends the values of the center as they existed when he left by actions which accord with the values which should be observed. In the *Cid,*
the return of the hero and his recognition by the king indicates the res-
toration of true values to the court. Hero and king are once again in harmony and the epic center resumes its normal function. As always, the hero
cannot regard himself as successful unless he secures the approbation of
those at the center, even though their conduct towards him has verged
on the brutal. The defeat of the evil advisers allows the king to remain as

the theoretical embodiment of the virtues of the epic center, even though his earlier conduct has indicated the contrary. It is his judgment which restores the Cid to society and the alliance of the Cid's daughters to royalty confirms the identification with the values of the epic center.

In Germanic "heroic" literature, there are two traditional centers, the court of King Gunther at Worms and that of Attila the Hun. The former invariably has the functions of an epic center, since its values are those by which its heroic characters judge their conduct. Yet the literary application of that function varies sharply with the tradition in which the work is written. If the sympathies of the author are with the "northwestern" tradition, in which the Burgundians struggle against the brutal and cruel Attila, Gunther is the dominating figure, Hagen is secondary and definitely a liegeman, even if related to his sovereign, and both die to defend the values of the center. Such are the majority of the Scandinavian representatives of the tradition. If the author writes in the "southeastern" tradition, however, a different situation arises. Although the values of the center remain valid, they are represented not by the weak king Gunther but by the subordinate, Hagen who, like Guillaume or the Cid has to save the values in spite of the actions of his master. This feature is particularly evident in the poems on Walter of Aquitaine.

The southeastern tradition presents some anomalies, particularly since it is often grafted on to northwestern material. Attila's court is the epic center not of a series of poems whose heroes regard him as an arbiter of conduct but of works whose principal character is an exile who has found refuge with Attila, namely Dietrich von Bern. Attila is always portrayed as a pagan, and the best that can be said of him is that he is the ruler of wide domains who is generous and kind to those who serve him. In no sense can he be said to set or represent the standards of conduct which govern the actions of Dietrich, who is a Christian warrior deeply concerned with the moral aspects of his prowess. Nevertheless, in most of the Dietrich epics the court of Attila looms large because of the hero's responsibility to it. He is the vassal of a great king, and it is characteristic that the death of Attila's two sons in *Rabenschlacht,* for which he is technically responsible, raises the question of what action the king will take against him. The situation, in other words, is a great deal more primitive than in the other epics we have discussed, since the basic relation of the hero to the center is one of loyalty, not of observance of moral and social standards set by the center. Nor does the question of the approbation of the center arise. Dietrich the exile serves Attila in recognition of his kindness in taking him in. (The same may be said of Walter of Aquitaine.) He appears to set his own standards of conduct.

This lack of any set of values in the southeastern epic center is particularly evident in the *Nibelungenlied.* The court of Attila has drawn into its orbit a large number of people, all of whom have different standards of morality and conduct. It has drawn them for one reason only, the power and wealth of its prince. Dietrich, as we have seen, is an exile, Ruedeger a vassal who owes all he possesses to Attila. Kriemhilde has married the king entirely because his power will enable her to carry out her plans to avenge the murder of Siegfried. It is Gunther, Hagen, and the Burgundians, who bring with them the values of the northwestern epic center, who provide the only examples of conduct motivated by an accepted set of values. The only reason, in fact, for the journey of the Burgundians to Attila's court is their feeling that honor demands that they accept the invitation; in other words, that their courage would be suspect if they were to refuse. The power of the "code" is such that it can overcome in other members of Gunther's court the objections of Hagen, who is prepared to risk his reputation by rejecting the invitation and flying in the face of the values of the center. Hagen's failure at this point is particularly striking in view of his reputation both earlier and later in the poem as the very embodiment of the virtues of the center and the principal source of wisdom. It is he, once the decision has been made, who insists on the ruthless prosecution of the standards of the center whatever may be the consequence to individuals.

When the final conflict develops, the groups of combatants are in a strange situation. The Burgundians have brought with them the values of their own epic center. They are unified not because each, as an individual, agrees with all the others—this is palpably not so—but because they all know the values which apply in the situation in which they find themselves. The ultimate logic of this position is seen in Hagen's decision to sacrifice his king so that the values of that king's court will not be defamed. Quite the contrary is true of their opponents. In the absence of any set of values, each is obliged to settle for himself (or herself) the problems of confrontation. For some it is easy. Bloedelin makes his assult purely for gain, Hildebrand entirely out of personal regard for the dead Ruedeger. Kriemhilde is motivated by considerations of revenge and, as is made abundantly clear by the attitudes of Ruedeger, Hildebrand, and

even Attila, her relentless pursuit of this revenge in defiance of the role
set for women in the center from which she came constitutes her greatest
sin, exceeding even the fact that her revenge is taken on her own brothers. In other words, the values of the epic center she abandoned are still
valid for her in the judgment of most of the participants, and her individual defiance of them constitutes a graver fault than the deed she is avenging.

For those permanently attached to Attila's court who are men of conscience, the problem which faces them is insoluble. Ruedeger is bound
to Attila's court only by considerations of the loyalty due to a generous
overlord. He does not share with that overlord a sense of values which
justify the relationship. Ruedeger is the only one of those who are technically Christians whose conduct seems to be guided by his religion. His
dilemma is not the classic "heroic" one of having to choose between loyalty to his chief and loyalty to a relation or even a friend. It is much more
subtle. His conscience and religion tell him that Kriemhilde is wrong in
enforcing revenge and in particular in causing the deaths of innocent
people. He admires the Burgundians because they are closer to him in
ethics than the court which he serves. Yet he has sworn an oath to
Kriemhilde and is reminded of his duty by the unedifying spectacle of his
king and queen on their knees before him, a subject. It is impossible to
imagine Hagen or even Gunther sinking so low. The utter lack of any
code of values could hardly be better expressed. In the end Ruedeger finds
himself caught by his Christian conscience, his oath which he can never
foreswear.

Dietrich's problem is different. Although he shares with Ruedeger an
admiration for the values of the Burgundian epic center, and for the individuals who represent it, he has sworn no oath and is bound to Attila
only by the loyalty which comes of gratitude to the king who had taken
in a friendless exile. Although, according to his reputation, his interference at any stage could have been decisive, he does not feel called upon
to take a part in the conflict, nor does either Kriemhilde or Attila ask him
to do so until all else has failed and his own followers have perished under the leadership of Hildebrand. When he does defeat Gunther and
Hagen, and takes them prisoner, the lack of guiding rules of conduct becomes painfully evident. Dietrich recommends that they be spared by
Kriemhilde, but she, following only her own assessment of the situation,
has Gunther killed and cuts down Hagen with her own hand, only to fall

victim herself to Hildebrand's anger and disgust. The end is primeval chaos, a complete breakdown of organized conduct.

It is, I hope, clear by now that the historical court which established certain values for those attached to it developed in literature to an epic center. The values of such a center determine conduct. Still more, they determine what is meant by honor, the socio-ethical standard by which a hero's status is to be judged. An epic center like Attila's court, which does not possess such values, becomes merely a topographical point at which events take place, not an epic center in the true sense. In the Arthurian romance the historical and topographical elements become utterly unimportant.

The development of an epic center around the person of Arthur who, if he existed at all, was an inconsiderable Celtic leader of the sixth century, illustrates the tenacity of the epic center idea. It will probably never be possible to determine for sure whether French poets merely took over from Breton minstrels an interesting person who became the center of a superior culture, or whether it was the deliberate choice of Geoffrey of Monmouth to set up Arthur as an anti-Charlemagne figure which gave Arthurian romance its most important stimulus. In either event the result was much less the glorification of Arthur as a person than the designation of his court as a major epic center. It might even be speculated that Arthur was probably a greater person in the pre-romance tales than in the romances which developed from them. When he appears in the works which we call Arthurian, it is more often as a middle-aged and rather pathetic figure than as a heroic warrior, as a person who is too old, too tired, too apathetic, and too feeble to carry out the actions, including the rescue of his own wife, which the values of the epic center he rules would demand from him.

It is a commonplace of Arthurian criticism that Arthur's court is always to be found where the story requires it. It has no permanent, fixed existence—even its most famous location, Camelot, seems to be a combination of two words and certainly could not be found on any map. It is equally true that it has a code of manners and morals which guides the actions not only of its own members but of all those who aspire to true chivalry. Although this code of morals is by no means so fixed as some critics would have us believe and certainly is not something of philosophical derivation which could be consulted before action (or before writing a romance), it is certainly well known to the characters in the romances and sufficiently comprehensible to the reader to allow him to determine when those characters are behaving well or ill. No Arthurian works earlier than those of Chrétien de Troyes are extant in which the "Arthurian" code can be observed, but it is usually assumed that there must have been a considerable number of lost romances which familiarized the audience with this Arthurian convention. Romances may well have been lost, but nothing more than the work of Geoffrey of Monmouth and its poetical adaptation by Wace would have been needed to establish Arthur's court as an epic center. Groups of stories, even though they were not romances, could also have contributed to the idea. The convention of the epic center was already so well established in narrative poetry that it would have found ready acceptance amoung a courtly audience.

Once established, the Arthurian epic center became the most important in medieval literature and, in a curious reversal of the historical process, its values were accepted by later generations as those of an earlier historical period. Functionally, the Arthurian court is always the center of narration in the most literal sense. Action begins there and ends there, so that the hero or heroes in almost every case move from Arthur's court to an ill-defined area in which they find adventure and then return to the court after their successes. Some heroes—Galahad and Perceval—are born away from the court but make their way to it before their adventures really begin. It has thus been possible to describe Arthurian romance in terms of quests, of physical departure and return, and to see in the final solution of the stories of *Erec* and *Yvain* in particular a physical and moral departure from the Arthurian court and Arthurian values and a return to them at the end of the story. Such an evaluation is to regard the epic center as little more than a physical court. All Chrétien's works, however, show a constant state of tension between the values of the epic center and those of the maturing individual, a tension which is no less present because the hero is not completely aware of it. At the beginning of the career shown in the poem, none of the heroes is shown as questioning in the least the values of the court. There is complete surface harmony. The first part of *Yvain* and *Erec* shows the hero acting entirely in accordance with the dictates of the epic center and then committing an offence against those dictates which causes a physical departure from the epic center and a series of adventures in which the hero rises above the standard of conduct set by the center while still, apparently, conforming to its rules. The effect is achieved by contrasting the standard concept of adventure as a purposeless employment of leisure time to obtain the approbation of the epic center with adventure in a new sense, the employment of physical strength and nobility of character to help the distressed and in particular women who have been unfairly treated by apparently conformist members of Arthur's court, including Gawain himself.

Thus the values of the epic center take on a new meaning. They are treated by Chrétien with irony and are represented at their worst by Kei, at their best by Gawain, but neither personifies such high values as those of the hero of the poem. The struggle with Gawain which occurs in almost every poem is not merely to show the hero as excelling in Arthurian virtues but as rising above them. There are other ways in which doubt is cast on the values of the epic center. Arthur's position is overshadowed by that of his wife Guinevere. While she decides, Arthur sleeps. When he is abducted, Arthur is at a loss. Female influence is, in fact, preeminent at the court and in many instances that influence is not that of the female heroine or of the best women at court. The *Lancelot* is the most obvious example of the malign influence of the feminine, as it is the best example of Chrétien's ironic treatment of the values of the epic center, but it is not, as some have believed, an exception to his usual method but a more intense, perhaps crasser example of his normal attitude. The female element which dominates Arthur's court is always compared unfavorably with the highest manifestations of the feminine as represented by Enide, Lunete, and even Laudine. Chrétien's works are largely studies of the various ways in which women can influence those dependent on the Arthurian epic center, whether for good or evil. The female standard of the center itself is always treated with irony, whether it be in the comedy of *Cligès* or the satire of *Lancelot*.

In changing the values of the epic center from a purely masculine-warrior basis, as they are in the epics, to a largely feminine orientation, Chrétien (or his predecessors, according to one's point of view) determined the course of Arthurian romance for a large number of later writers. The Vulgate cycle, with its concentration on the relationship between Lancelot and Guinevere, which is partly justified by the adultery (on the same night as that in which the lovers consummate their passion) between Arthur and Camille, provides an epic center of a very different kind from that found in the earlier writings. Although the court of King Arthur is still spoken of as the center of chivalrous culture, in practice the reverse is true. Knights behave as they believe a knight of the Round Table should, but Arthur himself, Lancelot, Bors, and others continually break the code by which they should live—and they are conscious of their lapses. The same, it may be added, is frequently true of the knights and ladies in Malory's work. True love of the kind found in the earlier romances is hard to find there. The feminine orientation of the epic center has led to an excessive emphasis on love in the erotic sense and a corresponding decline in moral standards. It is highly significant that in all the Grail romances the Arthurian court is rivaled by a new epic center, the Grail castle, and that in the Vulgate cycle and Malory's work the new hero, Galahad, is neither a product of the center's instruction nor an example of its values.

The Vulgate cycle, indeed, marks its departure from the medieval narrative tradition by its failure to exploit the tension between individual and epic center and by the use of the technique of "entrelacement," whose effect is to show action as a continuing complex rather than an altercation between an individual hero and selected persons who are introduced to test him, whether consciously or not, and to elicit responses from him, in terms of the values of the epic center. In this respect, apparently, there is a marked difference between prose and verse.

The Grail romances inevitably introduce a new epic center, the Grail castle. The much-debated question of the antecedents of the castle and its connections with various traditions, whether they are Celtic, Christian, or Oriental, is of little importance structurally. The earliest version we possess, that of Chrétien de Troyes, is unfortunately the one which tells us least about the new epic center. The Grail castle, like Arthur's court, appears to move, it is awesome and occupied by a group far different from the knights of the Round Table. Its king is courteous but not courtly in the narrower sense. We do not see the castle again after Perceval's first visit, but its emissaries emphasize its strangeness and remoteness from courtly life. It can hardly be doubted that Chrétien intended to introduce into his poem tension between two epic centers rather than between the epic center and the hero. The Gawain plot shows us in almost parodistic detail a normal plot of tension between the hero and the feminized Arthurian court, a passage through young, innocent love which is nevertheless fully aware of the social prestige attached to the service of a champion, to the mature and fleshly love of the sister of the king of Ascalon. The later scenes of encounter with the scornful lady are a pretty combination of slavish obedience to the feminine Arthurian values and purposeful, if somewhat fanciful adventure. Gawain's ultimate marriage with his lady has little in common with the final scenes of *Erec* and *Yvain*. There has, in fact, been no true tension between the hero and the epic center because Gawain is not the hero. He illustrates the values of the Arthurian court but he does not test them, or himself. What Chrétien intended to do with the new epic center, the Grail castle, is not clear, since we are told little of the king and his company. It is clear, however, that Perceval's aspirations were to be changed from a desire to become a knight of the Round Table to a yearning to be Grail King. This new aspiration must inevitably have included a far stronger religious motivation than is to be found in those whose aim is acceptance at the Arthurian epic center. The groundwork was thus laid for a new structure which, in one form or another, is found in all the Grail romances but is most marked in Wolfram's *Parzival*—the tension between two epic centers, the Arthurian court and the Grail castle.

Wolfram makes this tension very clear. Those who belong to the Arthurian epic center have complete freedom of movement, and their conduct is determined by social and superficially moral considerations. The values of their epic center are easily interpreted as conventions, and this is what Perceval in fact does. The Grail company, on the other hand, cannot leave the castle except on specific duties, which include the ruling of lands left leaderless. Children of female Grail attendants must return to the castle. Of the males there, only the king may marry. The sharp contrast with the feminine-oriented Arthurian center is obvious. Parzival attains his Grail kingdom through tension with the Arthurian center caused by ignorance of worldly conventions followed by tension caused through his uncomprehending yearning for the Grail. He thus passes through and beyond the classic pattern of conformity and transcending to aspiration for a higher goal. The quest is ineffective in this new sphere, even when it involves purposeful adventure, for in the hero's move from one epic center to another is mirrored the more general opposition of the two epic centers themselves, between two completely different approaches to life. The difference between the two centers is reflected most obviously in the female members of each. Those of the Arthurian court are active, almost relentless in their demands on the knights and the encounter between one of them, Orgeluse, and the Grail king Amfortas, has already caused a tragedy before the poem opens. Gawain finally effects an accommodation with Orgeluse, so that she accepts the "normal" status of a lady in the

Arthurian court. No such adjustment is necessary for Parzival, since his wife belongs to the other center or, perhaps more accurately, moves naturally into it. Wolfram makes it very clear both from the narrative and remarks made in his person, that Kondwiramurs is far removed in manners and morals from the ladies of the Arthurian court. Sigune too, after her initial error, demonstrates the Grail qualities of passivity, chastity, and humility. It has been rightly pointed out that the women are of the inner sanctum of the Grail castle and that is is through the female line that its values descend.[1] Wolfram leaves us in no doubt of his own opinion of courtly women, and there is no poet who contrasts the values of the two epic centers more sharply.

In the Grail romance of Chrétien and Wolfram, the contrast between the two epic centers appears to be deliberate. It is, of course, impossible to determine whether Chrétien introduced this tension, but in any case he, and still more Wolfram, recognized its potentialities and exploited them. Some of the later writers of Grail stories followed them. It should be noted, however, that a contrast of two epic centers is more likely to lead to an allegorical treatment than tension between a center and an individual. When the values of two centers are being opposed, those who represent them are in grave danger of becoming typical figures and this fate does overtake Galahad and others in several of the prose romances.

Interest in the love-affair between Tristan and Isolde and the absence in many of the Tristan romances of an obvious epic center such as Arthur's court has obscured the fact that the tension between hero and center is as marked in these works as in other medieval narrative poems. The *Tristram und Isalde* of Eilhart von Oberg is not concerned with the relationship of the two lovers so much as with the effect of love on Tristram's duty as a knight, that is, with his conformity with the values of an epic center. His love-affair causes him to enter into a conflict with these values in which one of the most important, loyalty, is disregarded, and Tristram's death is a direct result of this conflict.

The situation in the work of Thomas of Britain reflects concern with an epic center of a different kind, the court dominated by feminine values which we have noted in the work of Chrétien de Troyes. Although there is still a marked conflict between loyalty to Mark and love for Isolt, the interest concentrates on the degree to which the two lovers can fulfill the demands posed by the feminized values of the epic center without suffering oblivion at the hands of Mark. It is unfair to judge Thomas by the extant fragments of his work, which refer to incidents late in the story and by the translation of Brother Robert into Old Norse, but it does seem that he was concerned to show the love affair as an example of the fatal attraction of beauty. Thomas' most significant addition to the tradition in his description of the figures of Isolt and her court made for Tristan in his exile, figures so lifelike that he could imagine the physical presence of his beloved without difficulty. Thomas does not seem to depict love-service by Tristan for Isolt. Their love is mutual in the sense that each is prepared to make sacrifices for it, and it clashes rather with the fact of Mark's marriage to Isolt than with the values of Mark's court, which are not clearly defined. The impression is that Thomas approves of the love affair as an example of the invincibility of love.

In the work of Gottfried von Strassburg, the conflict between the attitudes of the feminized epic center and the conduct of the two lovers is very marked. Gottfried explicitly states in his prologue that he is writing for a small and select group who will be able to understand his lovers, sympathize with them, and be edified by their example, and throughout the poem he makes it clear that the tension in his work is between a group, represented by Mark and Brangaene for good and Melot and Marjodo for evil, whose values are determined by the courtly concepts of the epic center. Not only do these people, except Brangaene, put difficulties in the way of the lovers on social grounds, but all of them, including Brangaene, utterly fail to understand the artistic-intellectual basis of the love between Tristan and Isolde. Gottfried has thus set up tensions on several levels of interpretation between his lovers and the epic center implicit in the poem and represented physically by the court of Mark. There is personal tension between uncle and nephew, the constant search for proof of disloyalty and adultery, a tension found in every version of the story. On a higher level there is in Brangaene and, in their early career, in the lovers themselves, the desire usually found in the first part of Arthurian romances, to conform to the norms of the feminized court and conduct an intrigue like that of Lancelot and Guinevere. This attempt is due to a failure to understand their own love. It is superseded by another tension, the most important of all, between the love which is understood by the epic center and conforms to its conventions, and the higher desire which expresses itself not only in physical union but also in a spiritual and intellectual harmony reflecting the divine harmony of the world. This love is made manifest by the scene in the grotto of love, separated from the court by wood and wasteland. The formal epic center is distant in time, place, and conception, so far indeed, that the grotto can be regarded as a timeless allegory and is so interpreted by Gottfried himself. When the values of the epic center once again intrude, as they do with the arrival of Mark's hunting party, the refuge has lost its value, and the conflict between "Tristan-love" and the values of the epic center must be continued, first at court and then in exile.

Gottfried is one of the few authors who states explicitly that there is a conflict in his poem between the values of his principal characters and those of the epic center. The prologue to the poem, that is, the episodes concerned with the love of Tristan's parents, is devoted to an examination of the values of the epic center at Mark's court and the relation of Tristan's parents to it, so that the audience can be fully aware of the values of that court and their deficiencies from the point of view of the higher values sought by Tristan and Isolde. The courtliness of the epic center is on numerous occasions specifically rejected, not only so far as its values for love are concerned but because of its obsession with artificial love-service, formal combat, and particularly intrigue. Chrétien's irony has developed into specific rejection.

We may conclude this survey of works which illustrate the epic center as structural determinant by a study of *Gawain and the Green Knight*. Standing as it does almost at the end of the line of Arthurian romances, it might be expected to represent the ultimate development of the literary use of the epic center. The opening is conventional enough, with its assembled court and monstrous intruder, but the hesitation to accept the Green Knight's challenge, Arthur's reluctant decision to defend the honor of his court by accepting, and Gawain's saving of his king show that all is not well. The epic center exists indeed but its values are not, apparently, a force cogent enough to inspire its members. There are many ways in which the poem can be interpreted, but it is undoubtedly possible to regard the poem more as a trial of the values of the Arthurian court than as a trial of Gawain. For it is the values of that center which arm Gawain for his test at the castle of Bercilak and they fail. In a tension between appetite and social convention, they will serve well enough, and Gawain has little difficulty in resisting the advances of his host's wife, while at the same time maintaining his reputation for courtesy. When a more significant moral problem arises, the values he has learned fail him. He accepts the scarf not, as would be customary for an Arthurian knight, as a token of a lady's favor but as a talisman against death or, more bluntly, against fear of death. The hesitation which all the knights of Arthur's court and Arthur himself had shown in accepting a challenge which might lead to their death is shown in the end to be just as much a part of Gawain's character. The court had moved so far from its original basic quality of fearlessness and defiance of death that even the one member who apparently still upheld the tradition is shown to have lost it. The outwardly inhuman Green Knight is closer to its original spirit than any of the members of the court, for he is aware of Gawain's anguish and is merciful in his power.

Gawain is, of course, aware of his failure but his awareness is not due, apparently, to any tension between him and the epic center. The reception he receives on his return to court makes this clear. The scarf which he wears as the sign of his own dishonor is taken up by the court as a mark of solidarity with him. To the court it is little more than a token, since it is clearly impossible for them to share Gawain's feelings of guilt, and their very readiness to wear the scarf shows their inability to appreciate Gawain's failure, but for author and audience the wearing of the scarf must surely represent the failure of the values of the epic center in Gawain's own failure. In this last of the great Arthurian romances, the epic center itself is put on trial in the person of its chosen representative and found wanting.

The individual works we have surveyed cover a great span of time, and their use of the epic center structural form is remarkable in its persistence. The form is not derived from classical antiquity, for the classical epics do not achieve their effects by tension between a hero's behavior and the values of an epic center to which he belongs. On the other hand the earliest medieval verse narratives show it in a highly developed form. The epic center has a great deal in common with a very widespread motif, the center of light and culture surrounded by primeval darkness, but such a motif does not account for the essential element of dialogue and tension between a hero and his own epic center. It would appear most likely that the roots of the epic center form are to be found in the conditions of early medieval society. The group of warriors around the chief, whether Celtic or Germanic, and the demand for absolute loyalty seem to have given rise at an early stage in oral literature to the classic "conflict-of-loyalties" dilemma, which finds its clearest expression in the *Hildebrandslied*. Increased literary sophistication retained the conflict while minimizing the personal element. The center ceases to be an individual to whom loyalty is due and becomes the court of an individual king, such as Arthur or Charlemagne, to which a set of abstract values is attached quite independent of the character of the ruler himself. The relation between the individual hero and the epic center is the common feature of virtually all medieval narrative poetry, whether it be categorized in literary history as popular epic, *chanson de geste* or romance. Each of these types does indeed develop certain characteristics in its treatment of which the most striking are the strongly feminized court of the Arthurian romances and the development of tension between two epic centers in the Grail romances, but the epic center always remains the structural determinant, and the dialog between it and the hero the most satisfying approach to the study of the works. Just as the form of the classical epic invariably showed a beginning of the narrative *in mediis rebus,* so the medieval epic shows a form built around an epic center, a form which authors could manipulate as they saw fit and which was sure of recognition by their audience.

NOTE

1. See Herbert Kolb, *Munsalvaesche: Studien zum Kyotproblem* (München: Eidos, 1963).

8

Time and Space
in the *Ludus de Antichristo*

MOST OF THE critical discussion of the Tegernsee *Ludus de Antichristo* has been devoted either to its position in relation to the large number of medieval and Renaissance Antichrist plays or to its treatment of the Emperor Friedrich Barbarossa.[1] Although he is never mentioned by name, it is clear that the portrait of the Holy Roman Emperor given in the play is influenced by his reputation and by the concentrated propaganda put out by contemporary apologists in support of his efforts to unify the secular dominions of the emperor and to extend his power over the spiritual lives of his subjects.[2] Interesting though they are, these references to imperial ambition are only a small part of the play. It was not written to provide a framework for one more piece of imperial self-justification. Quite the contrary. The Tegernsee *Antichrist* is a very well-organized dramatization of one of the most important episodes in the whole history of Christian salvation,[3] and it is designed to throw light not only on the behavior of politically organized Christendom but on the way in which God proposes the ultimate merging of all peoples into a unified *Christianitas* and the conversion of those parts of the world which are not Christian. It would be impossible to study all these themes in the course of one essay, but a study of the way in which space and time are used in the play will throw a great deal of light on its unity and on the purposes of the author.

It is clear from the scheme which is provided in the manuscript that the author was interested in the question of space. The distribution of the thrones is, in fact, a division of the world according to traditional views, with the East containing all holy shrines—the Temple at Jerusalem in which Christian activity culminates and the Synagogue. The presence of the (Latin) King of Jerusalem in this position is determined by his role as temporary secular guardian of the holy places, but he is an offshoot of Western Christendom, as is made clear by his return to the West on his expulsion by Antichrist.

This Eastern, religious end of the axis is balanced by the secular, political end at the West, which is occupied by the powers of Western Christendom, the Holy Roman Emperor, who takes over the place assigned to the German king after giving up his powers, and the King of France. Significantly, there is no throne set aside for the Pope or for Ecclesia.[4] The Pope is mentioned at the first entry of Ecclesia, but he never speaks and is treated as an appendage to the Western powers; nor does he accompany Ecclesia when she transfers to her true location in the *Templum Dei*. She returns to his *sedes* when driven out of Jerusalem by Antichrist. This failure to provide a throne for the papacy and the fact that there is no transfer to Jerusalem seems to be a clear indication that there is no permanent place for the papacy in the ultimate design of the world and that it, like the empire, will lose its status when God's design is completed. The evidence is negative indeed but not insignificant.

The East-West axis is thus the view of Christendom which is enshrined in the design of so many churches. The position of the other two thrones is harder to explain. It is not difficult to see why the throne of Gentilitas, the pagans, should be in the South. Western Christendom had very confused ideas about the Moslem religion and identified it with paganism in general. The worship of idols was commonly attributed to the Moslems, and they could easily be included in a description of polytheistic worship. Since pagans and Moslems were thus confused, it was easy to set their abode in the South. It is much harder to explain or even identify the position of the throne of the King of the Greeks—"ad austrum." The exact meaning of *auster* is doubtful. Classical references frequently make a direct opposition between Aquilo and Auster, in the meanings "North Wind" and "South Wind," and seem to use *auster* and *meridies* indiscriminately as words for "south." Yet the wind Auster can be wet and cold as well as hot and dry. The best information is given by Isidore of Seville,[5] who distinguishes between *euroaustrum* and *austroafricum*—southeast and southwest. But later he says that Eurus is directly opposed to Boreas, the Northwest Wind. The evidence would seem to show that *Auster* may well be somewhat east of south or at least flexible in that direction. It was, after all, a wind, not a compass bearing. The intention is probably to show that the Greek king is situated in an area between the (southern) pagans and the (eastern) Christian areas. The West had, notoriously, a very poor opinion of Constantinople. The assigned position bears out this view.

The positions of the various rulers and powers on the stage are thus set in accordance with their functions in God's plan for the universe. Geography is a secondary consideration. The simultaneous stage and the positions of the *sedes* on it reflect the *ordo mundi,* an order which has no permanent place for Antichrist. It will be noted that he and his followers are never mentioned in the distribution, and the reason for this is simple. They are simply transitory shadows of true beings who come and are gone. We should also note one other important fact about the stage. One side of it is completely open. This was presumably the side facing the audience or, if we reject the idea that the audience sat only on one side, an area where only members of the audience were to be found. The audience thus completes the space circle. The fact is important, since those who occupy the various *sedes* are called upon from time to time to move from one place to another and in one or two cases, particularly in that of Ecclesia, to make moves which at the time seem permanent. The audience does not move, but it is obliged to shift its point of concentration; and it is this shift which constitutes the most important spatial function in the play.

There would clearly be no dramatic action if the principals merely occupied their *sedes*. There is considerable movement in the play and for the most part it is formalized. Although there was clearly a space, a *platea,* between the various thrones, it is never mentioned as a place of action. It is hard to see how such actions as the various battles could be depicted elsewhere, even at a minimum level of representation. However this may be, the directions call for movement between *sedes,* since the object of the play is to illustrate the relationships between individuals and groups, not to provide action or the appearance of it. An account of the space relations makes this clear.

The play begins with the entrance of the various figures and their procession to their individual *sedes*. Where do they come from? There is nothing in the play to indicate their starting point, but a likely guess is that they move from among the audience. The resemblance to the Introit is obvious. The various figures take up their positions and identify themselves and thus provide the picture of the *ordo mundi*. When the action begins, all movement is concentrated on the Emperor. He sends ambassadors to each secular ruler in turn to enforce the unity of secular Christendom. The King of France has to be compelled to yield by force of arms, but in the end he conforms to the pattern—each secular ruler comes to the imperial throne and is confirmed in his position but only as a liegeman of the Holy Roman Emperor. All movement is ultimately centripetal. The Kings of France, Constantinople, and Jerusalem are at this point shown as satellites, and space is seen as Christendom concentrated about its secular head. All the movement is concentrated in a western direction, not to the spiritual center in the East.

This unified movement contrasts sharply with what follows. The King of Babylon attacks Jerusalem, that is, a secular power moves east, and, at the request of the Latin King of Jerusalem, the Emperor intervenes and defeats him. The Emperor must, of course, move from his throne to do this; but when he returns to it, the King of Babylon does not come with him to yield his crown and thus conform to the pattern. He has been beaten and driven away but he has not become part of secular Christendom. The space-unity which was in process of being forged is thus destroyed or at least left imperfect, with important consequences for the next part of the play. The centripetal pattern closing on Western Christendom is shattered by the centrifugal action of the pagans.

The movement of the Emperor and the figure of Ecclesia from the West to the *Templum Dei* in Jerusalem is thus premature. The focal point of Christendom should not be moved from its secular to its religious center until all secular matters have been brought to a conclusion. In other words, the concept of Christian space has not yet been fully realized. It is true that Synagoga is topographically in the same place as the *Templum Dei*, but she has not yet been converted and there is no evidence of any intention to convert Synagoga by arms. The new Christian center of concentration thus lacks two important elements, one spiritual and one secular, and this imperfection has dire consequences at the coming of Antichrist.

When the second part of the play opens, the three major divisions of religion once again identify themselves. Their substance has not changed, since the secular victories of the Emperor have had no effect on two of them. While they are thus engaged, the precursors of Antichrist move about "captantes favorem laicorum." It is not clear where this attempt to win over the laity takes place; but since it happens while singing is going on at the *sedes,* it is a fair presumption, and one which is dramatically plausible, that they would start by moving among the audience and slowly concentrating on the site of Ecclesia and the King of Jerusalem. The attack on the unity of Christendom thus comes from outside, and its movements are totally erratic and differ sharply from the clearly centripetal movement of the first part. The deposition of the King of Jerusalem takes place at his throne. There is no invasion in the narrower sense of the term. He, and later Ecclesia, flee to the German king, the ex-Emperor, thus reversing the movement of the first part and destroying the Eastern Christian focal point. But this does not mean that the focus returns to the West. The German king does not at once take up arms against Antichrist as he had against Gentilitas. Quite the contrary. It is now Antichrist who goes through a series of actions which amount to a parody of those of the Emperor in the first part, although the words he uses are often parodies of those of Christ. Antichrist has no *sedes* and indeed no spatial existence except in so far as he imitates and parodies others. This is made clear in the winning over of the Kings of Constantinople and France, which follows the same spatial pattern as that in the earlier scenes but which brings the kings to the spiritual center of the *ordo mundi* set up on the stage, not to its secular center and does so in the name of a false belief. Antichrist puts a religious mark on his liegemen before giving them their thrones and uses the methods of terror and bribery to convince them rather than historic proof and superiority in war. What he has done in fact is to use the spiritual center as a site for his own secular power.

The dealings with the German king are very complex. The attempt by the emissaries of Antichrist to bribe him have as little success as the Emperor's earlier efforts to win over the King of France without war. They involve movement by the emissaries of Antichrist to the throne of the German king but no movement by the King himself. His firmness in the face of Antichrist's efforts is thus confirmed. The forces of the other kings are summoned to the throne of Antichrist and ordered to undertake what can only be described as an anticrusade against the King of Germany. It will be noted that the first part of the play saw an attack by Gentilitas, the one power outside the Christian orbit, on the spiritual center, Jerusalem, and its defeat by the Emperor. The attack is now made from a false spiritual center by forces won over to a false belief upon the one survivor of the Christian secular orbit. The spatial moves are thus in

themselves anti-Christian in that they move away from the Christian concentration and Christian unity which had already been achieved. The
German king sees his victory as one for the imperial idea, even though
he returns to a German king's throne.[6]

The spatial movements thus reflect the confusion and anarchy of the
regime of Antichrist, and those that follow are more confused still. There
is no statement anywhere that the King of Germany leaves his throne,
nor Antichrist his, yet both are present at the healing of the sick and the
raising of the dead. When the King is won over by the miracles, "ascen-
dit ad Antichristum." This is the expression used of those kings who have
yielded. It seems clear, therefore, that the King must have come into the
presence of Antichrist, even though there is no direction to that effect. It
is hard to offer any logical explanation for the omission, and it is probably due to careless writing; but it is interesting to note that the move to
the presence of Antichrist would be the only movement from one throne
to another which is not the result of a request from a superior power or
a challenge. The German king is not forced into dependence on Antichrist
but yields as an act of belief, albeit in a false power. His position as an
"unbeaten" secular Christian ruler is thus maintained.

The German king does not return to his throne after this incident but
commands the forces collected by Antichrist against the pagans. The spatial movement here is significant. In the first act, Gentilitas had marched
against Jerusalem, that is, inwards towards the Christian center, which had
been shattered but not subjugated. Now the movement is, quite properly, outward against the pagans. If the force behind the move were Christ,
not Antichrist, the direction would be right; but after the defeat of Gentilitas the King of Babylon is pardoned and, like all the other kings, is
returned his throne as a spiritual and secular subject of Antichrist. There
is thus no concentration whatsoever. The whole disposition of Antichrist's
world is a move out from Jerusalem and away from a spiritual center, a
disposition which contrasts sharply with the markedly centripetal movement of the first part.

The "conversion" of the Jews involves little spatial movement, since it
takes place at Jerusalem and, although the restitution of the "promised
land" is mentioned, no actual territory is involved. The breakdown of the
domination of Antichrist begins, as might be expected, with movement
from outside the system of control which he has set up. Enoch and Elijah, who had never died, now return to the secular sphere and persuade
Synagoga to renounce her allegiance to Antichrist. They act like the an-

gels in the *Chanson de Roland* and the *Jeu de Saint Nicolas* of Jean Bodel
in intervening in moments of crisis and thus show that the secular sphere
is not self-contained but subject to powerful movement from outside. The
performance of the play presumably reflected this by introducing the two
prophets from an area away from the sites of the thrones, possibly from
the unoccupied north side. Whatever system was adopted, the stage takes
on a new dimension by the revelation of an extra dimension, and that the
most important of all, for it should be noted that Synogoga is converted,
at least to the extent of recognizing the Trinity. This is the first true spiritual change in the play and it takes place without secular interference.
The secular reply is the martyrdom of Synagoga and the prophets; but
the triumph is shortlived.

   All the kings are summoned to the throne of Antichrist, and this is the
final movement of the play, a converging of all temporal power, presumably including Gentilitas, on the spiritual center, Jerusalem. The converging is a repetition of the triumph of the Emperor at the end of the first
part, but it purports to be spiritual and is therefore a parody of the true
converging of spiritual forces on Jerusalem which should take place at
the Second Coming. The mockery is made clear by the words used by
Antichrist and repeated by his followers:

> Cuncta divinitus   manus una firmavit,
> Suos divinitas   hostes exterminavit.
> Pace conclusa sunt   cuncta iura regnorum,
> Ad coronam vocat   suos deus deorum.
>   (II.10.3 ff.)

This last movement is one toward final unity, but it is the unity of evil,
not good. Again, the decisive movement comes from outside the stage:
"Statim fuit sonitus super caput Antichristi et eo corruente et omnibus
suis fugientibus, Ecclesia cantat. . . ." Divine, not secular power has
triumphed, and Ecclesia emphasizes the fact by her sarcastic "Ecce homo"—
behold the man who did not take God as his helper. Antichrist has concentrated all the earthly powers at Jerusalem and thus carried out God's
purpose in spite of himself. All return to the true faith, and Ecclesia accepts them. There is no reference to their returning to their original *sedes*.
Secular power has been eliminated, and all Christians are unified, spa-
tially as well as spiritually, at Jerusalem.

   It is clear that spatial movement on the stage, whatever form that stage may have taken, is in conformity with a religious pattern. The movements of the first part are all designed to show concentration on the secular center of Western Christendom and the subordination of all secular power to that center. The failure to force the final subjection of Gentilitas means that the concentration is imperfect, since one power has avoided the centripetal movement. Thus the time for the concentration on the spiritual center is not yet come. The handing over of power to Ecclesia by the Emperor is an empty gesture. Nevertheless, the East, the spiritual center, has now become the point of concentration, and the original attack on it by Antichrist is carried out by "spiritual" means. Once he is established there, however, he attempts to produce a pattern similar to that of the first act, but his success is incomplete. As we have seen, the pattern of movement is fragmentary and disrupted, and the apparent spiritual unity is based not on spiritual values but on a parody of them, in combination with force and terror. Antichrist's regime survives the challenge of secular power and even of the prophets who had never died (though with great difficulty), but it falls apart when challenged by true divinity.

We should not forget that the audience is a participating, although silent part of this drama. They complete the circle in which the action takes place and they are part of the people represented by the Western secular powers. What goes on concerns them intimately. It is through them, too, that a point of view is maintained, for none but a Christian audience could appreciate what is going on, and the attitudes towards Synagoga and Gentilitas must be those of Christian observers. Furthermore, the audience constitutes an essential part of the circle within which all spatial movement must take place. They are on the circumference of that circle and thus capable of appreciating those centripetal and centrifugal convergences and dispersions in which they and the characters are involved.

The time-pattern of the play is even more complicated than that of space and is better documented in the speeches of the participants. It is significant that the first group to enter and introduce itself is Gentilitas:

> Deorum immortalitas
> Est omnibus colenda,
> Eorum et pluralitas
> Ubique metuenda.
> (prologue, ll. 1–4)

The very first words spoken in the play thus broach two concepts, immortality and plurality, and the rest of the speech is little more than *amplificatio* of these two ideas. The pagan gods are eternal in the sense that they have always been there since the beginning of time. Their time is therefore that into which Jewish time and Christian secular time are fitted, but it is not eternity in the Christian sense of the term. The gods are creations, whether they are regarded as figments of the human imagination or as evil spirits. Their time is therefore longer than Christian secular time but does not and cannot correspond to Christian eternity. Their plurality makes them the exact opposite of Christian *simplicitas,* that unity which is in God and which is the goal towards which Christians strive. Nor is immortality the same for all the gods. Time for the pagans is thus very long, extending indefinitely backwards. There is no move towards any new point in time—the Day of Judgment—nor any move to unity, simply an indefinite and pointless prolongation of secular time. The pagan gods are as much subject to secular time as their worshipers.

The views on time expressed by Synagoga are less explicit but equally significant. The expressed hope of salvataion lies with God, not with man or with Christ. The contrast is between the continuation of life and the hope of eternity. Synagoga's time is the same as that of the Christian before the birth of Christ; it is a period of waiting for the Messiah. Time for the Jews is thus shown as parallel to but outside time, in the sense that it continues indefinitely the time of the Old Law, already in fact superseded, and thus comes no nearer to ultimate salvation, since, from the Christian point of view, a time which is moving towards unity and the end of secular time has already been established.

Christian time is in sharp contrast to these. It combines unity with diversity, eternity with time. The verses sung by Ecclesia and by the chorus both emphasize this in their vocabulary and in their style:

> Unum te lumen credimus
> Quod et ter idem colimus
> Alpha et O quem dicimus
> Te laudet omnis spiritus.

The emphasis is on the triumph of life over death, whereas in the speech of Synagoga there is no such belief. Christian time is at once progress toward salvation and toward spiritual eternity. It will be observed that it differs from pagan time because it concerns the spiritual as well as the secular world, with which latter the pagan world is entirely concerned, and from Jewish time because it has already started a new time from the true Messiah, while the Jews still wait. If I may use a paradox, Christian time is at once linear, because its secular elements proceed toward salvation, and circular because its ultimate end is the same as its beginning ("sine fine principium").

The various Christian kings who ascend their thrones represent the secular aspects of Christian time, and the importance of this is stressed in the very first lines of the dramatic action:

> Sicut scripta tradunt   hystoriographorum,
> Totus mundus fuerat   fiscus Romanorum.
> (I.1.1–2)

The Holy Roman Emperor bases his claim to the obedience of the other kings on historic grounds, on his being a ruler in direct line from the classical Roman emperors. We are witnessing the continuation of the last of the great secular empires, the completion of whose allotted span will signal the approach of the Day of Judgment. It is thus vital for the author of the play to establish the continuation of secular "Roman" time and the legitimacy of the Emperor's actions in unifying Christendom. His actions are not those of a conqueror but of a man restoring unity in time. The Emperor thus acts as a symbol of continuity from the time of Christ's birth to the time before Doomsday. Although he is a different person, he is still the Emperor and ensures that continuity. Furthermore, he is conscious of his role and apparently also of his place in the continuum, since his action to bring about unity and thus conclude secular time is quite deliberate. All the Christian rulers are as aware of this as he is, and the only resistance, from the King of France, is based on historical argument, namely: Who is the true successor of the Romans?[7]

The Emperor makes no effort to interfere with non-Christian time. There is no mention of any relations with the Jews in the first part of the play, and the battle with Gentilitas is brought about by an attack on Jerusalem by the pagans. It is preceded by the rather cryptic stage direction "cum iam tota ecclesia subdita sit imperio Romano." The meaning is presumably that the Emperor now had all *Christianitas* under his control, an event which would mark a definite point in Christian time. Rex Babylonis again stresses the "novelty" of Christian time, its being a late-comer so far as pagan time is concerned. His desire is to set human existence back into pagan time, a retrogressive act. It stands in sharp contrast to the actions of the Christians. The words of the embassy sent for help to the Emperor could equally well refer to God and the references to Jerusalem either to the secular or the eternal city:

> Defensor ecclesie   nostri miserere,
> Quos volunt inimici   Domini delere.
> Venerunt gentes   in dei hereditatem,
> Obsidione tenent   sanctam civitatem.
> (I.4.13ff.)

To make the point absolutely clear, there is, for the first time, intrusion from outside the time-framework of the play. The angel appears from Christian eternity to reassure Jerusalem. The final act of the play will be of a similar nature.

The battle is fought. "Finito responsorio" is perhaps no more than a stage direction but it does link the battle in time with the timeless words of the responsory. The defeat of the King of Babylon does not abolish pagan time. He is put to flight, not captured or brought into submission, and his concept of time thus continues. It is secular Christian time which appears to end here with the Holy Roman Empire, and the Emperor hands over his power to Ecclesia. From now on, it should be Ecclesia's time which rules, an interval between the end of Christian secular time and the Day of Judgment.

The first part is an imperfect resolution of the time problem. The only change effected is within *Christianitas,* which has been unified and pre-pared for the Day of Judgment by the abolition of Christian secular time through the demise of the Empire. Jewish time and pagan time are, how-ever, unaffected, a fact made very clear by the exact repetition of their opening statements at the beginning of Part II. Their time is still running parallel to that of Ecclesia. One important difference from the situation in Part I should be noted. In Part I, all the characters move onto the stage as they sing their characteristic verses. In Part II, they are already in position in their *sedes* and, according to the first stage direction, "Ec-clesia et Gentilitas vicissim cantant." This is not the order in which they actually sing, and the exact meaning of *vicissim* is not clear. "In their turn" is probably the best translation, for the idea of opposition is present. The important point, however, is that the precursors of Antichrist are not described as having any time of their own, any more than they have space of their own. They "use" the time of all three of the religions. The direction specifically states, "Tunc, cum Ecclesia et Gentilitas et Synagoga vicissim cantant"; the present tense indicates time at which or within which, and here means the time of which the supporters of Antichrist take advantage. Significantly, it is the King of Jerusalem who first yields to their blandishments, as he had been the last to join the Roman emperor (without a struggle). He thus allows Antichrist himself to take possession of the city which is at once the symbol of time and of eternity and begin the process of reversing the movement of time which we saw in the first part. Antichrist's perversion of time has begun.

As Antichrist says in his first speech, his purpose is to substitute his own worship for that of Christ. He stresses that it is the world *(mundus)* which is to adore him, and all his actions make it clear that he is thinking of himself as a ruler in the secular sense and in secular time, even though he uses spiritual signs and Christ's own words to describe his power. His subsequent actions are designed to reverse the time-pattern as he does the space-pattern. By taking over the spiritual center at Jerusalem and expelling both the King and Ecclesia, he restores Christian secular time as it had existed before the emperor's deposition of power. Yet this time cannot continue in the true sense, since the Roman Empire, which defined it, has ceased to exist. The result is chaos, with France and Constantinople respectively bribed and terrorized into becoming part of Antichrist's retrogressive pattern. The deposition of the crown of the Holy Roman Emperor is specifically reversed by the offer of it to the King of the Greeks by Antichrist. The constant verbal parallels to the words of the Gospels used by Antichrist, his followers, and those who yield to him equate his advent not with the second coming of Christ but with the first. Time for Antichrist is time in reverse.

All the actions of Antichrist are those which Christ himself had specifically rejected as means of gaining power in this world or winning converts for the next. None is more specific than Antichrist's use of miracles in persuading the King of the Germans. When the King is persuaded, time has run so far backwards that the King has unilaterally resumed his function as Holy Roman Emperor after his defeat of Antichrist:

> Ius dolo perditum   est sanguine venale.
> Sic retinebimus   decus imperiale
> (II.5.59f.)

It is thus as Emperor, not as King, that he makes his submission to Antichrist:

> Cum autem venerit coram eo, flexo genu offert ei
> coronam cantans:
> tibi profiteor   decus imperiale.
> quo tibi serviam,   ius postulo regale.

The words are the same as those used by the King of the Greeks, but the situation is different. The King of the Germans *is* Emperor. Time is now totally reversed.

Antichrist now goes beyond the opening scene of the play by moving against Gentilitas. The pagans are defeated by Antichrist's army under the leadership of the King of the Germans. Although his refusal to yield is based entirely on his rejection of monotheism, his admission of defeat and request for the return of his kingdom makes no reference to religious faith. He simply acknowledges Antichrist as his secular overlord:

> Tibi profiteor   decus imperiale.
> Quo tibi serviam,   ius postulo regale.

There is thus no overt advance in Christian time. It is the conversion of the pagans which marks progress toward Judgment Day, not their subjection in the secular sense. Once again we have reverted to time as it was at the beginning of the play, when the German emperor was establishing his military supremacy.

Antichrist follows the normal order of events in turning next to the Jews. Several new ideas are introduced into the speech made by Hypocritas to Synagoga. It will be remembered that there was no attack on Synagoga by the German emperor, nor indeed any negotiations. Hypocritas begins by praising the Jews for their persistence in the faith and their long suffering in exile while awaiting the Messiah. The stress is on the length of time and remoteness of space. This time is now at an end, and a new time has come:

> Hec exspectatio   reddet hereditatem,
> Iocunda novitas   mutabit vetustatem.
>   (II.7.9f.)

He announces the birth of the new king, who is the Emmanuel prophesied by the Scriptures, in language which is a careful compilation of the language of the Old and New Testaments. The speech makes it clear that the birth of the new king is the culmination of Jewish time, and Synagoga accepts without question statements made by Hypocritas in the words of the Bible which she had refused to credit in their original form. When she approaches Antichrist, the future tense used in the lines quoted above is replaced by the present:

> Ades, Emmanuel,   quem semper veneramur
> In cuius gloria   nos quoque gloriamur.
>   (II.7.23f.)

Jewish time has apparently culminated in the coming of the Messiah, but the judgment of Synagoga is false. The time is still secular time, and the Jews are still where they were at the beginning of the play, in spite of the effort of Antichrist to show them that they have reached the promised land.[8]

The prophet scene which follows is, from the point of view of time, one of the most interesting in the play. It opens with a statement by the prophets entirely in the past tense, which affirms the Incarnation of Christ, the inability of the Jews to recognize His divinity, His Crucifixion, and the freeing of the patriarchs. This statement is one of facts. It combines with the future in the line, "Hic surrexit non moriturus." The past, Christian revelation which the prophets recognize, merges with the future, the function of Christ in salvation. The next line summarizes the temporal function both of Christ and the prophets, "Regnat semper in proximo venturus." The present is the "perpetual" present, borne out by the juxtaposed "semper," and the next three words refer to the impending completion of time so that it will merge into eternity. All the succeeding verbs, except those in the first two lines, are in the future tense, but they refer to one event only, the end of the world and the Day of Judgment, the completion of secular time. The appearance of Antichrist is a designator of this point in the future, and he is about to act as if he were Christ at the Last Judgment—a situation summarized in the line, "Malos dampnans bonos glorificabit." The final couplet links the Last Judgment with the present of the prophet scene and the unbroken life of the prophets' writings and of Enoch and Elijah, who never die. Elijah himself confirms this:

> Illi nos sumus vere,
> In quos fines   seclorum devenere.
> (II.8.27f.)

They show that Christ has already fulfilled their prophecies and that Antichrist is false. Synagoga is immediately persuaded, recognizes the false
nature of Antichrist, and is converted. Except for a statement that "we
were deceived by Antichrist," all verbs are in the present tense, and the
identification of the Jewish Adonai with the three persons of the Trinity
is made evident. Jewish time, which was indefinitely prolonged in awaiting the coming of the Messiah, now merges into Christian time by the
action of the prophets. True Christian time, moving towards the Day of
Judgment and into eternity, has incorporated Jewish time. Secular time
has been taken over by Antichrist, who has incorporated pagan time and
reversed the movement of Christian secular time toward eternity. Two
time-systems are now opposed, that of Christian/Jewish time linked by
the prophets, and secular time represented by Antichrist. The clash culminates in Antichrist's attempt to anticipate Christ at the Last Judgment.
He proclaims himself as the sole front of religious authority and as the
opponent of worldliness, using the words of true religion in a false sense.
The prophets reply with a truth, an eternal truth consisting of descriptions without verbs, which again brings forth from Antichrist an explo-
sion of offended authority in Old Testament terms. The most significant
line is "Pereant penitus oves occisionis," a perversion by Antichrist of the
concept of the Lamb of God and a clear statement that he regards the
faithful as mere sacrifices to his authority.
  Synagoga's next speech is neatly ambiguous:

> Nos erroris penitet,   ad fidem convertimur;
> Quicquid nobis inferet   persecutor, patimur.
> (II.9.31f.)

This could be construed as a confession to Antichrist, but the audience
knows it is not, firstly because of the word *persecutor,* but chiefly because
the two parties are on a different time-scheme. Synagoga and the prophets are now moving towards eternity, whereas Antichrist is still engaged
in reversing secular time. Ecclesia confirms this interpretation by taking
the Jews to her bosom with the words of the Song of Solomon, the Old
Law interpreted in terms of the New.

The last action of Antichrist is to produce his version of the end of time, a bringing together of his subject kings to inform them that peace has come. The terms used are carefully selected. Antichrist desires to be worshiped, and his use of the word *gloria* bears this out. There follow four lines which are uttered successively by Antichrist, his messengers, and those who approach his throne:

> Cuncta divinitus   manus una firmavit,
> Suos divinitas   hostes exterminavit.
> Pace conclusa sunt   cuncta iura regnorum,
> Ad coronam vocat   suos deus deorum.
>
>   (II.10.3–6)

These four lines are deliberately ambiguous. Antichrist, of course, speaks of himself as "manus una," one hand, a single person, and as "divinitas." The peace he refers to is that gained in secular warfare by the kings under Antichrist's direction. All the laws are laid down and the kings are called upon to acknowledge his throne and himself as god of gods. Such is Antichrist's concept of the end of time, an indefinite prolongation of secular domination in which control is exercised by superstition. In Christian terms, however, the four-line passage states eternal truths about the power of God. The peace referred to is that which will end all strife and end all secular powers, the unshakeable final peace, and the *corona* is the crown of glory which awaits the faithful. But the most significant difference lies in the tenses. Antichrist regards his work as complete and uses the perfect tense in the first two lines. In the last two he is talking about what he regards as a permanent phenomenon in his secular world. In Christian poetry, all four lines would be in the future, since they refer to the final judgment of God on the human race, which will bring secular time to an end. Antichrist has brought time in a circle. He is in the same position as the Holy Roman Emperor in the early scenes of the play, even though he has put an end to Jewish time and pagan time and has attempted to incorporate them in his own concept of indefinite secular time. The same remarks apply to Antichrist's final speech. Again he speaks of himself as the man foretold by the prophets, calls upon all those who have deserved it to share his glory with him, and speaks of the "pax et securitas" which have come after the fall of those who have fallen victim to the world (*vanitas*). Again all verbs but one (*fruentur*) are in the past, even though in Christian terms the events are still to come. He utters the words "pax et securitas universa conclusit" and is immediately struck down, presumably by God's thunderbolt. His time comes to an end. The statement made in his last line is now made Christian fact by Ecclesia's reception of everyone into the true faith. (The "omnes" presumably includes pagans and Jews.) Christian time is now established as the only time, and the events of the play have set it on the true course to eternity by destroying all others.

The time of the *Ludus de Antichristo* is thus determined by the concepts of time inherent in its participants. The span covered by the action of the play begins with a survey of time-concepts of pagan, Jewish, and Christian religious beliefs. Each, in its statement of identification and creed, makes its standing in time clear. A time circle is thus established which, like the circle of space, must also be thought of as including the spectators, who, for the purposes of the play, are viewing events from eternity. The action of the play, however, moves at first in linear fashion, since the deeds of the Holy Roman Emperor are designed to bring Christian secular time to an end. The apparent success of his actions causes the church to take over in Jerusalem and institute nonsecular Christian time, that is, the time of waiting for Judgment. But neither Jewish nor pagan time has been abolished. They continue to exist as parallels to Christian time. In the second part time is turned back on itself, and Jewish and pagan time are forced or cajoled into integration with secular, Antichrist time. It is by direct divine intervention that this time is brought to an end and the position at the end of secular Christian time restored and Jewish and pagan time eliminated. The play which began with a rehearsal of the enormous diversity of the time-concepts of the various groups thus ends its own time with total unity. The Christian secular time unified by the Emperor is merged with the Jewish and pagan time shattered by Antichrist into a total *simplicitas*. Time in the play, like time for *Christianitas*, is in suspense and awaits the Second Coming.

We may apply very similar criteria to the study of space. The position of the *sedes* on the stage is far less important in absolute than in relative terms. Movement is from centers to points on a circumference, but the center itself shifts in sympathy with the movement in time. The play ends with no change in the absolute positions of the abstractions representing secular powers but with a major shift of center. The two movements of Ecclesia to Jerusalem are, as we saw, the indicators of a time-shift, and they perform the same function for space. There is, however, one important modification: there is no continuing linear movement in space as there is in time. There are no beginnings or endings in the sense that characters appear or disappear. The movement is entirely within a circle, so that, in spite of the action of the play, the universe as represented on stage remains unchanged in its relative physical relationships but, at the end of the play, is totally changed in its focus of attention and in the links which bind it. Instead of a number of separate centers a group is formed which concentrates on the Emperor, and attention moves to Jerusalem. The center is first shattered by the discursive and dispersing actions of Antichrist, then re-formed about him in a false sense. The concentration he effects, by moving all elements (except the audience) from points on the circumference to Jerusalem is simply a duplicate of the actions of the Emperor, with the important addition of Gentilitas, and it contributes to the final solution, when Antichrist is eliminated by divine action.

In both space and time the author represents the circularity of the world by his positioning and movement within space. In both space and time, the linear movement is always to attain an end within the circle, a circle of which the audience is an essential part.

NOTES

1. I have used the expanded text given by Karl Langosch in his *Geistliche Spiele* (Darmstadt, 1957), pp. 181 ff., notes pp. 267 ff. The expansions, which seem to me sensible suggestions, play little or no role in my argument.

2. For a convenient summary of the literature, see Paul Lehmann, *Das literarische Bild Karls des Grossen* (Munich, 1934; reprinted 1959).

3. For a detailed study of the theme as it appears in drama, see Klaus Aichele, *Das Antichristdrama des Mittelalters, der Reformation und der Gegenreformation* (Den Haag, 1974).

4. Langosch assumes that they share the throne of the German emperor, but the text does not state this.

5. *Isidori Hispalensis episcopi Etymologiarum sive Originum Libri XX*, W. M. Lindsay, ed. (Oxford, 1911), xiii, 11.

6. The language is not altogether clear. The German king says "Sic retinebimus / decus imperiale." Langosch, who translates "Wir werden so den Glanz des Kaisers wieder erringen," appears to think that the King is talking in terms of the recovery of the imperial power he has given up, a reversion to earlier, secular, time. The passage could mean "these are the methods by which we shall keep up

imperial power," i.e., supreme power. It is "decus imperiale" that he concedes to Antichrist, in the sense of recognizing his possession of it. The King of Babylon uses the same phrase.

7. The use of the word *tributum,* perfectly natural in the context, inevitably recalls the biblical "licet nobis dare tributum an non?" (Luke 20:22; variants Matthew 22:17, Mark 12:14), which appears to give Christ's own approval to the Emperor's action.

8. All the speeches of Antichrist and the allusions in them point to his being treated as a derogatory allegorization of Christ, a kind of anti-allegory.

9

Pyrgopolinices Converted:
The Boasting Soldier in
Medieval German Literature

SINCE THE BEGINNINGS of Western literature man seems to
have been divided between admiration for the heroic stature of the
great soldier and contempt for those who used the reputation of their
profession to gain personal advantages. Both attitudes are well exempli-
fied in the literature of all ages, but it fell to the Athenians, those urban
and urbane civilians, to crystallize the dislike and contempt of the suffer-
ers into a clearly distinguishable and permanent literary type. This figure,
the αλαζών, is best known to us through the dramas of Plautus and Terence but he is essentially a character of the Greek New Comedy. For in
him we see that infringement upon the norms of social conduct which is
characteristic of all the figures of that comedy. His vices are exaggerated
projections of all that a civilian found least attractive in the military. The
core of his character is excessive vanity, a vanity so colossal that it does
not know even when it is being mocked. Of this vanity his boasting is
only one manifestation; he is led into traps by his lechery and his stupidity, most of all by his inordinate appetite for money and bribes. Thus we
see him in Plautus' *Miles Gloriosus,* easily persuaded of the love of a neighbor's wife for him and always eager for pecuniary gain. In spite of this
stupidity, Pyrgopolinices is a powerful man and knows it. And it is this
very element which provides the essential feature of comedy—discomfiture at the hand of the weak and socially inferior. The type was soon well
established and there can be little doubt that, on the decline of legitimate
comedy in Rome, it was taken over by the *mimi.*

Since the appearance of Reich's book,[1] the use of the word *mimus* raises many questions and few people would agree with his extreme interpretation. The words *mimus, histrio, ioculator* are often used interchangeably and there can be no question of the survival of the theatrical *ludus mimicus* as such. Yet the persistent references in church decrees to the scandals of acting, the prohibition on participation of the clergy in marriage feasts where they were present indicate that there were actors, who would provide entertainment for those who could pay. These actors must have had an oral tradition, a stock in trade of parts and characters handed down from one generation to the next. The persistence of such types in the folk drama of modern times demonstrates how strong this oral tradition was and is still. It is therefore altogether likely that many of the types portrayed were those which had been found popular in the ancient theater and which, suitably adapted to contemporary traditions, could be relied upon to produce their effect. That such a figure as that of the *miles gloriosus* would be among the most popular of these types is very probable. In a society essentially military and feudal, the portrait of the braggart soldier could not fail to appeal. The actors who portrayed him would have no idea of his descent, no idea of the connection with Plautus and Terence. To them he was simply a stock character in their act. The connection with classical antiquity lies entirely in an oral acting tradition. The object of the representation, however, remained unchanged—to satirize those aspects of the military mind and of military behavior which appealed least to the civilian. Thus a literary type and a theatrical tradition would coincide. The soldier becomes a character whose very appearance prepared the audience for laughter of a special kind, for a demonstration of exaggeration and distortion which would flatter the soldier in the audience and soothe the civilian.[2]

This survival, this persistent tradition, was not, however, the only influence which was affecting the figure of the soldier in literature. The growth of feudalism and in particular of the conception of knighthood was leading more and more to a close association between the ideas of a perfect Christian and a perfect soldier. It was no longer sufficient for a soldier to demonstrate qualities of physical courage and to give obedience to a secular code. He had to exemplify in his own person those virtues most closely associated with Christianity. He had to become the *miles Christianus*. Now it has been correctly pointed out by Preissl that some of the earliest and clearest evidence we have of the crystalization of the type of *miles christianus* is to be found in the tenth century in the plays of Hroswitha of Gandersheim.[3] Concerned as she was with the propagation of Christian virtues, with offsetting the sinful beauties of Terence with Christian purity in contrast to pagan vice, she is careful to depict her heroic soldiers as following the rules for the *miles Christianus:* "tueri ecclesiam, impugnare perfidium, sacerdotium venerari, propulsare pauperum iniurias, pacare provinciam" (to protect the church, to fight unbelief, to respect the priesthood, to relieve the wrongs of the poor, to make peace upon earth). His virtues are a formidable catalog: "spes, pulchritudo, fides, charitas, nobilitas, ingenuitas, bona fortuna, cautio, iustitia, severitas, liberalitas, beneficentia, religio, veritas, misericordia, innocentia, reverentia, pietas, fortitudo, securitas, constantia." Virtuous indeed was the knight who combined in his own person such a mass of good qualities. But the list is important, for it is of great influence on the characterization of the heroes of the courtly epic and in particular of Parzival. More important for our purpose is that Hroswitha's artistic sense caused her to seek for an opposite type, a black background against which the purity of her heroes or heroines could stand out more sharply. The most clearly drawn of these is Dulcitius, the one truly comic figure in Hroswitha's work. His basic characteristics and his actions are already present in the story, found in the *Acta Sanctorum,*[4] upon which Hroswitha drew. But he is infinitely more alive in the play—vain (for he thinks the girls must like him), lecherous, cunning (note where he imprisons them), blustering (they won't get away with this), and above all disrespectful to the church. In him we see personified the opposites of the Christian virtues—"luxuria, cupiditas, infidelitas, calliditas, crudelitas, ignavia." Now these are the very vices or qualities of the *miles gloriosus* or of his equivalent in the mime and it is tempting indeed to see here a deliberate effort on the part of Hroswitha to discredit classical comedy by selecting a story of martyrs in which there appeared a character very close to the *miles gloriosus* of classical comedy. Did Hroswitha have some experience of the mime version of the *miles gloriosus?* Had she seen the black-faced, cowardly, and lustful soldier brought to disgrace and ignominy by his own vices? She mentions the charm of Terence's style, but in spite of the raptures of some critics there is little evidence that she made any attempt to imitate it,[5] and one has the feeling that her ideas on Terence may ultimately have been colored by the crude representation of the *mimi.* This question cannot be answered, but what is certain is that Hroswitha formulated clearly a type of *miles antichristianus* in which she incorporated those elements of the *miles gloriosus* tradition which corresponded neatly with the "sins" in the *Lasterkatalog*, directly opposed to the virtues of the true Christian soldier.

It is in the poems of the Arthurian cycle that we should expect to find a fully developed type of *miles antichristianus* and we do indeed find those characteristics in the opponents of the heroes of the Round Table. But here the source material, and especially the legendary and mythological elements, color the characterization and development so strongly that any attempts to isolate those elements which are derived from the *miles gloriosus* tradition are foredoomed to failure. But one feature of the Arthurian epics deserves attention. Sir Kei was originally, that is, in the Celtic tradition,[6] one of the Round Table. There was little trace of those unpleasant characteristics which made him the butt of all later writers. How did this violent change come about? It is obvious that it dates from that period of the development of the Arthurian cycle when the stories were in the hands of the professional story tellers, and that the writers of the epics in French and German took over a tradition already established. It is clear from all the epics that Sir Kei is the very type of boasting soldier; his treatment of Iwein in the matter of the night of the fountain,[7] his challenges to Parzival and Lanzelet,[8] and his subsequent discomfiture reveal him as a braggart and not even an efficient one. But perhaps even more significant is his more lengthy appearance in the *Krone* of Heinrich von dem Türlin.[9] The scene is one of the numerous tests which the unfortunate knights and ladies of King Arthur's court were so often called upon to endure. A cup is passed round from which only the chaste lady and the man of untarnished honor can drink without spilling. Again and again Sir Kei laughs and mocks at the successive proofs of misbehavior— only to be made ridiculous before the whole court as his own wife fails the test with éclat and he himself is proved even lower than those around him.

Why was Sir Kei thus treated? The answer is as much sociological as literary. Sir Kei was a steward and thus in direct charge of the *ioculatores* who haunted the courts. Such stewards were probably not the best loved officials in the eyes of the wandering minstrels and it was in revenge for insults suffered and misery endured that the transmitters of the Arthurian legends foisted upon the steward the character they had ready to hand— the boasting soldier, always ready to outdo the world in talking but falling both literally and figuratively over his own excessive vanity. It is no accident that Sir Kei has more broken limbs than any other Arthurian knight and that he falls so grotesquely. He is the heir of mimic slapstick.

Sir Kei reflects the resources which were at the command of the wandering actors but he is not the *miles antchristianus*—rather the *miles non christianus*. We may find numerous instances of the *miles antichristianus* in the Arthurian romances—Valerin and Meleogranz in *Lanzelet* for example. But to see the clear development of the type, we must again turn to the drama. Here we are fortunate in having a developing series of plays in which the emergence of the type can be traced. Now the events in the life of Christ which form the subject of the drama, Christmas, the Passion, and the Resurrection, were all in some way involved with pagan soldiers. The slaughter of the Innocents by the order of Herod appears in the Christmas plays; Pilate and his minions are the villains of the Passion and particularly of the Crucifixion. It is in the representation of these characters that fusion between the comic soldier still played by the professional actors and the Christian picture of the pagan bringing martyrdom to the innocent could be most easily carried out.

For once again our problem is at least in part sociological. There can be little doubt that the comic elements enter the religious plays when professional actors begin to be employed. The Mercator scene is obviously deeply rooted in tradition, not even Christian tradition. But the soldiers were easier to play. There is biblical authority for their presence on several occasions in the life of Christ,[10] but their role is a small one. It was the clear duty of any professional to make these roles into occasions for the use of business he knew was popular and stock characters of certain appeal.

The development is slow at first. If soldiers appeared, they were silent. Their earliest "appearance" as speakers is in a play written in Latin, the *Klosterneuburger Osterspiel;*[11] they sing a chorus together and dance to the refrain: "schouwe, schouwe propter insidias." The song they sing has little comic force and merely repeats in substance the orders they have received. But its presence in the play and the dance that accompanies it are indications of the increasing influence of the secular and the comic— and hence of the professional actor. It is interesting to note that the *Krämerszene* also appears here and is even more developed in the parallel play of Benediktbeuren. But even so it would be futile to maintain that there is here, at least in the text, any embellishment or development of the bare theme that the soldiers at the grave were bribed and that the power of the angels crushed their disbelief in the Lord's resurrection. The play is still essentially controlled by the sacred elements, even though the germs of the comic scenes are there. The soldiers are thus anti-Christian but only in a formal sense. Dramatically they are still in embryo.

The same situation prevails in the *Wiener Osterspiel*. But the conduct of the soldiers is more boastful and they betray their mimic origin by the sacrilegious song they chant about Jesus' resurrection as they move to the grave.

> wir wollin tzu dem grabe gan:
> Iesus der wil uf irstan.
> ist das wor, ist das wor,
> zo sint goldin unser hor![12]

Mockery of Christianity had been characteristic of the mime in classical times and here its influence may be plainly seen. It is in the scenes with Cayphas after the soldiers have returned from the grave that the comic elements begin to appear most clearly; the financial negotiations are realistically tightfisted.

YSAAC *dicit:* Ir seyt esil und affin!
Welch tewfil hot euch geschaffin,
das ir seyt also blint?
euch hilft dach keyne login hint!
ir seyt rechte logener!
is wirt euch noch czu swer:
ir habet genomen gobin
und en weg lossin tragen!
DER ANDIR RITTER: Sweigit stille, ys wirt euch gut!
PESSAG *dicit:* Jo, gummen, das ir uns icht tut!
gebit uns wedir unsern solt,
beyde silber und golt
unde vil drote czu der stunt,
adir wyr benemen euch ewern gesunt!
ISAAC: Ouch sweiget stille dorczu,
ee wir euch nedir slon alz eyne ku!
TERTIUS MILES: Das welle wir vorsuchen nw!
. . . .
ir herren, nw rucket ewer swert!
slot an sy, sy seynt sin wol wert![13]

Obviously the dialogue brings us close to those scenes where the soldiers' misery is completed by a hail of buffets, blows, and insults at the hands of persons themselves despised—as it was at the end of Dulcitius. The professional actors have taken over the scene and to it have adapted these scenes of low soldiery which were part of their stock in trade. All this is clear enough but it should be emphasized—and this has been frequently overlooked in facile statements about the introduction of "derbe Realistik"—that these scenes serve a definite dramatic purpose. For the object is not merely to amuse the groundlings but to present upon the stage the anti-Christian element and to ensure its defeat. It is with the high priest and his followers and with Pilate, all anti-Christian characters, that the soldiers quarrel. The reduction of these characters to a ridiculous level was best attained by grafting upon them the characteristics of stock comic figures already well-known to the audience.

As the sacred drama becomes more developed, and incorporates more comic elements, the identification of the boasting soldier type which had been introduced with the *miles antichristianus* becomes increasingly clear. The boast that Christ will not rise again while they are watching, that any disciples who appear will be given rough treatment, and a great deal of mutual admiration and moral back-slapping, all these contrast sharply with the abject terror at the angels or the miserable apologies of the return when they announce the failure of their mission. The boasters are deflated, their hollowness exposed. The characteristics of the boasting soldier are made to correspond with those mentioned earlier—stress is laid on his ignorant disregard of the virtues of the Christian knight, or his deliberate flouting of them. In both cases his fault was equally great, for he had the opportunity to learn better and willfully disregarded that opportunity. Far from protecting the church, he attacks it, he rejoices in perfidy instead of combatting it, he mocks not only the priesthood but Christ himself. What once were mere stage directions now become scenes with differentiated personalities. Nowhere is the utter depravity of the soldier better brought out than in the Donaueschinger Passion Play. Here the soldiers vie with one another in the cruelties they can inflict and the jokes they can play on the unresisting Jesus. At the scourging and crucifixion they fill the cup of evil to the brim. The deliberate prolongation and intensification of the agony of Christ and their callous demeanor *(crudelitas)*, their dicing for the garments, and their quarrelling over the spoils *(avaritia, cupiditas)*, their boasting over women in the *Alsfelder Pas-*

sionsspiel (luxuria), all stand in marked contrast to the knightly virtues we have already mentioned and agree only too closely with the thundering condemnation of Bernard of Cluny, who years before had described the anti-Christian soldier:

The fierce soldier who plunders and tortures, pilfers, oppresses the poor,
Those he touches he crushes, gnashes his teeth at them, bites them
Driving and striking, burning, o'erturning, racking the country
Consuming as flame, and twice as destructive . . .[14]

This is Bernard's view of the *miles antichristianus* and we have no difficulty in seeing that the drama too illustrates these vices but in a form which was infinitely more effective for popular consumption. Mere description of these vices would have produced little effect in the somewhat hardened sensibilities of the common man. So a type was selected with which everyone was familiar—the boasting soldier. He was inserted in the story in those scenes where there was some slight biblical justification for his existence and made to demonstrate the unchristian vices. How far the introduction of such scenes, and in particular of the players who were to act them, was a deliberate attempt to utilize the minions of the devil, namely the *ioculatores,* in the service of the church is a question which is unlikely ever to be fully answered. Certainly the evidence points to such an attempt, for it is hardly likely that the professional actors would have been allowed to take part in the plays on any other terms. If such was the intention, it was a dubious success. For the type got out of hand. There was little to prevent the ambitious producer of sacred plays from giving more and more prominence to those comic or crude elements which appealed to the less sensitive members of his audience. Even when the intention was to impress upon the hearer the monstrous villainy of the forces opposing Christ, the very realism of the representation would be more likely to impress itself upon an uncultivated audience than the more somber truths which underlay that realism.

But there was another factor. With the decline of chivalry in the thirteenth and fourteenth century, the alleged *miles christianus,* the ideal knight, had more and more the appearance of his unchristian counterpart. The writers had probably good reason to know of this degeneration and could make excellent use of the *miles antichristianus* type as a parody, a parody which would be amply appreciated by fellow victims in a predominantly

bourgeois audience. Thus the boasting soldier returns to his original role—
he satirizes the militarism of his day in all its aspects. Even as early as the
thirteenth-century Muri Easter Play the references to the soldiers of the
court are unmistakable:

SERVUS: Here, als du hast gedaht,
           so choment si gelihe,
           die huoter güetelihe.
PILATUS: Sint willechome, ir heren mir,
           selfiu got, nu sagent ir,
           waz geschalles ist bi iuh gewesen?
PRIMUS CUSTOS: Da sin wir chume genesen!
           wir waren vil nah alle tot
           und sin endrunnen mit not,
           und wie uns geshehen ist,
           daz sage ih dir in churcer vrist:
           do wir hinaht lagen,
           als wir des grabes phlagen
           mit vil grozem vlize,
           do cham en engel wize,
           der begunde zuo zuns gahen,
           und du er uns wolte nahen,
           do cham uor im en tonrshal,
           da von ershein da uber al
           von dem blicheshoze en viur:
           da von wart da so ungehiur,
           daz wir vil chume endrunnen sin.
           ih sprihez uf die triuwe min,
           daz wir des gelihe iehen.[15]

The use of courtly language is unmistakable and it offered a good opportunity to pillory the reliance of the knights on physical force and their
overwhelming interest in the acquisition of wealth by any means, fair or
foul.

Thus in considering the character of the boasting soldier we are once
again faced with one of the eternal problems of literature—that of the
boundary between literary invention and life. It is clear that the *miles gloriosus* type springs from a deep human feeling, present in every age, of
revolt against the particular form of militarism current at that time. But
the mere presence of such a feeling is not in itself enough to give birth

to a literary type, particularly such a well-defined type as the boasting soldier. It was the definition of that type by the Greeks and its later modifications by the Roman comedy and mime which provided subsequent literary tradition with the material with which it had to work. The matter ceases to be social and becomes typological. It becomes established in the popular and literary mind and can be relied upon to produce certain reactions in an audience merely by association. As such the type becomes timeless, one of the aspects of the human comedy which are ever present. But for effective use in literature it must be brought into relationship with the vital themes of its time. And this is why we must speak of Pyrgopolinices converted. For it is as the *miles antichristianus* that he appears. His characteristics suited so perfectly the picture of the soldier lost to all Christian virtues, causing by his wickedness grief to the martyrs and anguish to the faithful. Brought into the drama to act as a foil to Christian virtue, he grows and flourishes until he monopolizes the attention whenever he is on the stage. For the boasting soldier in medieval literature represented then as he does now that desire to see the collapse of "those sanguine cowards and abominable misleaders of youth," as the most famous of them all was called. For Falstaff, Shakespeare created sympathy, but for the medieval braggart soldier there was little but mockery and contempt. He paid the penalty of his opposition to the church by earning the hatred of all good Christians and the penalty of his character in the laughter which accompanied his inevitable collapse.

NOTES

1. H. Reich, *Der Mimus* (Berlin, 1903).

2. See for example the stage direction in the text of the *Visitatio* of Sainte Chapelle in Paris: "Surgant milites, si ibidem fuerint et faciant quod eis bonum faciendum." In K. Young, *The Drama of the Medieval Church* (Oxford: Oxford University Press, 1933), I:288.

3. F. Preissls, *Hroswitha von Gandersheim und die Entstehung des mittelalterlichen Heldenbildes.* Erlanger Arbeiten zur deutschen Literatur, vol. 12 (1939).

4. The story is based upon the "De Sanctis sororibus Agape, Chionia, et Irene," to be found in *Acta Sanctorum* (Paris, 1866), Aprilis I:245–50.

5. Especially the French ones.

6. See Ulrich von Zatzikoven, *Lanzelet,* Webster and Loomis, tr. (New York: Columbia University Press, 1951), note 99 and the references therein.

7. Hartmann von Aue, *Iwein,* F. Bech, ed., Deutsche Classiker des Mittelalters, vol. 6, part 3 (Leipzig, 1873), lines 810 ff.

8. Wolfram von Eschenbach, *Parzival,* E. Hartl, ed. (Berlin: 1952), 290, 3 ff.; Ulrich von Zatzikoven, *Lanzelet,* K. A. Hahn, ed. (Frankfurt/Main, 1845), lines 2990 ff.

9. Heinrich von dem Türlin, *Die Krone,* G. H. F. Scholl, ed. (Stuttgart, 1852), Bibliothek des literarischen Vereins in Stuttgart, vol. 27, lines 1239 ff.

10. Matthew 27:62–66; 28:2–4, 11–15.

11. *Das Drama des Mittelalters,* E. Hartl, ed., Deutsche Literatur in Entwicklungsreihen (Leipzig, 1937), 2:35.

12. *Drama des Mittelalters,* 2:80 (336.11 ff.).

13. *Drama des Mittelalters,* 2:91 (311.3 ff.).

14. *De contemptu mundi,* H. C. Hoskier, ed. (London, 1929), Book 2, lines 315 ff.

15. *Drama des Mittelalters,* 2:276.

FOUR

ALLEGORY AND ROMANCE

10

Allegory and Allegorization

T HERE ARE few words in literary criticism so abused as allegory. A work whose meaning is obscure—and there are many such—can often be raised to a high level of literary dignity by designating it as an allegory. Every action, every nuance of character, every detail of description, every feature of the milieu can be "interpreted," and the method has the superb advantage that the critic himself can determine the frame within which the interpretation is to take place. Is he a social realist? Then every detail can be referred to class struggle, to environmental influences. Is he a man of deep religious feeling? Then the story refers to man's relation to his God. Of "psychological" interpretations it is hardly necessary to speak. Every page of the most innocent story is found to be littered with Freudian symbols.

It may easily be argued that medieval writers allegorized freely and that they constantly interpreted anecdotes from the classics and even works of doubtful morality as parables of Christian revelation. No reader of the *Legenda aurea* or the *Gesta Romanorum* would deny the charge, but one important factor must not be overlooked. The interpretation was always within the framework of Christian revelation. The theologically acceptable reading of the Old Testament as a foreshadowing of the New, the acceptance of certain incidents, for example, Daniel in the lions' den, as foreshadowing Christ's descent into Hell, meant that by extension secular material could also be interpreted as reflecting God's purpose. Since all human acts and all events in some way reflect the divine will, they can be interpreted as referring to Christian revelation.

The danger of such a practice lies in the fact that it is uncontrolled, in the sense that the events allegorized may be so obviously immoral or at least superficially unchristian that to interpret them as Christian revelation is distasteful. Yet there remains the control that all the allegorizing is done with reference to Christianity. The interpreter cannot use any frame of reference he feels inclined to use. Such allegorization as this is found very largely in the theological commentaries, where it is widespread, or in moral and didactic works. The sermons on the *Song of Songs* by Bernard de Clairvaux are the best twelfth-century examples of this detailed application of the techniques of allegorization.

To say that these allegorizing methods passed from theological to secular literature is a little inexact, since they seem to have originated in the Greek allegorizations of Homer. Yet for the Middle Ages it is true to say that allegorization was felt to be a theological technique which could be applied to secular works. It is also true that many medieval readers of such secular works would be able to apply the training they had received and see in the events and characters of the romance the reflection of a higher secular ideal. The most obvious example of the application of such allegorizing is in the *Tristan and Isolt* of Gottfried von Strassburg. Here indeed is the secular counterpart of theological allegorizing. A cave with its smooth walls and high roof, its crystal bed and guarded door is allegorized in terms of the accepted method of relating the church building to the Church of Christ. Thus there is a double allegory, a parody of an allegory, for if the cave can be allegorized in the same way as a church, then there must be some relation between the frames within which the allegories operate, the church of love and the Church of Christ.

Let us stress once again that this is allegorizing, not the literary genre which we call allegory. Gottfried's cave is a cave. It has walls and a room, and its location is described in detail. Tristan and Isolt live in it. Its attributes, however, are features whose allegorical value was already well established—the wild mountain with its tiny favored spot like an earthly paradise, with trees of special types and the bird song of the love-lyric. The likelihood of an allegorical interpretation is clear. Gottfried, however, does not ask us to allegorize the scene for ourselves—he does the interpreting for us, leaving us only to make the important shift, namely that the allegorization he makes parallels that of Christianity. The ultimate generalization is again made by Gottfried—that the cave exists in the hearts of all *edele herzen* or "Tristan lovers."

Gottfried's *Minnegrotte* scene stands midway between allegorization and medieval allegory as a literary genre. For the two are quite different, and it will be the principal purpose of this essay to show what the essential features of the allegory type are. Let it be said at once that allegory does not need to be allegorized. By its very nature it performs the essential act of universalizing, of expressing the general by means of the particular, the universal by the individual.

The books of rhetoric do not mention allegory as a type.[1] Their definitions of it are based on such classical statements as that of Quintilian, *De institutione oratoria* VIII.6.44:

> At allegoria, quam inversionem interpretantur, aliud verbis aliud sensu ostendit ac etiam interim contrarium: prius fit genus plerumque continuatis translationibus ut
>
> > O navis, referent in mare te novi
> > fluctus: o quid agis? Fortiter occupa
> > portum . . .
>
> totusque ille Horatii locus quo navim pro republica, fluctuum tempestatem pro bellis civilibus portum pro pace atque concordia dicit . . .

Such a definition clearly refers to metaphor, and Quintilian makes it clear that he regards *allegoria* as a sustained metaphor in which the sequence of metaphorical expressions is not broken by any explanation. Such a sustained metaphor can easily be lengthened into a prolonged series of personifications. Even in such a brief example as the passage from Horace just quoted, the allegory is controlled by the conditions of seafaring, so that it can be interpreted only in a limited way.

If we compare this definition with that given by Isidore, *Etymologiae* I.xxxvii.22, the contrast is marked:

> Allegoria est alieniloquium. Aliud enim sonat et aliud intellegitur ut Vergilius *Aeneis* I. 184: Tres litore cervos conspicit errantes, ubi tres duces belli punici, vel tria bella punica significantur. . . . Inter allegoriam autem et aenigma hoc interest quod allegoriae vis gemina est et sub res alias aliud figuraliter indicat, aenigma vero sensus tantum obscurus est et per quasdam imagines adumbratur.

Such a definition as this clearly opens the way to any kind of interpretation. If allegory is simply saying one thing and meaning another, any statement may be treated allegorically and may be used to illustrate Christian and other truths.

Quintilian and Isidore represent two different traditions of the definition of allegory. Bede follows Isidore, as might be expected (*De Schematis* II.12): "Allegoria est tropus quo aliud significatur quam dicitur." The examples he gives are all arbitrary interpretations of biblical passages, e.g., the two sons of Abraham representing the Old and New Testaments.

Neither of these two definitions can be said to be clearly connected with the development of the literary type we call allegory, except in the very general sense that allegory is an extended metaphor. Allegory (which will be capitalized in this essay when it refers to the literary type) stems from a number of rhetorical devices and in particular from personification. It is unnecessary to labor this point or to do more than point out the well-known classical examples—Rumor in Vergil and Ovid, Virtus and Clementia in Statius. The principle of such personifications is clear. An abstraction is made to talk and act like a human being or a god (which in the classical tradition amounts to much the same thing) and is furnished with attributes, such as numerous mouths or wings, which intensify its characteristics and explain its behavior and role in the work. Such personification is a long step on the road to Allegory, but it is by no means the decisive step. This step is taken when the personified abstractions become the only participants in the action or when the appearance of human beings is confined to the participation of the author himself or his *persona*. The earliest such work which survives is the *Psychomachia* of Prudentius (late fourth century), and it was one of the most influential of all works for medieval literature.

All the characters in the *Psychomachia* are abstractions and all are female, partly because their names are grammatically feminine, partly because of the long tradition in classical literature of female virtues and vices— and advisers such as Diotima in the *Symposium*. Their names and qualities reflect the growing tendency in Christian literature to isolate the various qualities of human behavior and show them as opposing virtues and vices. The characters in Prudentius' work do not conform exactly to the later cardinal virtues and seven deadly sins, but there is considerable correspondence. The work is cast in the form of single combats, a natural contrivance if human existence is to be regarded as an unremitting struggle between the forces of good and evil. Much more important, however, for any understanding of the nature of medieval Allegory is recognition that the *Psychomachia* uses and relies on the conventions of the Vergilian epic. The fact is so obvious that its importance for the subsequent development of Allegory has not been appreciated.

The work assumes, as does the Vergilian epic, a struggle between the two opposed views of existence—the new Trojan and the old Italian in the *Aeneid,* the combats between brothers in the *Thebaid* of Statius, and it assumes also the possibility of the resolution of the struggle between these forces by the outcome of one titanic conflict. In the *Psychomachia* this battle is fought for and perhaps in the human soul, but its trappings, physical description, and methods of combat are all those of the classical epic. Ditches are dug by Fraus, Superbia rides a huge horse, sword and spear thrusts dispose of the combatants. No device of rhetoric is spared to impart to the participants the characteristics of dress or behavior which will illustrate their nature and identify them for the reader. In making abstractions human, Prudentius has taken them beyond humanity into the larger-than-life world of the epic.

No one in Prudentius' day thought of war and battle in the terms he describes. The Roman army was a practical and successful military machine which did not rely on obtaining a decision by the individual victories of selected heroes. By using these epic techniques, Prudentius lends to the Christian's daily struggle with evil the grandeur and majesty as well as the authority of the epic. The Vergilian frame and the epic convention are as important for Prudentius' work as the fact of personification. The implication of an "epic" struggle dignifies the effort to make virtue conquer vice and universalizes it. No allegorization is necessary, for here are set out in the most general terms the universal truths which allegorization seeks to determine from specific incidents. *Superbia* is not an example of Pride but all Pride everywhere, and in defeating *Luxuria, Pudicitia* destroys all sexual depravity. Such a universalization would have little aesthetic appeal were it to be presented in the bald form "Luxuria defeated by Pudicitia." Only by making abstractions alive, by endowing them with behavior, can they be made believable. Yet such abstractions simply cannot move into everyday life, for they would lose their effectiveness. Only by giving them a milieu outside everyday life but within the experience of the reader can they be made real. Such a combination could be achieved only by the use of an established literary frame.

Another popular and influential work of late classical antiquity illustrates the necessity felt by the writers of Allegory to use an established frame. Martianus Capella (c. 375) wished to describe the nature and function of the seven liberal arts. Rather than follow the simple method of describing them *in abstracto,* he chose to incorporate his description in an elaborate Allegory which, to judge from the numerous medieval commentaries on it, struck the fancy of readers. The form chosen this time was the marriage feast of the gods, a widespread type of which perhaps the best-known classical example is the *Marriage of Peleus and Thetis* of Catullus. Conventionally such a poem gave wide latitude to the author to insert topics not directly connected with the narrative. Martianus Capella follows this tradition by making the seven liberal arts into goddesses who are attendants at a marriage feast where their appearance is particularly appropriate, that of the god of the arts, Mercury, and Philology, a lady who is a newcomer to the Olympic pantheon.

As a work of art the *Marriage of Mercury and Philology* leaves a great deal to be desired. It is mentioned here only because it illustrates the compelling necessity which Martianus Capella felt to put his universal treatment of the seven liberal arts into the frame of a well-known poetical form. Neither to him nor to Prudentius is it a matter of concern that the frame belongs to pagan literature. The Vergilian grandeur is the point at issue with Prudentius, the classical tradition of learning with Martianus. Each author imparts authority to his work by his choice of frame.

How did this frame tradition develop during the Middle Ages? It was long in developing. There are numerous examples of personification, but they occur mostly in debate poems or other brief pieces. There is no full-scale Allegory in Latin or the vernacular until the thirteenth century; in other words, until the courtly romance had developed a new set of values and a new frame. This is not the place to discuss the nature of courtly values or the motifs which went into the making of the romance, but the facts as they appear in the extant works are not disputed.

The milieu is a world either of remote classical antiquity or of a civilization unknown to the author, for example the Britain of King Arthur, which could be adjusted to suit the ideal situation it was intended to portray. The hero was not essentially a member of an army or a liegeman of a great king but an individual hero seeking a balanced way of life in a community with a well-defined set of values. The work consists in every case of the quest for these values and for their reconciliation with the hero's own life-situation. This is the true meaning of the word "adventure" in the romance.

The knight of romance, as is well known, seeks the goal of adjustment and purposeful living in two ways: proof of manhood with his fellow knights in the world of combat and with the opposite sex in the field of love. Even where the author was primarily interested in only one of these, as most writers of the Tristan romances were, he could not afford to ignore the other aspect completely, and it is significant that in those romances where love is the main quest (the Lancelot-Tristan groups) or where adventure for personal fulfillment is all important (the Grail stories), the result is in one way or other the destruction of the individual and the ultimate collapse of the society to which he belongs.

The adventure, used in the fullest sense, is the means whereby the individual comes to grips with the problem of his place in society. The larger question—the salvation of his immortal soul—is not treated in the romances, not even in the Grail romances. In order to come to grips with the problem, the knight must move outside the direct influence of his normal society into a place where its values are suspended or not known. Thus he will be able to experience the true value of the virtues which are taken for granted in Arthurian society. The courtly code, to use an inadequate term, is realized in a series of incidents in which different aspects of it are treated. An obvious example is the series of incidents by means of which Yvain is made aware of the true values in the relationship between knight and lady. He had assumed it to be a matter or superficial love service, but his efforts on behalf of the lady of Narison, of Lunete, of the wronged heiress, and of the proposed victim of the giant Harpin reveal to him the full scope of love.

It may be asked what the connection of all this is with the *Roman de la Rose* (c. 1236). Firstly, the work is an adventure. The lover is in his own world at the beginning and is taken out of it by two events. The convention of making him fall asleep removes him from the bonds of time and space and allows him to participate in a world where such problems no longer exist. He will be able to come to an understanding of love by observing its universalized manifestations and not its appearance in individuals. The significance of this dream element is stressed by the author, and the authority of the dream experience maintained. The *Roman* (the word is used by the author) begins within the dream, not before it, and it opens with the May topos, the idealized spring landscape which indicates the season for love and adventure. Arthurian romances frequently begin at Pentecost, for Arthur, with praiseworthy perspicacity, developed the custom of not sitting down to dinner before the opportunity of adventure presented itself. The renewal of life meant the renewal of the spirit of adventure, the move from court to world. But the formal love-song also began with the *Natureingang,* the spring opening, and for a slightly different reason. The urge to love came with spring, but this was an idealized spring, a May which signified flight from reality to an idealized world.

The *Roman de la Rose* takes account of both these conventions. The lover will start out into a new world and (though he does not know it yet) will pursue love in its highest form. Here we should note another point of resemblance between the hero and the Arthurian knight. Each is, if one may use the term, uncommitted. Although Erec and Yvain, to name only two, are at the Arthurian court at the beginning of the romances which bear their names, they are not of that court in the fullest sense of the term, since they have not experienced either love or adventure in any meaningful way—at least so far as the author lets us know. Indeed, their subsequent experiences would be meaningless if anything similar had happened to them before.

The purpose of adventure is to remake the hero in terms of the milieu of the court. In the *Roman de la Rose* he comes immediately to the walled garden, the *hortus conclusus.* The use of the wood in the Arthurian romance as the place in which adventures occur is too obvious to need stressing, and it is clear to any reader that such woods have two faces, one grim (the wasteland), the other magic, often friendly. Common to both kinds is the idea of exclusion of the outside world and the suspension of the normal rules of time and space. Examples of the use of these two wood conventions can be adduced from the romance and from lyric poetry. The grotto of love in Gottfried's *Tristan and Isolt* is particularly appropriate since it presents both faces. It is surrounded by rock and wasteland and unbroken trees, thus presenting to the outside world a gloomy and threatening exterior. It is repellent and deliberately so, since no person should be allowed to approach who is not prepared to brave the formidable obstacles to love in order to appreciate love's true nature. In the lyric, the debate between Phyllis and Flora provides an excellent example. The first part takes place in the kind of spring setting normal in such poetry, but the judgment is given by the classical god of love. To reach him the ladies mount steeds of mythological origin which, transcending time and space, take them into a wood where Cupid and his court live on. The treatment is ironic but the convention is clear. In the paradise garden there is no passage of time and thus only the eternal features of love can be present.

It is not implausible that the wall around the garden in the *Roman de la Rose,* with its representation of qualities inimical to love, is intended to represent the wild wood, the obstacle to the attainment of true love. If the exterior represented the interior, there would be no point in the lover's wishing to enter the garden, for the pictures would turn away anyone whose heart was set on love but who did not notice, as the dreamer does, that within the garden there must be beauty, for the birds sing and there is joy. Since he realizes that the inner face of the garden is the true one, he looks for an entrance, finds it and is admitted by the first of the personifications, Oiseuse. It is, of course, right that love should begin with ease or leisure, just as it is appropriate that the next characters we meet should be associated with pleasure—Leece, Cortoisie, Deduiz—for they are the outward and superficial characteristics which attract people to love. In the same way Erec and even more Yvain are attracted by outward beauty and fail to realize the deeper implications.

The next stage in love's pilgrimage is marked by the description of the arrows of the love god. They do not, at this point, affect the lover. The participants in the dance of love which the dreamer watches are personifications of those qualities which make love possible, Franchise, Largece, Cortoisie, and Jonece, and each is given those attributes which are appropriate to her qualities, even if this means that Franchise has to attend the dance in her underwear. The dreamer does not himself participate in the dance. He thinks of love and watches its rituals but he is not yet a lover himself. He visits all of the garden without definite purpose, but the god of love is on his trail and his call to Douz Regarz shows that a turning point is near. The entry of love is through the eyes, and the lover will be led into the toils of love through images which he sees.

The function of the pool of Narcissus should be thoroughly understood. The story of Narcissus was well known in the Middle Ages and was the *locus classicus* for a particular kind of love. Ovid's story emphasizes that Narcissus had been deaf to the pleadings of Echo, who loved him. She therefore remains only as a voice to haunt him. He himself is punished through his other sense, sight. He sees what he considers to be perfect beauty in the pool, falls in love with it and when he finds out that he is in love with his own reflection, he perishes. It should be emphasized that there is no question of narcissism in the modern sense. When

Narcissus finds out that love is impossible because it exists only within his own imagination, he is lost. This is precisely the situation of many lovers in the *canzon* and the *Minnelied,* even, though to a lesser extent, of many of those in the romances. They know that they are in love with the lady's image but they cannot be sure that the actuality corresponds to their image and still less can they know whether she returns the love they feel. This is the "Narcissus situation."

The lover in the *Roman de la Rose* knows of the Narcissus experience, but he cannot avoid it. He has entered the garden and watched the formal game of love, the dance. He desires love (signified by Cupid's lying in wait). In other words, he is in the situation of the knight who believes that love is going to be a pleasant experience which need not be taken too seriously but who finds that love is part of his responsibilities, something which must be harmonized with adventure if it is to be fully experienced. This is the initial impetus towards love which corresponds, say, with Yvain's first sight of Laudine.

The lover sees the rosebud reflected in the pool of Narcissus, not directly. It is therefore with his own conception of the rosebud that he falls in love, not with the actuality. The pool, as he says, is deceptive. He does not know whether he can pluck the rose, he does not know at all what is involved. Discovery comes quickly. The love god's arrows pierce him and he swoons. The arrows are Biautez, the first impact of love through the eyes, Simplece, the untouched unsophistication of new love, and Cortoisie, the atmosphere that makes love possible. It should be noted that he falls in a swoon, as do Erec and Yvain at turning points in their respective romances. He is now in the service of love and receives from the love god advice which shows him how to perform his service and which also makes clear that he has now left the path of joy forever. His love will indeed bring him happiness, but it will be mixed with the deepest sorrow. The whole dialogue between the lover and the love god is filled with the technical expressions and imagery of the love lyric. Yet this scene is reminiscent of a scene which occurs in many romance groups, namely the instruction of the young hero by an older or more experienced person. The stress laid on the need for politeness and readiness for service, the advice to imitate Gawain and not Kai, the need for humility are all typical of this kind of instruction. A lover, like a knight, should practice feats of arms and be skillful in music and the dance. In other words, a man must prepare to be a lover as he does to be a knight.

The subsequent actions of the lover, so far as they are related by Guillaume de Lorris, constitute a series of adventures in the service of love, and each is designed to show the failure of one or the other approach. Yet their cumulative effect would be to prepare the lover for his ultimate success, as the various adventures of a knight prepare him for his full realization of the meaning of love and adventure.

The first of these adventures is brought about by Bel Acueil. The first pleasant meeting leads to overconfidence, too close an approach to the rose and to an encounter with all the qualities which are inimical to love—Dangiers, Male Bouche, Honte, Peor, and Jalousie. It will be noted that all these are not courtly qualities, in fact the exact opposite. They are like the enemies any knight encounters on a quest. The lover must learn to deal with them, not necessarily by attacking them but by understanding and circumventing them. He has to find help, particularly from Franchise and Pitié, and Venus herself helps him to a kiss. This apparently pleasant event proves his undoing. Jalousie is aroused by Male Bouche, and all the personifications of female reticence combine to thwart love's intentions. A castle is built about the rose, Bel Acueil is imprisoned. Here is the peripety which we find in all the romances, the apparent success followed by the plunge into failure. It is at this point that the poem breaks off, at the low point where the lover can do no more than hope that Bel Acueil will not forget him.

The end of Guillaume de Lorris' work is not therefore a mere breaking off in the middle of the story. It is the conclusion of what is normally the first part of a romance. Had Guillaume continued, he would have had to show the lover gradually acquiring through various trials a different attitude towards the rose, that is to love itself, and gradually overcoming those qualities which oppose his union. Jean de Meung's "continuation," therefore, does not really continue Guillaume's poem, because he either did not grasp the necessary connection between romance and Allegory, or more likely, because he chose to disregard it. As in much work of the later thirteenth and fourteenth centuries, the superficialities of love and adventure are preserved (castle storming, etc.), but the careful structural effects which lead to the rehabilitation of the hero are abandoned. The actions described by Jean are largely arbitrary, intruded into the narrative by third-person determination.

We may now turn a third type of Allegory which depends on a framework of a different sort. *Die Jagd* of Hadamar von Laber does not follow a literary convention. There are no poems which are devoted entirely to a description of a hunt, but the use of the hunt as an incident and of hunt imagery was widespread in myth (the deaths of Adonis and Diarmaid), in epic (the hunt of Dido and Aeneas), and in occasional poetry (*Cynegetica* of Nemesianus).

In medieval works it was common to introduce a hero to a stranger king by showing the young man to be a master in hunting skills and even more in the very elaborate rituals which governed the chase. The emphasis is always on unusual knowledge rather than on mere skill. The *De Arte venandi cum avibus* of the Emperor Frederick II is proof that a text book on falconry was not beneath the dignity of the greatest prince in Christendom, but more relevant for our purpose are those works which describe the conventions of the hunt and particularly of the hunting of the deer. Two early ones are the *Moamin et Ghatrif*, which is a translation from the Arabic, and Guicenna's *De Arte bersandi*, both of which were prepared for the court of Frederick II. The earliest extant work to deal with the conventions and ceremonies of the hunt was *La Chace dou cerf*, an anonymous work of the late thirteenth century. The best-known work in English, the *Master of Game* by Edward, Duke of York, is largely translation of an earlier French treatise and dates from about 1413.

Since hunting is extremely conservative in its conventions, it is safe to assume that much of the etiquette and ceremony described in these works would be applicable to the early thirteenth century and certainly to the period in which Hadamar wrote his poem (about 1340). The hunt in the poem begins, as might be expected, with an early morning departure and the setting out of dogs at strategic points along the proposed line of hunt. The first view of the quarry naturally corresponds to the act of falling in love. Thereafter the various hounds are loosed and attempt to bring down the quarry. Many of them correspond to the qualities personified in the *Roman de la Rose*—Glück (Fortune), Rat (Raison), Scham (Honte), Hoffe (Esperance)—but the abstractions are clearly not derived from this source, for they are used in quite different ways, but rather from the vocabulary of the *Minnesang*. Typically, one of the most important hounds is Herze, the projection of the poet's own desire.

Although there is a line of action, even a peripety if we think of the wounding of Herze or the escape of the quarry in this sense, it cannot be said that the work follows the pattern of a romance. It uses the conventional events of a hunt after noble game and thus brings in several human but unnamed characters—the wise old hunter who has already pursued the same quarry almost to the end and the brash young man who pursues ignoble game by ignoble means. The author is, in other words, using a nonliterary framework for his Allegory. So far as he can, he keeps to the hunting conventions. Yet his work is not successful, and the reason is not far to seek. The idea of a "hunt of love" is at first sight very attractive, and Hadamar was by no means the only person to try it. There was, however, a basic contradiction which no amount of literary skill could overcome. The object of a hunt was to have hounds catch a deer and tear it to pieces. Such an ending was clearly impossible within the conventions of the *Minnesang* or indeed the conventions of any love poetry. The lady either remained completely unattainable or she was to be won by gentle means. Hadamar therefore had to conclude his poem lamely with the assurance that he would go on eternally hunting with virtually no hope of success. The frame of the Allegory is thus broken, for the conclusion of the poem is incompatible with its conventions. Hadamar had in any case found the situation hard to handle and had fallen back on the device of long conversations with the other hunters he encountered.

Other poets used the hunt frame to contrast true and false love (the noble and the ignoble quarry) and noble and ignoble means (with dogs and with nets). Nowhere is the hunt allegory really successful, and the reason is clear. The authors were using a set of conventions from life, not from literature and were therefore obliged to attempt an adjustment of those conventions to their love poetry. If the type had persisted, a way might have been found to produce a literary "hunt conclusion," but apparently it was too much of an effort. Once again it is demonstrated that an Allegory is very much at the mercy of the frame it chooses to adopt. The hunt frame proved unworkable and was abandoned.

It may be objected that there are many allegorical works where there is no frame, literary or otherwise, or that they have at most a convention such as a journey or a dream which could hardly control the development of a literary work. On examination these works prove to be allegorical but not Allegories, that is they contain features which are used in Allegory—personification of abstractions, allegorization of situations and events, persons and objects—but they do not adhere to these features throughout the work. A few examples will suffice to make this clear. The *Minnegrotte* in Gottfried's *Tristan and Isolt* is allegorized as if it were a church.

Its proportions and concrete features—smoothness, straightness—are allegorized as qualities of "Tristan love." By reference to the frame of traditional allegorizing we are made aware that this is a temple to a love religion, which in its turn exists in abstract form in the human heart, as Gottfried himself informs us. All this, however, is included in a story about people, about Tristan and Isolt. They may be regarded as examples, as martyrs to love, but they are not personified abstractions.

Similarly in *Piers Plowman* we have a typical allegory, beginning with the dream convention and the journey convention. Throughout the poem there is much use of abstractions and personifications. Yet the dream convention merely serves the purpose of allowing the author greater freedom. Most of his characters are people, not abstractions, and the allegorization is spasmodic and not consistent. Again we have a descriptive didactic poem in which the author uses allegorical techniques when they are of value to him but does not attempt a consistent Allegory.

In his letter to Can Grande, Dante calls attention to the allegorical nature of his poem. He also tells us, by implication, that it is not an Allegory, for he makes it clear that the work must be allegorized in order to be understood. We find the conventions of the journey, of the mysterious wood, of the learned guide, of the *paysage idéal* and numerous others. Many of the named individuals can be "interpreted" as personifications of abstractions. Yet all this proves that the *Commedia* is not an Allegory, for if it were, interpretation of this sort would be unnecessary.

The evidence produced seems to support a definition of Allegory rather more precise than that advanced, for example, by C. S. Lewis. Allegory as a literary form depends on a framework derived from a literary genre already well known to the audience for which the Allegory is intended. The structure and conventions of the "parent" genre were regarded as binding for the Allegory and are to be assumed for any real understanding of it. Ideally, all characters should be personified abstractions and no human beings should intrude. In practice the *persona* of the author is often a character in the work.

This ideal type of Allegory could be modified in several ways. Another frame, such as the hunt, the cloister, the besieged castle could be substituted for the framework provided by the literary genre. Such a procedure was less satisfactory since the frame was less clearly defined and its conventions less strict. Thus there was a greater possibility of the intrusion of human characters. Many works which are not themselves Allegories contain passages which use the tradition of Allegory for a particular purpose.

I am aware of no medieval definition of Allegory, but there are many of allegorization. This has led to an assumption on the part of critics that we must think in terms of allegorization whenever we talk of Allegory. The reverse is true. For Allegory is one of the few medieval types which need not be allegorized. The author has done it for us.

NOTE

1. The following books and articles are of service for the understanding of various aspects of allegory and allegorization. Most of them are concerned with the techniques of biblical exegesis. E. Auerbach, *Typologische Motive in der mittelalterlichen Literatur* (1953); M. W. Bloomfield, *The Seven Deadly Sins* (1952); E. R. Curtius, *European Literature and the Latin Middle Ages* (1948); H. R. Jauss, "Form und Auffassung der Allegorie in der Tradition der *Psychomachia*," *Festschrift Walther Bulst* (1960) and *Genèse de la poésie allégorique française au Moyen-Age (de 1180 à 1240)* printed separately but also a chapter in *Grundriss der romanischen Literaturen des Mittelalters* (1962); C. S. Lewis, *The Allegory of Love* (1936); H. de Lubac, *Exégèse médiévale: les quatre sens de l'écriture* (1959); J. Pépin, *Mythe et allégorie: les origines grecs et les contestations judéo-chrétiennes* (1958); P. C. Spicq, *Esquisse d'une histoire de l'exégèse latine au moyen-âge* (1944). More bibliographical information is to be found in these works.

II

The Nature of Romance

I T IS, perhaps, a pity that the romances of Chrétien de Troyes have come to be regarded as the standard by which others should be judged. For it is clear that his work is the product not only of genius and an ironic temperament but that it can be understood fully only if it is assumed that the audience was aware of a tension, an interplay between the conventions and standards of a narrative genre which we can call "romance" and the poem which Chrétien himself wrote. Such an assumption means that there had been established by 1160 an idea of what the romance should represent. But what is the evidence for its existence?

The word "roman" itself is of no help whatsoever. A term applied to works so dissimilar as *Le Roman de la Rose* and *Le Roman de Renard* could have little genre significance, even if it were in contemporary usage when the works were composed, as distinct from the time when they were copied. It is clear, however, that writers of the Middle Ages had a strong sense of genre, even when no theoretical definition of that genre existed—or at least had not been recorded. The survival of such works as the *Anticlaudianus* of Alanus de Insulis and the *De mundi universitate* of Bernardus Silvestris shows that the genre we now call allegory was known and was being written, yet medieval theorists never define *allegoria* as a genre but always as a figure of speech, as it had been defined by the author of the *Ad Herennium* and by Quintilian.[1] To seek for the definition of the genre through the origin of its themes and motifs, as the Celticists and others have done, is equally pointless, since the same themes and motifs are found in works which are not romances. We would be better advised to approach the genre problem of the romance in the same way as we approach that of the medieval lyric—by the way in which it treats a theme and the terminology and imagery which it uses.

The existence of the idea of genre has much in common with the concept of the independent existence of the *verbum*. The concept of the existence of an idea, a theoretical being expressed by a word, is at least as old as Plato's *Republic*. In practical, human terms such a concept could not exist apart from the word which expressed it, so that the word stood not only for the often imperfect physical manifestation of the idea but also for the perfect theoretical form with all possible associations of that perfection. The concept of the *logos* as an independent entity is expressed in Christian terms by the *verbum*, which is at once the entity itself and, perhaps more important, the means of its communication to men. Through the *verbum* God reveals the totality of his message for mankind, but the understanding of that message depends on the use of the intelligence with which he has provided mortals to understand it. The word, therefore, is always more than the material objects or the events which it describes. The exact realization of its meaning will depend on the context—and on the interpreter.[2]

The *Etymologiae* of Isidore of Seville follows the same principle. His explanations of the etymologies of words are less concerned with their origin than with the connection of ideas, with the persistence of a concept through whole groups of sounds. A group of sounds possesses an innate meaning which it cannot lose, even when the group is joined to other sounds. The word thus develops an existence of its own, an existence whose outward form is fixed but whose significance may vary enormously. The word in this sense is not only a single expression, a *vocabulum*, but also a *locutio*, an expression, and, by extension, a combination of words, a literary work, as the Bible is the word of God.

The aspect of the independence and many-sidedness of the word and the genre which has received most attention from medieval and modern critics is that of allegorical interpretation. This type of interpretation of literary works had been formalized by the Greeks in their studies of Homer long before it was taken up by Jewish interpreters of the Old Testament and later by Christians. Typological and allegorical interpretations of individual words, of events, and of whole stories are nothing more than an extension of the concept that the word contains within itself all possible implications and ramifications, that it is not limited in time or space, and that its meaning may be different for different readers in differing contexts. The dangers of such free interpretation can easily be seen, on the one hand, in the often ludicrously strained allegorizations of the *Gesta Romanorum* and *Legenda aurea* and on the other hand in the efforts of modern critics to see Christian allegory in even the most secular work. Absurd as some of these interpretations may be, the freedom of meaning implicit in the concept of the *verbum* must inevitably allow them, and it is doubtful whether a theorist of the twelfth century would have disagreed with the procedure, even if he rejected the result.

As I have pointed out elsewhere,[3] allegorization, to be convincing, needs a context, a framework within which the process may operate. For the Middle Ages, this framework was the Christian religion, and this fact has led modern interpreters to believe that this framework can—indeed should—always be valid. By such a procedure a vital fact is obscured— that a secular work, by the independence of the word, may have its own context of interpretation, its own rules, and its own existence. The romance does develop precisely this independence. It has a code of behavior of its own, a set of values, a set of ideals which are, in fact, unreal in the sense that they are not directly connected with the life of twelfth-century France. This independence, this life-of-its-own has caused critics many difficulties. Some have sought to regard the details in the background of the romances as representing characteristics of twelfth-century France, some have sought to demonstrate a connection between behavior in the romance and the ethics of Aristotle, of Cicero, of the pseudo-Guillaume de Conches, of Wernher von Elmendorf. There are, of course, reflections of moral systems of various sorts in the romances, just as there are reflections of medieval fashion in arms and dress. But before a satisfactory understanding of the nature of romance can be achieved, it is necessary to dismiss any thought of attempts to portray "reality."[4]

Unreality, in fact, is the first principle of the romance genre. It is this unreality which gives it that independence and flexibility of morality and imagery which are its greatest glory.

Unreality may be achieved in various ways, some of them surprising. The earliest extant French romances are all on classical subjects. The stories they tell are well documented from other sources and, from the medieval point of view, were historical, but they are remote from French history. They can be and are manipulated for the purpose of constructing the romance's own world. The *Roman d' Enéas* may serve as an example. The *Aeneid* of Vergil sets forth a very specific set of public circumstances:

a Trojan of semi-divine descent escapes from the Greeks and is commanded by Jupiter to set up a Trojan kingdom in Italy from which the
Roman state will take its origin.[5] In the course of his wanderings he loses
his wife Creusa at Troy, is almost seduced into staying at Carthage with
Dido, and marries Lavinia for political advantage. The poem, like most
great epics, is concerned with public events and public virtues. Creusa is
lost because Aeneas has to be free to marry Lavinia. The affair with Dido
is designed to show the dangers of allowing personal feelings and sensual
desires to interfere with public duty.[6] However we may be affected by
the Dido scenes, there is no doubt that, in the structure of the poem,
they are designed to show the hero's weakness.

What do we find in the *Roman d'Enéas?* A total reversal of this situation. The public affairs in the poem are little more than a framework for
the interplay of personal relationships. The divine mission of Enéas is of
little importance for an author whose main concern is to contrast two
types of sexual attraction, one crassly sensual in which both partners are
the victims of a blind force, the other a more sublimated but still erotic
connection which rises above sensuality and is as much a matter of the
imagination as of physical attraction.

The most remarkable feature of the poem is the concept of a love at a
distance. It will be remembered that there is a deliberately organized
physical separation between the two lovers, when Lavine is in a tower
which is being besieged by the forces of Enéas. This convention of love
which depends purely on a glance, on a meeting of the light from two
pairs of eyes, is clearly unreal. Whatever its origins, whatever its dependence or nondependence on the developing love-mystique of the Provençal *canzon,* the result for the romance was an unreality in the depiction
of love between the sexes which became a characteristic of the genre. The
verbum "amour" has developed a new meaning, one appropriate only to
the romance. The subsequent ramifications of this independent life are
worth exploring.

There is no developed concept of love-*service* in the early classical romances. Enéas does not perform any tasks or adventures for Dido or Lavine
(unless we include the killing of Turnus!). Nor does Achilles for Po-
lyxena or even Troilus for Briseida. To state that the concept of love-
service was adapted from the *canzon* is unprovable, particularly since the
form of service in the *canzon,* praise in song, is not characteristic of the
romance. It is far more likely that the concept of love-service developed

its own rules from the unreal love situations already described. If the lover is enslaved by the mere sight of the lady, it is likely that he will do anything to honor her, anything to decrease the distance between them. The method of serving which developed is the adventure.

In spite of the large amount of ink which has been spilled on the subject, it is often not realized how radical a departure from earlier narrative poetry the "adventure" is.[7] In epics, feats of arms, battles, and combats all take place within the pattern of public behavior, to support or save a society of which the performers form a part. The most superficial study of Western epics from Homer to *Beowulf* and the *Chanson de Roland* proves this. Acquisition of fame by the hero is, of course, important, but it is fame among his peers, gained in pursuit of public objectives, not recognition by a lady. The idea that the fruits of combat should be female recognition was so extraordinary, so contrary to any sense of history, that a special court had to be created for the romance where such a concept was acceptable, namely the court of King Arthur.

The evidence that the Arthurian court was artificially created for literary purposes is overwhelming. It is clear from the distribution of events that Geoffrey of Monmouth designed his *Historia regum Britanniae* as a framework within which the ideal age of chivalry could be depicted. Certainly there is no love service in Geoffrey's work, but there is a court which had realized a degree of civilized behavior never attained before or after in the history of the Western world. The reasons for this construction are not altogether clear, but the work is clearly designed to present an ideal if unhistorical court.[8]

It is, of course, perfectly possible, if unprovable, that the romances which are no longer extant had already created the Arthurian court and that Geoffrey adopted it. In any case there can be no doubt that by the time Chrétien de Troyes began to write there was an established tradition of an unreal court with unreal traditions and values. At this court, two situations predominate, intimately connected with each other—love-service and adventure. These two are entirely personal matters, affairs which cannot by any means be called public or have any social significance in normal society. Yet the Arthurian court, as it is portrayed in the fully developed romance, exists only as a stage for these exploits, not as a political entity. It does not rule a land—or if it does, that rule is of no significance. It fights no wars, it has no political enemies. It also differs from the ruling center in any epic poem in being completely stable. In all the great twelfth- and thirteenth-century romances the Arthurian court is precisely the same at the end of the work as at the beginning.[9] This stability is all the more remarkable since the court has no obvious derived code of morals or religion. Certainly Arthur's court is ostensibly Christian. Its members go to church and references are made to God, Christ, and the Trinity, but such actions are no more than lip-service. Christianity does not affect Arthurian behavior.[10]

The court is governed by a self-generated set of rules which are peculiar to itself and whose intention is to allow the romance to work out its purpose, the glorification of love between the sexes and the self-realization of the individual. Both these objects were so far removed from the themes of epic poetry that a new milieu had to be constructed within which they could operate.

It will be noted that we said "a set of rules." These rules are far from being a moral or philosophical code. It is true that certain qualities appear to be demanded of a knight if he is to be a worthy member of the court. The usual epic virtues of bravery, loyalty, and generosity are among them, although again they are employed more for gaining a lady's favor than in a heroic society. More interesting are mercy to a defeated enemy, moderation and balance of virtues, and good manners. Yet we would search in vain for any clear-cut statement of these so-called courtly virtues in any romance. The nearest approach to a listing of them is in *Der arme Heinrich* of Hartmann von Aue, which is not a romance but a legend. Significantly, the virtues are ascribed to a hero who has all the secular virtues but lacks true religious faith. The romance qualities with which he is so bountifully equipped prove useless in the face of a real test of his morality. Hartmann demonstrates that these romance virtues are irrelevant to the Christian world.[11] They are not created for Christians but for romance heroes.

The organization of Arthur's court as it appears in twelfth- and thirteenth-century romances, is highly significant. At its head is Arthur, a king whose whole behavior is middle-aged and who is seen, when he is seen at all, hunting, taking the kiss after the hunting of the white stag, grieving on numerous occasions for an abducted Guinevere, or just sleeping. Never do we see him carrying out any significant public action. He never fights himself but sometimes arranges opportunities for others to engage in adventure. His function is basically that of an arbitrator of individual prowess. In other words, he is a literary king.[12]

Beneath him there is a studied hierarchy. Gawain represents the best in the Arthurian world. He appears in most romances, not usually as a hero but as the criterion against which others are to be measured. His virtues are entirely secular—courage, loyalty, good breeding, and chivalry both to men and women. It is significant that he has more ladies to serve than any other knight. Sir Kay represents the other extreme and the position given to him in the romance shows the constructed court at its worst. Kay manipulates the rules for his own benefit, exercises his privileges as a knight without deserving them, and behaves as if he alone were capable of carrying out and interpreting the rules. His function is important, for he becomes a parody of a knight, seeking to demonstrate individual qualities he does not possess in a milieu designed only for the display of those qualities. Seneschals all seem to partake of Kay's qualities. While regarding themselves as the most knowledgeable persons at court, they demonstrate their unfitness for the society they represent.[13]

Thus by the time Chrétien de Troyes began to compose, the romance had developed a form peculiar to itself, not, be it noted, in structure, for which there are many parallels in the epic, but in milieu. It had a setting peculiar to itself designed entirely for the demonstration of individual prowess, chiefly concerned with the impressing and winning of a lady, and which had no other social or moral significance. Had the romance not progressed beyond this point, it is doubtful whether it could have become a serious genre.

Chrétien de Troyes, however, saw an opportunity of utilizing the conventions which had been established. As we have said, the world of the romance had become an entity in itself. Chrétien saw that it must now be compared with reality. Yet in making the comparison Chrétien could retain the advantage given to him by the independence of the genre, namely that his expositions still belonged to the world of the romance and hence need not conform to the historical conditions of his or any other day nor with those of epic poetry. A few examples will suffice to show his purpose and method.

Erec's encounter with Enide is brought about by a typical Arthurian situation, an attempt to avenge an insult to Guinevere—not a personal insult but conduct which could be so construed. It is to avenge this insult that Erec performs "love-service." His choice of Enide as the "lady-to-defend" at the tournament of the sparrowhawk is motivated entirely by a desire for revenge, not by love for Enide. In other words, he performs love-service which is not *love*-service. His relation to her has been negotiated with her father and has nothing to do with love. The marriage between Erec and Enide is thus brought about by a romance convention of honor, not by love. The physical relationship which follows this almost accidental marriage binds the two lovers very strongly but it comes near to breaking because of another, quite irrelevant romance convention. Erec's men take umbrage at his apparent lack of interest in adventure, that is, in pointless combat. Enide is disturbed by what she feels to be a breach of the standards of romance behavior, namely that she has prevented her husband from participating in the pursuit of adventure. Her anxiety is entirely due to the force of romance, that is literary, convention, and Erec's reaction to her words, half heard and completely misunderstood, is conditioned entirely by the romance tradition that a knight conducts adventures for the honor of his lady. Because he believes that Enide is yearning for her husband to perform for her the love-service she never received, Erec's wrath is aroused and he sets out to give her the adventure for which he thinks she longs. Each partner believes, wrongly, that the other is seeking fulfillment of a romance point of honor but in carrying out his part of the bargain, Erec deliberately and cruelly flouts another rule of behavior in subjecting his lady to the hazards as well as the honor of the adventure. Yet it is this natural act which brings about mutual understanding and reconciliation. In contrast we are offered the theoretical romance situation pushed to its ultimate absurdity in the "Joie de la cort" episode. In exercising her power over Mabonagrain, his lady has placed his destiny and her own at the mercy of knights seeking adventure. Her will and his love-service produce entirely negative results. This artificial life and Erec's misunderstandings are strongly contrasted with the true and natural love which emerges for Erec and Enide after their trials. To love truly they must abandon the romance conventions.

It hardly seems necessary to comment on the extravagances of *Lancelot* and *Cligés*. In the latter Chrétien openly mocks the conventions of love-service in the scene at court between Alixandre and Soredamors and still more in his parody by exaggeration of courtly love relationships between Cligés and Fenice. True love is attained apparently only by deceiving a husband and feigning death, living in adultery in a tomb, and finally by fleeing to Arthur's court at which similar behavior is quite usual. While it is true that Cligés' uncle has betrayed his trust, the resulting incidents are far less concerned with the public results of this faithlessness (for example, the birth of an heir who would exclude Cligés) than with the facts of sexual attraction between Cligés and his uncle's wife, Fenice. Public policy is sacrificed entirely so that the sexual union can take place in a decent, if not precisely legal fashion. Such an order of priorities is possible only in the unreal world of the romance. Of the *Lancelot* it is only necessary to state that it shows the degree of moral degradation which ensues if the conventions of the romance are pushed to their logical extreme. An adulterous queen is prepared to reward her lover, the greatest of knights, only after he has become the most abject of slaves. The *Lancelot* is not the zenith of love but its nadir—by any but romance standards.[14]

Yet even here, as in all Chrétien's work, there is true morality. It is to be found by comparing "romance behavior" with true nobility. Lancelot is noble despite the romance conventions because his intentions are noble. This point is made with the greatest clarity in *Yvain*. From the very beginning the artificiality of the concept of adventure is stressed. The incident narrated by Calogrenant took place years before the opening of the story, yet it must now be avenged at once. The giant herdsman, surely a representative of the natural world which looks so ugly to the romance dwellers, cannot understand the point of Calogrenant's search, although he performs every day tasks well beyond the knight's capacity. His good instincts are proved correct by the subsequent events. Calogrenant's self-centered actions deliberately destroy a natural harmony and Yvain's subsequent pursuit of the same ends not only disturbs the natural harmony, but results in brutal treatment of a wounded foe. The reason for Yvain's treatment of Esclados is made quite clear. Kay, the representative of all that is worst at the Arthurian court, must be offered evidence that Yvain has avenged his cousin's honor. Kay pays for his misconduct—but not so seriously as the dead king—and it is Gawain who again forces Yvain on to the true romance path. The love which Yvain so loudly professes for Laudine, a love which he had discovered in prison for the wife of the man he had murdered, is conceived in the most extreme romance fashion from the light of the lady's eyes and brought to birth by the dialectical skill of a lady-in-waiting. Yvain's love-service has been to kill his lady's husband. After winning her he vanquishes the lower element of the Arthurian court but yields to the higher one by abandoning quickly the love he esteemed so highly at the call of adventure. Up to this point Yvain has demonstrated impeccably what happens to a man who obeys the conventions of romance.

Chrétien does not deign to describe the adventures of Yvain and Gawain. The serious part of his poem consists in the rehabilitation of Yvain as a human being by separating him from the Arthurian world and allowing him, as the Knight of the Lion, to demonstrate natural principles of human kindness and charity to his fellow-men, not the artificial behavior of the romance hero.

The greatness of Chrétien de Troyes consists not in writing the "perfect romance," but in realizing that the romance had developed a set of rules for itself, that its life was a literary, unreal life, and in manipulating these rules and this independent existence for his own purposes. Those purposes were to examine the problem of sexual love in society from several points of view by using the romance conventions of love and adventure as a point of departure and to demonstrate the futility of those conventions either positively, as in *Erec* and *Yvain,* or negatively, as in *Cligés* and *Lancelot.* This is not to say that Chrétien's purpose was negative. In his treatment of the genre conventions, he elaborated a style of narrative poetry operating in an unreal world and thus possessing great flexibility which was able to discuss true values of chivalry and sophisticated behavior by contrasting them with the unreal values of the genre he was using.

There can be little doubt that a finished *Perceval* would have pointed sharply to the contrast between the amoral, rule-oriented Arthurian court and the world of the Christian religion. As it is, we must turn to the work of Wolfram von Eschenbach to see how explicit the contrast can be. Wolfram took over the most important feature of the poem, the contrast between the secular/courtly/sexual quest of Gawain and the religious/moral/social quest of Parzival. In doing so he made even more explicit than Chrétien the weaknesses of the Arthurian world by showing his innocent hero as almost corrupted by it and in insisting on the Grail company as a fellowship not only for the expiation of the sins of the individual but for the aid of those in distress as a result of accident or the action of enemies. In other words, Gawain's way is that of the individual, brilliant but without social conscience, Parzival's becomes that of the Christian king, the shepherd of his people.[15]

The Tristan story is unthinkable without the artificial courtly milieu of the romance. Even our most primitive extant versions stress the conflict between two loyalties and the degenerating effects of adultery on a noble character. Only the later versions accept in full the romance love conventions which present the Tristan story in the form in which it became most popular—the depiction of an overpowering love which struggles against overwhelming odds and results in the death of the lovers. The French prose versions show this attitude in its crudest form, while the poem of Gottfried von Strassburg is its most subtle exploitation, for here the weakness of the courtly morality is exposed not by opposing it to a highly religious love concept but by demonstrating the simple inability of a society allegedly organized for love and adventure to comprehend love when it is expressed in terms higher than purely sensual attraction. Gottfried shatters the whole romance conception by showing its adventures to be self-seeking and hollow pretence and its love-service little more than vulgar intrigue.[16]

In discussing the romance we are faced, as we said at the beginning of this essay, with a paradox. The romance as a genre developed a life of its own and certain rules by which its deliberately unreal life was to be governed. It also pursued as its principal motifs the pointless combat and love-service, both of no significance in a socially oriented genre. Yet when these game-rules were established, the way was open for them to be interpreted in any way an author chose and the great writers of romance chose, for the most part, to study individual behavior by setting it in the unreal world of the romance and showing how, by rising above the rules of the genre, the human being could fulfill himself, for the romance is the genre of the individual. It should not surprise us that critics have found much to allegorize in the romance, for it is the *verbum* in one of its many shapes.

NOTES

1. Quintilian comes closest to the idea of an allegorical genre, since he insists that *allegoria* is continuous metaphor uninterrupted by clarification. *Institutio oratoria*, ed. Rademacher, viii 44.

2. The subject is treated in great detail by Jean Pépin, *Mythe et allégorie: les origines grecques et les contestations judéo-chrétiennes* (Paris, 1958). See also the treatment of various kinds of beauty recognized by medieval writers set out by Edgar de Bruyne, *Etudes d'esthétique médiévale*, Rijksuniversiteit te Gent, Werke uitgegeven door de Faculteit van de Wijsbegeerte en Letteren, 97–99, 3 vols. (Bruges, 1946), pp. 213 ff.; and especially the following: "atque in hunc modum noster animus ex propria natura docetur quod visibilia ad invisibilia cognationem habent et similitudinem et quod ipsa visibilia imagines sunt et simulacra eorum quae visibiliter videri non possunt." Classical Greek and Latin criticism, which was chiefly concerned with the two factors of mimesis and rhetoric, does not stress

the independence of literary form. It sees the various genres as having differing relationships to mimesis and to social conditions. Plato comes closest when he speaks of mimesis as one of three forms—the idea, the sensible actuality, and the image, which can be literary as well as plastic (*Republic,* 598d ff.). It is often forgotten that, although Plato's "ideas" may have independent existence, that existence can be communicated only in words. The classical views of literature can be studied most easily in D. A. Russel and M. Winterbottom, *Ancient Literary Criticism* (Oxford; Oxford University Press, 1972), where the relevant texts are translated. See particularly the views of Strabo on myth, pp. 302 ff.

3. "Allegory and Allegorization," *Research Studies,* (1964), 32:161–175.

4. I am using the word here in the sense of the facts of historical society, not in any medieval-philosophical sense. The best summary of the arguments about the existence of a courtly code is to be found in H. Neumann, "Der Streit um das ritterliche Tugendsystem," *Festschrift für Karl Helm* (1951).

5. It should be remembered that Aeneas is not always such an exemplary character. In the *De excidio Troiae historia* of Dares Phrygius and particularly in *Frigii Daretis Yliados libri sex* of Josephus Iscanus, Gompe, ed., 6: 710–711 and 880 ff, he is a traitor to Troy and desperately eager to make capital out of his country's misfortunes. The tradition is followed in many vernacular Troy stories not dependent on Vergil's *Aeneid.*

6. Octavianus, unlike Antony, was able to resist the charms of the eastern seductress Cleopatra, a fact noted by Horace even more pointedly than Vergil.

7. "Aventure" in medieval French and German means both the facts which form the adventure and the story of those events. It is often hard to determine which meaning is intended—more likely both are.

8. It is highly probable that Geoffrey was setting up a British counterpart—perhaps even counterblast—to the image of Charlemagne's court as the ideal form of Christian monarchy.

9. Although it is true that the harmony of the Arthurian court is often disturbed by such events as the frequent abductions of Guinevere, that court returns to its former state when those events have been settled. There are no changes in attitudes. The Arthurian romances demand complete stability of the court to act as a scene for the exploits of their heroes. This is nowhere more evident than in *Gawain and the Green Knight,* where the court totally fails to comprehend what Gawain has suffered—and learned.

10. Hence the marked contrast made by Wolfram von Eschenbach in *Parzival.*

11. That is, they are irrelevant to the salvation of his soul and to spiritual as opposed to social relationships. The *Nibelungenlied,* in a quite different way, also shows the inadequacy of romance values. See Gottfried Weber, *Das Nibelungenlied* (1963).

12. He has none of the functions of a ruling king. In the absence of earlier romances we are, of course, compelled to assume that the Arthurian court shown by Chrétien de Troyes, in the Tristan romances, and in other late-twelfth-century romances had already been established as an essential in the romance form. The earliest extant romances would have made little sense to contemporary audiences if they had not been well acquainted with the Arthurian tradition.

13. Historically oriented accounts of Arthur do not show Kay as a fool and blunderer. This is a romance tradition. The seneschal parody is best seen in the *Tristan* of Gottfried von Strassburg.

14. C. S. Lewis, in *The Allegory of Love,* failed to grasp the ironical opposition between true love and Lancelot's behavior.

15. Not merely a pure Christian individual. This role is filled by Sigune, who responds to the hurt inflicted on her by Arthurian society by a withdrawal into spirituality. Her counterpart Orgeluse, who has suffered similarly, attempts revenge on that society by using its own conventions—which are unchristian.

16. See my *Anatomy of Love: The Tristan of Gottfried von Strassburg* (1971), where this theme is dealt with in detail.

12

Problems of Communication in the Romances of Chrétien de Troyes

IT IS A NOTORIOUS FACT of the literary history of the Middle Ages that the heroes of the national epics are inarticulate. They are, apparently, incapable of conducting rational conversation with their fellows, for their speech consists of rather lengthy statements of policy, gasconades about deeds either past or contemplated, or mere statements calculated to keep the action going. It is perhaps not too much to say that Charlemagne's problems in the *Chanson de Roland* stem from his inability to obtain a consensus from men who were incapable of nice argumentation or even a true exchange of ideas, and that much of the obscurity of the *Nibelungenlied* owes its origin not to a contamination of sources but to the incapacity of its characters to handle even the simplest of subordinate clauses.

How different is the romance! *Facundia*, the power of smooth and polished speech, is of the very essence of the characters. They are engaged in constant discussion not only of their own actions and reasons for action but also of the theoretical principles that guide their conduct. If there is no one available for such discussion, the characters are perfectly happy to talk to themselves, with a generous infusion of such abstractions or mythological beings as love, Cupid, their own hearts, their own eyes, and above all sorrow. Needless to say, the principal topic of their dialogues and monologues is love.

The earlier romances are instructive on the subject. Vergil has little to say on the love affair between Aeneas and Lavinia, and that little hardly

leads us to believe that there was a true love affair. The author of the
French *Roman d'Enéas,* on the other hand, shows us a developing passion. It cannot be conducted through the medium of dialogue, since the
two potential lovers are separated by opposing armies and a castle wall.
The dialogue/monologues, if such they may be called—for they are addressed to the other person even though they cannot be heard—are not
analyses of love so much as anticipation of its delights. They are highly
sensuous imaginings rather than esthetic evaluations.

It is to Chrétien de Troyes that we turn when we think of the love
monologue and love dialogue as principal instruments of exposition in
the romance, and it is fatally easy to assume that his technique is the same
in all his romances, when in fact this is far from being the case. Chrétien
does not treat love in the same way in all his works. Indeed, there is good
reason for believing that each of those works is an attempt to study the
love-phenomenon in a different way, and that his romances have as a
principal object the exposition, not always sympathetic, of the various ways
in which love can be treated. Perhaps we can throw some light on this
problem by examining the different ways in which the love dialogue appears. In making this brief study I shall assume, perhaps unwisely, that
Chrétien makes extensive use of irony in his Arthurian romances and that
we are not bound to take all his remarks seriously.

It can hardly be denied that in Chrétien's *Erec* we are presented with
love in its simplest and most attractive form. Erec's failure to realize the
importance of service as an attribute both of love and the knightly life
does not affect Enid's attitude to him. Her complaint, which her half-
bemused husband overhears and mishears, has no relation to her own
honor and standing in society; and throughout the poem her actions are
guided by one principle and one only—her husband's safety, prowess, and
honor. There is little in her attitude which could be called courtly. She
calls for no service; she exacts no tribute of adulation. Of all Chrétien's
heroines she is the most attractive and least demanding.

How is this most desirable of brides wooed? How does Erec fall in
love with her? When she first appears she is dressed virtually in rags—
and if the descriptions are to be believed and if such a thing is possible,
clothes made the woman even more in the Middle Ages than they do
now. But, as Chrétien shrewdly observes, the outside was poor but the
inside was beautiful. If we assume, as I think we may, that this description reflects what Erec observes, we have a man struck by a girl's simple

beauty, and this impression is confirmed by the author's comment: Erec was overcome with admiration. But there is no wounding of the heart through the eyes, none of the agonizing which accompanies the first sight of the beloved in other poems. Apart from normal salutations, they do not exchange a word, and this is not because Erec is so stricken that he cannot speak but because the real business of life goes on—Enid is taking his horse to the stable.

The wooing of Enid as shown by Chrétien must have been much closer to a normal wooing in noble families than were those which we usually find in twelfth-century romances. Erec needs Enid so that he may enter the contest for the silver sparrow hawk. She is surpassingly beautiful and deserves the honor. If her father agrees to her going, Erec will marry her and, to establish his right to do so, he tells of his birth and parentage. Enid is not asked for her opinion of the transaction. She is merely "very happy at being given this courteous knight and she well knew that he was a king and that she herself would be a crowned queen and loaded with honors." After the victory, Erec refused all offers of new fine clothing for Enid. The queen is to see her as she is and then herself make Enid beautiful. The contrast between the ladies of Arthur's court and Enid could hardly be more pointed. It is to Enid, the simple, unspoiled girl that Arthur gives the ceremonial kiss of the White Stag. In all this time Chrétien records no direct speech between the lovers, except of a most trivial nature, no love dialogue, no monologue on passion and the nature of love. They admire one another intensely, but their feelings are not verbalized. Chrétien is here, presumably deliberately, departing from the established tradition of love analysis by dialogue. We are invited to judge the lovers by their acts, not by their words. Now it is perfectly possible to argue here that Erec's love sinks into mere sensuality and that Chrétien intends by such a portrayal of love to indicate the lack of those social and spiritual features that should attend love in its higher sense. But even if we grant this, the fact remains that Enid's love is and remains a high and pure devotion and that Erec is brought to a realization of the nature of love not by discussion but by the evidence of Enid's devotion to him presented when she could not possibly believe that he was a witness to it. It is this conviction that there is such a thing as selfless love that causes him to undertake the adventure of the *Joie de la cort*. Mabonograin is the victim of precisely the love that Erec has avoided—a love of demanding service in which the male lover is utterly deprived of free will—and Erec has avoided it because of the nature of Enid. She expresses that nature clearly and frankly in her monologues, and I can find no hint of irony in them. Here, surely, more than anywhere, Chrétien portrayed his ideal lady and he did so without using the love dialogue at all, or indeed any of the artificial concepts of service normally expressed in that dialogue.

In *Cligès* we are provided with a total contrast. Although the work is a romance of chivalry, the concentration is entirely on the love-phenomenon. The first half of the poem is full of dialogue and internal monologue, and the descriptions of love given in these passages have made the work a *locus classicus* for "courtly love." Now the early discussions of love by Alexander and Soredamurs, which are naturally monologues, since neither dares to address the other, appear at first sight to be well within the tradition set out in the *Roman d'Enéas*. They describe the devastating effects of love's passion. Yet closer examination reveals that it is the effect of love, not of the beloved, which is being examined. Alexander assembles in his first love monologue almost every cliché and every figure which had by this time become the stock-in-trade of the troubadour, of what Kolb has called "die Mystik des Auges und des Herzen."[1] This untutored youth, Alexander, discusses eyes, light, mirror, arrows with a glibness which belies his previous innocence of love. When he does describe his love, however, it is in figures of significant sensuality. In all this there is little of what we could describe as love. The concentration is entirely upon a formalized analysis of his own feelings, which proves in the end to have little of service or even of reverence, as the last figure of the arrow shows, but to be thinly disguised urgings of the flesh. Soredamurs is equally concerned with self, for she says little of the man who has inspired her love but a great deal of her own position and the attitudes she must take. The scene in which Alexander understands that his shirt has been sewn with a hair of his beloved—surely one of the funniest in Arthurian literature—reduces the lovers' posing to its true level of inanity. For why should there be all this anguish? The two are of marriageable age, there are no impediments of social position, and when Queen Guinevere in pity brings them together, they are betrothed at once. One can only ask why the more direct methods of Erec and Enid would not be effective in this case. Are we to think that Alexander and Soredamurs are capable of *fin amors* and that Erec and Enid are not? If we take the indications of Chrétien's sympathy as a guide, the reverse would appear to be true, for he clearly regards the passion of Alexander and Soredamurs as laughable. The love monologues, then, would appear to be parody, parody of those we find in the *Roman d'Enéas* and still more of the sentiments of the troubadours. There arises a formal question—is the love monologue/dialogue itself an indication of parody, of a lack of serious belief in the love affair? I do not mean to imply, of course, that any dialogue between lovers indicates parody but that the formal monologue on love's symptoms and the formal dialogue of total submission may well be such an indication.

Fenice reveals her passion not to Guinevere but to Thessala, a specialist in black magic, who neatly sets up for her the very reverse of the Tristan love potion, for instead of making love inevitable, it makes it impossible. There is no real communication between Cligès and Fenice. Each allegedly is deeply in love with the other but for months their relationship is a kind of *amor de lonh,* both physically and spiritually. Cligès, we are told, fears rejection and hence does not communicate his love to his lady, but Fenice has, without his knowledge, already insured that there can be no true love between husband and wife and indeed no love at all. Their first dialogue is again couched in formal terms, this time the separation of heart and body motif which is found so often in the *chanson de croisade.* The dialectic is complex; the hearts, after much meandering, are finally in place; and now Fenice reveals to Cligès her true relations with her husband, not without a repetition of her earlier statement that she will refuse to be an Iseut la blonde. His suggestion that she go with him to Britain is rejected because she would then be regarded as an adulteress—far better to be an adulteress than to be thought of as one.

From now on the love affair between Cligès and Fenice is a series of deceits and technicalities, all of which are designed to preserve the fine distinction between being an adulteress *in esse* and an adulteress *coram publico.* Fenice has a nice taste in these matters which seems to accord ill with the power of love to deprive its victims of their rational faculties. Here, surely, is the ultimate absurdity of this secret love, the necessity of concealing it from the *jaloux.* Poor man, he does not even know that he has reason to be jealous. Preservation of the intact status of her body is very important for Fenice, and the scene in which the doctors are prevented from roasting it by a thousand angry ladies is an excellent commentary by Chrétien on female values. After all, Fenice was allegedly dead. Yet all the deception is in vain. The lovers do have to flee to Arthur's court in the end, and Arthur is perfectly prepared to take their side until the problem is solved by the emperor's death. All has come out right in the end—the lovers are united and adultery is justified. The trappings of love are here, but not true love itself. In the last resort, each of the lovers is concerned only with bodily satisfaction and with reputation, not with true service to each other or to their neighbors. Their communication, for all its elaborate figures, never rises above the lowest level, and their love, for all its dialectic, is sensual indulgence in an elaborate tomb.

In the *Chevalier de la Charette* the communication is of a very different kind. Nowhere do we find love analyzed in dialogue or monologue. Lancelot's musings are the contemplations of a mystic rather than the analyses of the love dialecticians. The communication between Lancelot and the queen is of a direct and peremptory nature. The queen commands and Lancelot obeys. His reception in the tower after the incident in the cart is notoriously cool, but the amount of conversation between the two is small. Lancelot is utterly unable to understand the queen's disdainful attitude toward him, for he has performed service for her, as several third parties remind him. There is no analysis of love between the two, only a statement of Lancelot's service to the queen. When the two lovers meet again, the problem is stated with a minimum of words: "You waited two steps." Lancelot asks for pardon and receives it. A rendezvous is made for the evening, and the two spend the night together. It is the fact of physical love which is important here, not discussions of the love theory. The rendezvous is, of course, more reminiscent of the *alba* than of the *canzon,* but this meeting is less characteristic of the love between Lancelot and Guinevere than is the stream of commands that pass from the queen to her knight. This romance is the story of love-service pushed beyond reason. It is not a love that can be expressed in dialogue, because dialogue should mean verbal communication on a rational level, and such communication does not exist between Lancelot and Guinevere. Nor is it the kind of "courtly love" that we found in *Cligès,* for there the love was at least mutual. In the *Lancelot* there is little evidence of true love on the part of Guinevere. She grants rewards to Lancelot, but she never says that she herself is in love, nor does she ever discuss the subject with anyone else. Lancelot's love expresses itself not in dialogue or indeed in any kind of verbalization but in action. He seeks the queen and finds her and in tournaments he wins or loses completely at her command. If service is the mark of the perfect lover, then Lancelot bears that mark. Yet this love is one-sided and ill-balanced. As Fenice and Cligès were in communication only on the level of sensual indulgence and discussed their relationship only from the point of view of making Fenice available without a technical loss of honor, so the love of Lancelot and Guinevere is discussed only from the point of view of service and reward. This is not to say that Lancelot's love was not sincere. He is, perhaps, the most deeply involved of all Chrétien's heroes, but his involvement is not expressed verbally. It is very significant that on the one occasion when Lancelot is shown thinking about love, we are not made party to his thoughts. Yet this absence of love monologue or love dialogue does not indicate the kind of love we find in *Erec*. The queen is the very opposite of Enid, for she uses her lover entirely to reinforce her personal sense of power. Communication through dialogue would thus be an impossible means of communication, for it implies give and take, compromise, and the possible recognition of another point of view, all of which would be quite impossible for the queen whom Chrétien portrays. The command is more natural.

It is, perhaps, in *Yvain* that the use of the love dialogue is most effective and most subtle. The love-problem is presented to us in this work, as in *Erec*, as a conflict between two aspects of the knightly life, but it is not, as has so often been stated, merely the reverse side of the *Erec* coin. Laudine's love for Yvain is never the same as that of Enid for Erec, either before Yvain departs on his tour of adventure or after his return.

Yvain's reaction on first seeing Laudine is not unlike that of Alexander on seeing Soredamurs. He is, he declares, hopelessly entangled in love. The first words of his monologue are: *Por fol me puis tenir,* and he is much nearer the truth than the cliché of the love monologue might indicate. Yvain follows the usual lines of the internal debate—his lady may hate him, he fears to approach her, her beauty is remarkable and should not be marred by sorrow. But this time, as Chrétien coolly remarks, Yvain is not a mere prisoner of love, bound in silken chains, but an actual prisoner in a space bounded by very substantial stone walls. His love is indeed mad by any logical standards, since he desires and knows he desires a lady whose husband he has just killed. Now according to Andreas Capellanus and certain Provençal and French lyric poets, the husband was an impediment, a jealous man who was better out of the way; Yvain has already put the husband out of the way but is liable to find him a more effective bar to love when dead than he ever was when alive. Yet once again social convention proves its strength. How can a widow accept her husband's murderer as a lover? (We have not yet reached the point of discussing Yvain as a husband.) At this point Yvain is as obsessed with his desires as were Alexander or Cligès. He has no thought of any larger issue or indeed of the lady's feelings. His desire is to possess beauty, and his monologue reveals that he thinks of the death of Laudine's husband merely as an impediment to desire and Laudine's possible objections to receiving him as being based formally on the fact that he had killed her husband.

Now in the dialogue between Lunete and Laudine that leads to the introduction of Yvain to his mistress, the word "love" does not occur. Lunete does not ask that her mistress should love Yvain but that she should take him as the defender of the fountain, as her lord, because he is clearly the best available candidate. This is a dialogue of reasoned matrimony, not of love, and it is very reminiscent of Erec's "wooing" of Enid. Laudine's monologue is rather casuistic proof to herself that her acceptance of the killer of her husband is a reasonable thing to do. A far cry, indeed, from the lovers in the *Roman d'Enéas* and *Cligès*. Again there is no mention of love, but when Lunete appears again, the question of rank and lineage is raised. Once the qualifications of Yvain—as a husband, not as a lover—have been determined, Laudine is impatient for his arrival. Laudine's description of her impatience is remarkable for its *double entendre,* its play with the vocabulary of love and medieval actuality. Yvain accepts the prison in its "love" sense, but Lunete knows better. He is taking his chance of actual prison if he does not please his mistress.

Yvain makes the formal acknowledgment of complete submission to Laudine. She asks whether this extends to her killing him. He says that it does. Now in the formal love dialogue such a remark would be perfectly acceptable, since to kill him would mean simply to make him die of love. But Laudine does not mean this. She means actual physical death. The love dialogue is being parodied in a grim tone. The parody continues as Laudine questions the reasons for his decision to come to her, carefully eliciting from him the required answers—his heart has made him do so, and his heart was forced by his eyes, and his eyes by her beauty, and all this led to a "love which is the greatest possible, so that my heart can not be separated from you and go elsewhere, so that I can think of nothing else, so that I love you more than myself, so that I would live or die according to your wish." And what is the reply to this passionate declaration? "And you would undertake to defend my fountain?" No word of love, simply of peace between them. There is considerable stress on the formal nature of the union, on the ceremony before the barons which made Yvain their lord. And Chrétien adds significantly: "the lady thought it more honorable to take a husband with the approval of her people, even though she would have done so without their prayers, at love's command." She has never said that she loves Yvain, any more than Enid had said that she loved Erec. There is no love-musing, no display of feelings, nor are we told at any time of love. The stress is rather on the externals of courtly entertainment. (It is perhaps significant that Gawain becomes Lunete's chevalier, promising her unstinting service, but is far away when she needs him.) Yvain's request to be allowed to go on an adventure tour is granted by Laudine before she knows what she will have to promise, and when she sets the term and says that her love will turn to hate if he exceeds it, she is merely continuing the contract on which all their relations have been based. Yet she is more thoughtful than Yvain, for she gives him a ring to preserve him from harm.

Yvain's adventures are mere games, but they are sufficient to make him forget his deadline. Just before the arrival of Laudine's messenger he is depressed by the thought that he has exceeded his leave, and well he may be, for events show that Laudine has been far more concerned about their separation than has Yvain, with all his protestations of eternal fidelity and love. His madness and thus separation from his earlier life is the introduction to a new and completely different phase of existence. During this period his attitude toward love is different. He is in despair and when he says that he will die if he cannot be reconciled with Laudine, he is speaking the literal truth. There are no shams, no dialogues of the sorrows of love, only a genuine desire to serve. The failure of Laudine to recognize him is not one more instance of the common medieval lack of visual memory. He is a different man, and his dialogue with Laudine is carried on in the person of the Chevalier au Lion, not that of Yvain. His request to her to intercede for him with his lady can be couched directly because he is not speaking as Yvain, and she can answer directly because she does not know that she is speaking to her husband and lover. There is, of course, irony in the condemnation of the hard-hearted mistress of the Chevalier au Lion, but Laudine is acting in precisely the same manner that Yvain had urged when he first made his exaggerated declarations of service. Now that he does indeed serve all women who need help, he need no longer make such protestations. His ultimate return is made in his new person and with the true humility that is characteristic of it. The dialogue is very far from the standard form. Laudine says that she is "entirely at his disposal; she would be willing to do what he wants and wishes only to do him good so far as she can." These words are addressed to the new Yvain, to the Chevalier au Lion, but they are to be applied to the old Yvain, to Laudine's husband. Laudine understands this perfectly well when it is revealed to her who the Chevalier au Lion really is and this is why she cries out that she has been tricked. Their agreement had again been reached on a utilitarian basis—the need to defend the fountain—and Laudine makes it clear that she is still not sure of Yvain's love and that there will always be a lingering doubt in her mind. But Yvain's repentance, which is not a declaration of love, is accepted.

At the end of the poem Chrétien has brought his hero to an understanding of the function of knighthood in the world and has also raised him to a degree of moral responsibility and social awareness far superior to that of the Arthurian court represented by Gawain. The relation with Laudine, which began with a totally conventional "falling-in-love," has thus served its purpose in bringing about the maturity of the hero. It may also be argued that his personal relationship to Laudine also shows more maturity, since he no longer thinks of her in terms of beauty only but as a woman to whom, as to the the other women he has helped, he owes a knightly duty. Yet Chrétien still does not show us any true communication between the two. Laudine accepts Yvain as her lord again, although she says that only her oath is making her do so. She does not say that she loves him and it is far from certain that she understands what he has learned since his madness and "rebirth." Her relation to him, in other words, is still formalistic. She feels that he has broken the agreement they made and that he should be punished. There is no evidence in Chrétien's poem that Yvain and Laudine will be happy ever after or even that Yvain's love-service has gained his mistress' love at all. He can only hope.

Hartmann von Aue, who wrote a German version of *Yvain* which keeps very close to Chrétien's poem, obviously felt that this lack of love and total reconciliation was a defect in the poem, for he added a scene in which Laudine flings herself at Iwein's feet and begs his forgiveness. The poem thus ends in total harmony, and the conventions have been satisfied. For the German hero, love-service has brought not only maturity but the love of his wife, and love is shown as merely one factor, if a major one, in bringing about the development of the hero. Laudine, for Hartmann, simply must accept her husband after he has fulfilled the necessary con-

ditions. Chrétien prefers to leave the matter to the imagination of his audience.

Since Chrétien never completed the *Perceval,* it would be unfair to draw
conclusions about the love of the hero for Blancheflur. Yet it is worth
noting that the conversation between the two is almost all of a very practical nature. They discuss what services the young Perceval can render,
and the lady apparently gives herself to him in exchange for the promised
services. In the Gawain incidents there is, of course, a great deal of parody. In the incident with the little girl, the communication with Gawain
is entirely formal conversation, in that with the sister of the king of Gav-
alon it is all action. Only in the long negotiations with the scornful damsel do we see the expanded love dialogue and it is, of course, largely an
exercise in futility, since the participants are working from different
premises. Gawain never muses over his love for the proud damsel—indeed, he never says that he loves her—but he accepts her commands as
Lancelot does those of Guinevere. His conversation with her concerns
those commands. Her conversation with him reflects her concern for the
defiling of her body which is really the cause of her unrelenting behavior
toward Gawain. She proves in the end not to be the cruel mistress who
exacts service from her knight but a woman who has suffered from the
system, who knows very well what the approach of a knight means. Her
apparent demand for unremitting and dangerous service is in effect an
attempt to prove to Gawain, the perfect knight, that if a woman really
demands service she can bring about the death of her knight, not his glory,
just as the cousin of Perceval had done for her lover. It is worth observing that there is a strong resemblance between Erec and Enid and Gawain and the proud damsel, with the roles, of course, reversed.

What conclusions can we draw? To me it is clear that Chrétien uses
the love dialogue, the characteristic of early romances, only when love is
not sincere in his sense. In other words, if Alexander and Soredamurs,
Cligès and Fenice are courtly lovers, then Chrétien wants no part of courtly
love. His real lovers never indulge in the love monologue or love dialogue when they are truly in love. The unregenerate Yvain is full of words
and mouths his statements with the best, but the repentant, experienced
Chevalier au Lion does not. Enid loves without words. Laudine loves true
service, and the dialogue is reshaped in her mouth to practical ends. Neither Lancelot in his infatuation nor Gawain in his patient endurance in-
dulges in words about love. Each demonstrates by his actions his devotion to his mistress, besotted though that emotion may appear to be. On

the basis of the use of dialogue, certain divisions of Chrétien's romances become clear. There are two in which love is commanded: the *Chevalier de la Charrette*, in which it is commanded for a woman's ego and is unhealthy and suspect; and the Gawain incidents in *Perceval* in which it is commanded by a lady who has suffered and who later repents of her commanding. Dialogue and monologue flourish in *Cligès* and yet, in spite of the many words, the only concern of the participants is bodily satisfaction. Love brings them no nearer to maturity. Finally there are two in which love is founded not on fine phrases but on the gradual evolution of mutual understanding. In both of these it is not love, courtly or otherwise, which is the prime force, but social needs and mutual help. The successful marriages are those in which the lovers do not protest too much.

Communication between lovers in Chrétien's romances is thus not quite so fluent as it may seem at a first reading. It would not be far from the truth to say that much of the verbalizing is noncommunication, since it consists of a series of shams, of fronts which prove to be unreal or, at best, evidence of a kind of love which Chrétien regards as unhealthy. Real communication in words is rare. None of the "true" lovers succeeds in expressing to the other what his or her feelings are. Had they been able to do so, much grief would have been averted, but the maturity which comes from suffering would not be attained. For Chrétien, the communication of real love, as distinct from the formalized games of the court, apparently came through action and through indirect communication of affection. He clearly mistrusted the rhetoric and dialectic of earlier romances as a method of representing love in its higher aspects and used them principally to parody the type of love he rejected. If we are right in assuming that he regarded married love as that which best fulfilled the aspirations of both man and woman, then we must also assume that he felt that such love needed no elaborate verbal communication. True love expressed itself in mutual trust, not in the artifices of cunningly wrought words.

NOTE

1. Herbert Kolb, *Der Begriff der Minne und das Entstehen der höfischen Lyrik* (Tübingen: Niemeyer, 1958), *passim*.

13

The Arthuricity of
Marie de France

THE WORKS OF Marie de France have suffered a fate at the hands of critics which is not uncommon when the author is regarded as being not quite of the first rank. They are used to make comparisons. Her fables are compared with the "Romulus" collection and with those of Alexander Neckham, her *Purgatoire St. Patriz* with versions in Latin, and her *Lais*, inevitably, with Arthurian romances. Marie has only herself to blame for the last of these critical positions. She constantly uses the word "Bretons" and "li Breton" in her *lais*, and it was therefore inevitable that the Celticists should ransack her work for analogues. They are not hard to find, but their discovery answers no questions. We must still ask where she found them and how conscious she was of their presence in the Arthurian romances, particularly those of Chrétien de Troyes, for they are the only *extant* French Arthurian *romances* (I exclude Wace from the list) which she could have known. The usual explanation of "a common source" is of no value. It does not throw any light on her relation to the romance as opposed to the raw materials. If we wish to compare her work with the romances, we should rather find out how she uses its genre conventions and what we somewhat loosely term the Arthurian ethic. It is to this point that this paper will be devoted and specifically to an examination of the most Arthurian of her *lais, Lanval*.

Before this more specific study, however, it might be helpful to characterize some of the general features of the *lais*. Most of them are concerned with sexual love, often with love that results in tragedy—*Laüstic, Yonec, Les Deux Amants*—or in long separation—*Guigemer, Eliduc, Milon,*

Chevrefeuille. Only two bring unalloyed happiness after pain, *Frêne* and *Lanval*. The chief aspect of love which these works share with romance, and particularly Arthurian convention, is the power attributed to it and the recognition that love overrides such matters as loyalty to a husband. Husbands, in fact, do not fare very well in the *Lais*. In *Laüstic*, *Yonec*, and *Guigemer* they are jealous to the point of insanity and possessiveness. As events prove, they have good reason for their mistrust, but the sympathy of the author is with the faithless wife and the adulterous lover. Their deception of the husband is regarded as natural. Only in *Eliduc* is the question of morality raised and then only by the first, abandoned, wife who founds a nunnery for herself to relieve her husband of the embarrassment of having two "wives." Love is undoubtedly dominant but it is worth noting that only in *Guigemer* and, to some degree, in *Eliduc* does the adulterous love result in lasting happiness. The *lais* with a happy ending are those in which the lover wins a lady against opposition, stays faithful to her, and ultimately marries her. Marie, like Chrétien, seems to have written a series of works about love in its various aspects. In all of them, love is the most important force motivating human conduct. The difference lies in the reaction of this force on the social circumstances in which the lovers find themselves. Thus the *Lais* and the Arthurian romances have an important common factor, the recognition of the importance of love in human affairs, and a common object, the examination of the social implications of love by setting it in a social context specially set up for the purpose, the Arthurian world or a reflection of it.

The supernatural is a part of this world, and Marie uses it very naturally. When the lady is locked away, her lover arrives by supernatural means—as a bird in *Laüstic* and *Yonec*, by magic ship in *Guigemer*. No stress is placed on these extraordinary happenings by the author, and they are not part of the main thrust of the story. In the same way, in *Lanval*, the way by which the lady knows of Lanval's desires and her means of arriving at Arthur's court are never discussed. The context for the *lais*, like the Arthurian court, is a fabrication, and there is no need to explain it. Nevertheless this cool assumption of the supernatural does impart an element of distance to the works, a confirmation that we are not thinking in terms of contemporary real life, whether medieval or modern. In spite of this distance it is wrong to speak of "idealized situations" in the *Lais*. The problems are real and the treatment often brutal. The characters are, in general, self-centered, even selfish, and are rarely concerned with the good of others, whatever lip-service they may pay to conventions of loyalty. Certain standards of formal behavior are demanded but they are little more than a mask for the real motivations of the characters. It is here that Marie de France comes very close to Chrétien de Troyes, and none of her works is more revealing in this respect than *Lanval*.

Lanval differs in many ways from the other *lais.* The most important feature which distinguishes it from them is its use of the Arthurian court. This is not simply a matter of the love conventions, of the supremacy of love in all matters, but of the actual composition of Arthur's court and the characteristics of its members. There are two "types" of Arthurian courts, that of the historically-oriented works of which Marie could have known only Geoffrey of Monmouth's *Historia regum Britanniae* and Wace's *Brut,* its Anglo-Norman derivative. In these works, Arthur is an active king, the true head of his court. None of his subordinates is of any particular importance and, although Gawain and Kei are mentioned, they are not differentiated. The court is highly civilized but it is not devoted to merely leisure pursuits, nor is sexual love the principal motivating force of the actions of its members. The court differs from others only in the outstanding personality of its king and the unusually polished manner of its court. The romances of Chrétien present a totally different picture. The king is weak—either petty or impotent—although he is a cultivated gentleman. His time is passed entirely in leisure pursuits and, except in *Cligès,* he has apparently no wars to fight. He is surrounded by knights, not by counselors, by self-seeking individualists, not by loyal subjects. In most of the romances, the court is dominated by Kei who, in spite of his crudity, ambition, and inability to treat anyone with kindness or even courtesy, is allowed to determine matters which should be the concern of Arthur himself. Both in *Yvain* and *Perceval,* tragic events spring from Kei's behavior, events which Arthur could easily have prevented merely by acting like a king. Gawain, on the other hand, represents the Arthurian court at its best. He is brave, generous, and always ready to recognize the good in other people. He is devoted to the code of love-supremacy and the pursuit of individual honor. It is impossible to determine whether Chrétien had any predecessors in this view of the Arthurian court. If he had, not a trace of them has survived. It should be emphasized that we are not discussing here the material of the romances, the stories which were used in its construction, but the artificial Arthurian court and its rules, which may very well have been a creation of Chrétien de Troyes and which was, in any case, refined and polished by him. The importance of this question for *Lanval* lies in the fact that Marie de France knows of Chrétien's concept of the court and relies on the fact that her audience understands it. *Lanval* has no point at all unless those who heard it knew of the petulant, weak Arthur, the Guenevere who betrayed him with Lancelot, the Gawain who was courteous above other knights, and the obsession of the court with leisure pursuits. Either Marie must have known Chrétien or she must have known some predecessor who treated the Arthurian court in the same way. The other possibility is, of course, that she arrived independently at the same ironical view of the virtues of the court as that reached by Chrétien. Such a solution is possible but unlikely, since the audience, too, must be aware of Arthur, *roi-fainéant,* if it is to understand the *lai.*

On chronological grounds it would not be impossible for Marie to have known the works of Chrétien. The "accepted" chronology would make it difficult for her to have known *Perceval,* of which there seem to be distinct echoes in *Lanval.* But the chronology of her works does not rest on an unshakable basis, and *Lanval* could easily be a late addition. The earliest extant manuscript is set in the mid-thirteenth century.

The general evidence thus would indicate that Marie knew either Chrétien or the works of someone whose views of Arthur's court were like his. But there is more precise evidence of acquaintance with Chrétien's works.

The opening is in tone and attitude very similar to the opening of *Yvain.* In Marie's work, Arthur is *pruz* and *curteis,* as he is in *Yvain.* The close resemblance of the two descriptions of Arthur would not in itself be particularly significant if it were not for the fact that in both poems the actions which immediately follow belie the description. In *Lanval,* Arthur is at Cardoel (Carlisle) because of the invasions of the Picts and Scots, who are specifically stated to be ravaging his country. He does absolutely nothing about the invasion but proceeds with what, in Chrétien's works, are normal Pentecost leisure activities. He distributes largess of various kinds but not to the one man who most deserves it, Lanval. Marie carefully states his qualities: *valur, largesce, beauté, pruesce,* the very qualities which were supposed to be characteristic of all the best knights of the Round Table. She adds a little later that Lanval "tant aveit le rei serui." Thus Lanval should be among the first to benefit from Arthur's generosity. Instead he receives nothing. Marie makes the reason for this that his qualities and deeds do not arouse respect but simply envy.

> ⌊Artur] ne l'en sovint
> Ne nuls des soens bien ne li tint.
> Pur sa valur, pur sa largesce,
> Pur sa beauté, pur sa prüesce,
> L'envïoent tuit li plusur;
> Tels li mustra semblant d'amur,
> S'al chevalier mesavenist,
> Ja une feiz ne l'en pleinist![1]
>
> (ll. 19 ff.)

This is the court of which the whole world stands in awe, and it is the whole court, including its king, which is here indicted.

The opening of *Yvain* is hardly more flattering. Arthur retires to his bedroom with Guenevere as soon as he has eaten his midday meal. His knights have nothing serious to do, and Kei soon succeeds in injecting bitterness and rancor into what was originally a harmless attempt by Calogreant to amuse the company by telling a story about himself which did him little credit. Kei is jealous of what he considers to be the honor or at least the reputation of the court whose behavior he purports to regulate. The fact that his own behavior does not conform to the standard he sets appears to worry him not at all. Moreover, it soon becomes clear as *Yvain* progresses that Kei *does*, in fact, regulate conduct. Guenevere cannot restrain him even when she rebukes him openly; Arthur sees in Calogreant's adventure one more opportunity for the court to indulge in its favorite pastime of purposeless fighting. Worse still, Yvain is so stung by Kei's abuse of his cousin that he cannot wait to attack the knight of the fountain and, when he has gravely wounded his opponent, he forgets Arthurian chivalry in a desperate attempt to secure "proof" that he has defeated the knight. The taunting figure of Kei is always in his mind:

> mes toz jorz a foïr entant,
> et cil de chacier s'esvertue,
> qu'il crient sa poinne avoir perdue
> se mort ou vif ne le retient,
> que des ranpones li sovient
> que mes sire Kex li ot dites.[2]
>
> (ll. 890 ff.)

It is thus Kei, mean, ungenerous, and envious, who is the driving force at Arthur's court, as Chrétien describes it. The same is true in *Perceval,* where Kei's actions override Arthur's good-natured but ineffectual efforts to prevent Perceval from fighting with the Red Knight.

> Vilonnie est d'autrui gaber
> Et de prometre sanz doner.
> Preudom ne se doit entremetre
> De rien nule a autrui prometre
> Que doner ne li puisse ou veille,
> Que le mal gré celui n'acueille
> Qui sanz prometre est ses amis
> Et des que il li a pramis,
> Si bee a la promesse avoir.[3]
>
> (ll. 1017 ff.)

In *Le Chevalier de la Charette* there is the same blustering Kei and the same ineffectual king, the same determination of the course of events by the lowest member of the court.

It is clear that a properly run court should not function like this, still less a court with the reputation which Arthur's ostensibly possesses. Both Chrétien and Marie are comparing a literary tradition known to their audience with a realization of that tradition which takes account of the differences in human personality and of the baser aspects of human nature. This is not a contrast between "idealism" and "reality" but the interpretation of a literary construct, created for the examination of certain conflicts between individual and society, in a manner calculated to make it more telling, even more relevant to the normal human condition. The method is to introduce into the Arthurian world qualities which are theoretically alien to it and to use specific characters who traditionally typify the best in the Arthurian world as examples of those qualities.

Lanval, as we have seen, is a perfect example of what a knight should be at Arthur's court but he is a stranger there. Marie describes him as "de halt parage / mes luin . . . de sun heritage." So were Gawain, Erec, Yvain, and other heroes. Foreign birth and coming from kingdoms far off should not hinder the progress of a knight. The foreign quality is of a different sort. Lanval feels himself far from home because he is alien to the behavior of the court, not because he is physically separated from his homeland. His situation is, in fact, very close to that of the lover who suffers "amor de lonh." He may be very close to the beloved physically and yet separated by an unbridgeable gulf or far away and yet indissolubly tied. The relationship is entirely dependent on a literary convention.

The alienation is illustrated by an interesting variation on the Arthurian theme. The knights of the Round Table never have to worry about costs. They all appear to have sufficient means to provide themselves with armor, horses, and whatever other accoutrements are necessary. Only occasionally do we hear of a person, like the *vavasour* in *Erec,* who has fallen on evil days and lives in poverty—far from the court. Lanval, however, because of Arthur's failure to reward his services, is reduced to extremes of poverty

> Tut sun aveir ad despendu
> Kar li reis rien ne li dona
> Ne Lanval ne li demanda.
> (ll. 30 ff.)

We are faced with the unmentionable—an Arthurian knight who is poor and who is poor because of the failure of Arthur to do what the literary convention demands. There is another aspect of this poverty. As Andreas Capellanus says to Walter, it is useless to think of love unless you have the means to afford it, and all the romances seem to support this statement. Certainly Lanval is deserted by male and female alike. There is no place for poverty, genteel or otherwise.

Thus it comes about that Lanval leaves the court because he is poor and has no friends there. As we all know, the classic opening of an Arthurian romance involves the departure of a knight seeking adventure. There is invariably an intrusion upon the apparent harmony of the court— the knight and dwarf in *Erec,* Calogreant's tale in *Yvain,* the abduction of Guenevere in *Le Chevalier de la Charette.* If the process seems different in *Perceval* it is because of the double intrusion of the knights into Perceval's rural life and the insult to Guenevere by the Red Knight. In *Lanval,* the hero leaves the court not to seek adventure but because the court has nothing to offer him. Its harmony is unbroken and even though it is Pentecost, the great day for adventure and although the Picts and Scots are at the gates, the surface tranquillity of the court is undisturbed. Marie's *lai* thus flies in the face of Arthurian tradition even as it is represented in the works of Chrétien de Troyes. The best knight rides out not to vindicate the honor of the court but because that court has no honor to offer him.

A move to an enchanted land on horseback is not uncommon in medieval literature and Lanval's horse shows its awareness of a supernatural
presence. More important, however, are the formal preparations which
the author makes for the erotic vision—the flowing water, the horse allowed to wander, the general malaise of the hero, his discontent with life.
Any reader of the *Roman de la Rose* will recognize them. He lies down—
it is never stated that he falls asleep—and sees two beautiful girls approaching. Leaving his horse, he goes with them to a tent in which he
sees a lady, dressed only in her shift, partly covered and partly exposed.
Now the interesting thing about this episode is the unusual concentration of the description on the dress—or undress—of the ladies. The two
messenger-girls "vestues fuurent richement / et lacies estreitement"—a detail
which does not occur often in romance. The lady in the tent, on the other
hand, calls attention to herself by her semi-nudity. Medieval ladies avoided
semi-nudity in public. Enide was ragged because she was poor, the amie
of the proud knight in *Perceval* was half undressed because she was being
mistreated, Isolde at her trial because she wished to excite the sympathy
which invariably went out to a noblewoman who had to appear without
the proper clothes. Here the object is to stir sensual desire. The lady knows
Lanval is coming and she is awake, unlike the poor lady in the tent so
rudely disturbed by Perceval. This lady, temptingly displayed in luxuri-
ous surroundings, is certainly the fulfillment of Lanval's erotic desires. She
is not only beautiful but possesses all the wealth for want of which Lanval is rejected at Arthur's court, the court where the dreams of love are
supposed to be fulfilled. Instead of riding out on adventure and gaining
a lady by love-service, Lanval is *taken* to her, she offers herself to him
without preamble or condition, and when he accepts, gives him a large
bonus—all the wealth he can use. We are here on the borders of a dream
world—but Arthur's court is a dream world too and there the standards
for which it was renowned were not being observed. Lanval, rejected by
it for no good reason, finds happiness elsewhere.

Now there are several instances of a hero meeting a lady on a bed in a
tent in the works of Chrétien de Troyes. Erec has such an encounter in
the *Joie de la Cort* episode and so does Perceval. In both instances the
result of the encounter is a fight with the knight to whom she is attached.
Erec fights him immediately, Perceval at a much later stage. There is an
element of magic in the incident, since the lady can clearly be regarded
as "bait" to tempt another knight. In the *Joie de la Cort* incident the
temptation is an essential part of the lady's plan to keep control of her

knight. In *Perceval* she is the unwilling recipient of the attentions of a crude boy, who has no understanding of the Arthurian attitudes towards women which his mother had tried to teach him. In Chrétien's romance the incident is comic, comic because of the boy's failure to grasp the advice given by his mother which refers to a set of highly artificial conventions. The result is tragic because the knight attending the lady, who should understand them and is supposed to obey his mistress in all things, proves to be a brutal tyrant who places no trust in the lady's word. Thus the episodes of the "lady in the tent" are in both cases an indictment of the alleged code of love and chivalry. In *Erec* the lady uses her person to enforce that code on her knight, in *Perceval* the lady is brutalized by a knight who pays lip-service to the code.

We should examine one or two details. It will be remembered that Perceval blunders into the tent because his mother has told him to enter any church or minster, buildings he will recognize by the cross upon them and their richness. The tent has on it a golden eagle whose outspread wings catch the sun and thus remind Perceval, who has little experience of these matters, of a cross. He has even less experience of ladies, either in tents or churches, and the richness of the interior is impressive enough.

> . . . il vit un tref tendu
> En une praerie bele
> Les le rieu d'une fontenele.
> Li tres fu biax a grant merveille:
> L'une partie fu vermeille
> Et l'autre fu d'orfrois brodee,
> Desus ot une aigle doree,
> En l'aigle feroit li solaus
> Qui molt estoit clers et vermaus
> Si reluisoient tout li pre
> De l'enluminement del tre!
> Entor le tref a la roonde,
> Qui estoit li plus biax del monde . . .
> Lor vient au tref, sel trove overt,
> Enmi le tref un lit covert
> D'une colte de paile voit;
> El lit toute seule gisoit
> Une pucelete endormie.
> El bos estoit sa compaignie . . .
> (ll. 638 ff.)

The tent to which Lanreal is led has some interesting resemblances. First it is extremely beautiful and of such rich stuff that neither Queen Semiramis nor the Emperor Augustus could have afforded it or even one panel of it. More significant is the fact that it, too, has an eagle at the top. Rich though it is, the concentration of the description is on its inhabitant and the beauty of her person, and at this point we should note a rather remarkable fact. Wolfram von Eschenbach's *Parzifal* is certainly based on Chrétien's work, even though Wolfram himself denies the connection. The German poet also has his hero blunder upon a lady in a tent (Jeschute) but he alters the emphasis of the episode. Whereas Chrétien wishes to portray the crudity and even stupidity of his hero and therefore stresses the description of the tent which no sensible person could mistake for a church, Wolfram wishes to stress Parzival's innocence. He therefore gives only a slight sketch of the tent and concentrates on the seductive beauty of Jeschute. There is a marked resemblance between his description and that of Marie, even to the detail of the fur covering thrown back from the body, a detail not in *Perceval*. Wolfram used many sources for details, and it is not impossible that he had heard this passage from *Lanval*.

What is much more significant is the way in which those authors, near contemporaries, have used the same motif of the lady in the tent. Chrétien contrasts Arthurian sophistication with adolescent boorishness, not altogether to the advantage of either. He is, at this stage, not particularly concerned with the lady's fate but later he uses the treatment meted out to her for ironical criticism of the Arthurian "love" ethic. Wolfram wishes to contrast his hero's naiveté in matters of love with the—to him—culpable love-relations encouraged at Arthur's court. Jeschute is seductive and had Parzival been anything but innocent he would not have parted so easily from such a prize. Marie de France uses the incident quite differently. The hero is young but, by medieval standards, a mature person. He is led to the tent and its richness and the beauty of its inhabitant are intended to appeal to a person who is poor and deprived of love. In other words, it is the fulfillment of his dream. Yet the point would be totally lost and the incident banal if it were not for the contrast with Arthurian mores. The lady offers herself, she does not require service, she openly uses sensual charms to attract Lanval, and she, not Lanval, provides the material goods. We have a totally different form of wish fulfillment, which places the lady on terms of equality with the man and even allows her to set an important condition for a continuation of their relationship, but there is none of the almost maniacal desire to dominate which we find in the *Joie de la cort,* in Gawain's relations with Orgeluse and, most significantly, in those of Guenevere and Lancelot in *Le Chevalier de la Charette.* In this incident, Marie is carefully preparing her ground for the subsequent attack on the Arthurian ethic. The lady in the tent, who remains nameless, gives to Lanval the rewards which the court has denied him. He has only to wish for her and the material goods she provides. She grants them for love, not service.

When Lanval returns to the court he actually takes over the functions which Arthur should perform:

> N'ot en la vile chevalier
> Ki de surjur ait grant mestier
> Qui il ne face a lui venir
> E richement e bien servir.
> Lanval donout les riches duns,
> Lanval aquitout les prisuns,
> Lanval vesteit les jugleürs,
> Lanval faiseit les granz honurs!
> (ll. 205 ff.)

These are the functions of a king, not a private citizen. Now that he is rich, he does not have to wait long for recognition and it comes to him in a conversation between Gawain and Yvain, a very suitable couple at this stage in the development of the romance:

> "Par Deu, seignur, nos feimes mal
> De nostre cumpainun Lanval
> Ki tant est larges e curteis
> E sis peres est riches reis,
> Qu'od nus ne l'avum amené."
> (ll. 229 ff.)

The order of adjectives is significant—*larges* before *curteis.* After all Lanval has always been courteous. So now Lanval is in the mainstream of life at Arthur's court, and the only other recognition needed is for him to be noticed by Guenevere. This happens at once.

Before discussing the incident we should note that the involvement of the Queen with Lancelot is not invariably part of the tradition. The *Lan-*

zelet of Ulrich von Zatzikhoven, which claims a French source, has no word about it. It does not appear in the works of Geoffrey of Monmouth or Wace. Once again, the earliest extant work about this love affair is the *Chevalier de la Charette,* where the Queen's behavior is not only adulterous but domineering to her lover and abusive of the very tradition she should represent. This is the tradition we find in *Lanval.* When Guenevere sees that Lanval is accepted by the knights led by Gawain, she is immediately attracted. His new wealth and his generous use of it have made him the most interesting figure at court or, to put it vulgarly, a prime catch. Guenevere is, characteristically, looking out of the window of a tower when she sees him, a picture familiar to readers of *Le Chevalier de la Charette.* The lady in a tower has to be rescued to be won, and the penetration of the tower by the hero is a stock symbolic motif of the romance—but Guenevere does not stay there. She descends, with selected ladies-in-waiting, to meet the group of knights, thus eliminating the necessity to penetrate the tower. The ladies are presumably to amuse the other knights, for the queen moves towards Lanval as soon as she sees him alone (actually far removed in thought from this assembly) and at once declares her passion for him in the most direct, even crude terms:

> "Lanval, mut vus ai honuré
> E mut cheri e mut amé;
> Tute m'amur poëz aveir;
> Kar me dites vostre voleir!
> Ma druerie vus otrei:
> Mult devez estre liez de mei!"
> (ll. 263 ff.)

If Guenevere had honored and loved him, she had succeeded admirably in concealing the fact up to this declaration.

There is clearly a parallel in Guenevere's offer of love with that made by the lady in the tent. Both break the convention of demanding love-service, but there is a great deal of difference between the two situations. Guenevere is the wife of the monarch, and she has had ample opportunity to know of Lanval's prowess and good service long before he became rich. Had she really loved him, his poverty would not have mattered. In fact, however, it is not his good qualities but his recently acquired fame which attracts her. Her attachment to Lancelot is of the same sort.

She has chosen him as the best knight in the world, and he must constantly prove the fact that he is. The lady in the tent approaches Lanval differently

> "Pur vus vinc jeo fors de ma tere:
> De luinz vus sui venue querre!
> Se vus estez pruz e curteis,
> Emperere ne quens ne reis
> N'ot unkes tant joie ne bien,
> Kar jo vos aim sur tute rien."
> (ll. 111 ff.)

The joy she offers is greater than anything on earth, if he is noble and courteous. We know he is. There is no mention of "druerie," and the lady is, so far as we are told, free from other love commitments. The most important point of her speech, however, is the allusion to her arrival from a far country. It is she who has suffered the pain of "amor de lonh" and who has taken action herself to cure her longing. The result is a frank and open union. Lanval simply agrees:

> Il l'esgarda, si la vit bele:
> Amurs le puint de l'estencele,
> Ki sun quor alume e esprent.
> (ll. 117 ff.)

There is no need for a long *amplificatio* of the topos of eyes and heart. Lanval replies courteously that he is willing:

> ". . . ne savrïez rien comander
> Que jeo ne face a mun poeir,
> Turt a folie u a saveir.
> Jeo ferai voz comandemenz,
> Pur vos guepirai tutes genz."
> (ll. 124 ff.)

It will be observed that Lanval offers total devotion and love-service but nothing is asked of him but silence about their love.

There can be little doubt that Marie sets up a deliberate contrast between Guenevere's crass offer and the behavior of Lanval's lover, but she is careful to keep it within the framework of expectations. If we know of the events in *Le Chevalier de la Charette*, we are not surprised at Guenevere's behavior, and we are struck by the irony that this love-court is little better than a barnyard. We can be equally but pleasantly surprised at a non-Arthurian lady who loves someone, asks frankly for his love, and rewards him. In both cases, worldly goods are important, but Guenevere is interested in Lanval only when he has them. The lady in the tent gives them with herself.

Lanval turns from Guenevere in disgust. His love for his own lady would have been enough to make him refuse Guenevere's advances but, unlike Lancelot, he has strong views about loyalty to his king and says so. It is thus ironical that the Queen, in her desperate efforts to avenge herself for his rejection should accuse him of being unworthy to serve the King because he must be a homosexual. To her disordered mind it is clear that any male who rejects her can have no interest in any woman. It will be noted that at this court dominated, allegedly, by consideration of love between the sexes, it never occurs to the Queen that Lanval might be in love with someone else or that, even if he were, he might wish to be faithful to that person even when offered the love of the Queen. The fine talk of constancy and imperishable affection is obviously not relevant.

The insult does, however, make Lanval reveal his own love. He does not say who the lady is, merely that the lowest of her serving-maids is more beautiful than the Queen. It is far from certain that he has revealed their love in any real sense, although he believes himself guilty and, at first at least, the lady regards him as guilty too. By his words he has set up a situation not unlike that at the court of Kaedin in the Tristan romances. Tristan explains his nonconsummation of the marriage to Isot aux blanches mains by saying how much more beautiful Isot la blonde is than she. He proves this by taking Kaedin to watch Isolde's retinue. Kaedin is overwhelmed by the beauty of her maids and ladies-in-waiting and forced to admit, when Isot finally appears, that Tristan is right. Guenevere, of course, is insulted by the rejection of her love but her appeal to Arthur for revenge cannot mention this. She falls back on the method of Potiphar's wife and produces the desired result in her husband, a ferocity and desire for revenge which he never displays over the real adultery of his wife. She is now using her power as wife and queen in an attempt to destroy a good man and is once again demonstrating that determination to dominate which characterizes her in *Le Chevalier de la Charette* and which is the negation of all the qualities for which women were lauded at Arthur's court. Arthur's legal position is correct. His honor has been impugned through the alleged insults to his queen, the worst of which, surely, would be the request for her love. The complaint made by the Queen is threefold: the alleged invitation to adultery, the vilification which followed her refusal, and his vaunting of the superiority of his own lady. No one comments on the strange fact that he asks for the Queen's love when his own *amie* is so superior. The Queen's list of complaints is nine lines long. Five of them are devoted to the last complaint, the comparison of beauty.

When the King states his complaint against Lanval he does not actually mention the Queen's accusation that Lanval asked for her love (although, in his reply, Lanval denies it) but dwells on the denigration of the Queen's beauty. The way is thus prepared for the virtual parody of a trial which follows. The barons all seem inclined to believe Lanval's statement, even though he makes no attempt to prove it. Gawain is prepared to stand as surety for him, as are his companions. When the day of the trial arrives, the complaint and the defense are heard by the entire group of Arthur's barons. Presumably complaint and defense are those already heard. Marie does not repeat them. In giving the judgment decided on by the barons, the Duke of Cornwall says:

> De felunie [li reis] le retta,
> E d'un mesfait l'achaisuna,
> D'une amur dunt il se vanta
> E ma dame s'en curuça.
> Nuls ne l'apele fors le rei.
> (ll. 439 ff.)

The meaning of this passage is not quite clear. Is Lanval accused of "felunie" and the boast of love or does his "felunie" consist in having boasted? Two manuscripts, incidentally, read "mesdit." From the decision proclaimed by the Duke, it appears that the second interpretation is true. There is no mention of the proposal to Guenevere, and all that Lanval is called on to do is to swear an oath of fealty if required and produce proof of his statement. This is a remarkable judgment. It ignores the basic question of an insult to the Queen and, by implication, to Arthur. The words, says the Duke, would not be an insult if they were true because the *intention* to insult would be absent.

> . . . E ceo fust veir qu'il en deïst,
> Dunt la reine se marist,
> De ceo avra il bien merci,
> Quant pur vilté nel dist de li.
>
> (ll. 455 ff.)

In fact, of course, the words could be just as much an insult if they were true, but Lanval is protected by the convention that a lover has the right to defend his lady's beauty against all comers. Guenevere is, so to speak, hoist with an Arthurian petard. Such statements, however, must be made with the knowledge that the knight must be prepared to defend them in combat against the other lady's champion, the Arthurian version of a judicial combat. No one comes forward to defend Guenevere in this way, and the decision of the barons calls for a judgment of a very different kind, something very close to a Judgment of Paris.

The main count of the indictment proves to be the relative beauty of Guenevere and that of Lanval's unknown lady. To settle it by a combat between champions would conform to the Arthurian tradition but it would not, in fact, prove anything. Erec's victory in winning the sparrow-hawk proves that he is a better fighter than his opponent but it does not prove that Enide is more beautiful than the other's lady. This is, of course, the basic fallacy of the Arthurian convention. A lady could be as ugly as sin but if she were Lancelot's or Gawain's or Perceval's lady, everyone would have to agree that she was the fairest. The beauty of a lady is seen only through the eyes—and strength—of her champion. Marie de France, to my knowledge alone of those who wrote in this tradition, arranges a direct combat between the women. The contest bears a close resemblance to those which take place between knights. We remember, for example, that Lunete is alone in her chapel, desperately hoping that someone will come to defend her but knowing that there is no one at Arthur's court who is willing to undertake the task. Lanval is in her position. He, too, feels abandoned, knowing that only the personal appearance of his lady can acquit him. Yvain appears at the last minute to save Lunete and the lady at the last minute to save Lanval. The scenario is well arranged.

In the Grail stories, the Grail is always preceded by a procession of women. In *Perceval,* they are of high rank and the last of them carries the Grail itself. In Wolfram's *Parzival* the hierarchical aspects are stressed even more. The rank of each succeeding group is higher, and the Grail itself is carried by a queen. There is a similar progression in *Lanval.* While Arthur is fuming with impatience to get a verdict from his barons, two maidens approach whose beauty is revealed rather than concealed by the one garment they are wearing. Not unnaturally, the barons break off their discussion to look at them and when they ask for lodging for their mistress, Arthur cannot deny them because to do so would be contrary to the conventions which he had himself established. The next pair attract equal attention and succeed also in postponing the barons' deliberations. The Queen (the other combatant in this conflict) is furious. She is like the seneschals in *Yvain* who are tired of waiting for their vengeance. Then comes the lady herself, the champion of Lanval, Guenevere's opponent! Her palfrey is of immense value and we observe once again the close connection between love and material goods. The description of the lady which follows is interesting in its relation to the topos of description of ideal feminine beauty:

> Ele iert vestue en itel guise,
> De chainse blanc et de chemise,
> Que tuit li costé li pareient,
> Ki de deus parz lacié esteient.
> Le cors ot gent, basse la hanche,
> Le col plus blanc que neif sur branche;
> Les oilz ot vairs e blanc le vis,
> Bele buche, nes bien asis,
> Les surcilz bruns e bel le frunt,
> E le chief cresp e aukes blunt:
> Fils d'or ne gette tel luur
> Cum si chevel cuntre le jur!
> Sis manteus fu de purpre bis,
> Les pans en ot entur li mis.
> Un espervier sur sun poin tint
> E uns levriers apres li vint.
>
> (ll. 559 ff.)

The first part of the description is *ad vestimentum,* not in itself surprising, since the description is the first thing which the audience at court would see. (The lady has already been described from the point of view of Lanval.) What is surprising is the detail. Instead of the usual description of the rich exterior, we are told of the guise: the lady's dress was such that the two sides were laced, revealing her naked flesh. Such an arrangement was unusual, to say the least, and it continues the pattern which we saw in the first description of the lady in the tent, a deliberate exposure to attract attention. After this opening, it is not surprising that when the actual description of the lady begins, it should reverse the usual order. It begins with the body instead of the head, and a body which is "gent," and mentions the unmentionable *hanche*. Then it jumps immediately to the neck, for which a conventional lyric topos is used. The lyric motif is continued in the concentration of the view on the eyes, mouth, and color of the face. The description finishes where it should begin, with the hair. This deliberate reversal of the "description of the lady" topos is intended to reflect first, the viewpoint of the males who are observing the lady and second the conflict which is to come. If we are to have a beauty contest, then description must concentrate on those elements which will produce an effect, not on conventional *amplificatio*. The last two lines of the description confirm this interpretation, for they describe the deliberate action of the lady in the use of her dress. The sparrow-hawk on the wrist and the greyhound are, of course, iconographical symbols of the lady in love.

This long and admirably organized description makes sure that both the reader and the audience at Arthur's court are won over by the lady before the contest has really begun. The procedure is simple. The lady stands in front of the King, lets fall her cloak, and invites everyone to judge whether Lanval was wrong when he said she was more beautiful than the Queen. The visual images multiply as she speaks, and neither Arthur nor the barons hesitate to pronounce Lanval free of all blame, even though, in her statement, the lady had mentioned the charge that he had made love to the Queen.

The contest is over and Guenevere has been defeated. Lanval, like the ladies in the normal Arthurian romance has stood by and watched his champion rescue him, and it is she who takes him on her palfrey to the Isle of Avalon where, presumably, the Arthurian writ does not run and practices in love are more fair. Of the reaction of Guenevere we hear nothing. She cannot, after all, be sent to a lady and be compelled to throw herself on her mercy as a knight would be under similar circumstances. The prospect is too frightening.

This brilliant parallel or even parody of the romance of love and adventure raises many questions. Marie de France has incorporated into it the conventions which we find in the works of Chrétien de Troyes and instead of using them ironically, as he does, she has turned them inside out. The court is dominated by love, and Guenevere is the representative of the dominant female, a domination which persists even in the face of real warfare. Yet it is soon clear that the love ethic of which Guenevere is the personification is not based on courtesy, bravery, or loyalty but on the possession of material goods. Love may conquer all but only if it is accompanied by the obvious signs of wealth. I know of no Arthurian romance in which the hero receives the assurance that his acceptance of a lady's love will bring fulfillment to his dreams of riches. Only when she sees the evidence of this material well-being is Guenevere interested in Lanval and prepared to sacrifice her honor as queen and woman to him. Guenevere's concept of love and by implication that of Arthur's court in general is thus clearly linked with material wealth and sensuality. Fine words about courtesy and honor are shown to be mere pretense. Worse still, love service is shown to be a sham. Neither Guenevere nor Arthur has the least interest in or respect for service rendered. Lanval goes unrewarded. The lady who loves him receives no service whatsoever. It is she who performs service for him. A man's honor is vindicated in a lady's beauty contest.

It will be noted that in concluding her story in this fashion Marie is not so much reversing the Arthurian ethic as pushing it to its logical conclusion. If women dominate the Arthurian court and determine its values, then it is they who should contest for the possession of man, not vice versa. Even in Chrétien's works the center of interest is always the emotional state of the male protagonist. The female protagonist is there to provoke that emotional state and, in some cases, to exploit it. Except in *Le Chevalier de la Charette*, the true decisions are made by the male and it is his "redemption" which brings the work to a conclusion. In *Lanval* the male has no influence on his own fate. His services are ignored. He becomes a lover because of the initiative of the lady in the tent. He is in danger because of the initiative of Guenevere. He is saved by a contest in the qualities for which ladies are renowned. He goes to Avalon not,

like Arthur, to be cured of his wounds, but to indulge forever the love
he has been offered—and to be at the mercy of his lady. If Hell consists
of the endless repetition of his favorite indulgence, he will be there.

We must now ask what Marie was trying to do. Write a short Arthurian romance? Certainly not. A parody of an Arthurian romance? Yes,
but is the object purely comedy? I think not. Many of the effects are comic
but the purpose is not. The Arthurian ethic is no doubt the result of a
desire to set up a fantasy world in which the crudities of medieval war
and medieval sexual life could be replaced by tournament exercises and
sexual play governed by an elaborate and artificial set of rules. This fantasy world was governed by a king who never was, who nevertheless set
a standard of chivalry which none could match. The aspirations of medieval society—and particularly feminine medieval aristocratic society—
could thus be realized in the romance as the hopes of their social inferiors
might later be realized in Heaven. Later generations saw in the romance
a standard of conduct worthy of imitation. Contemporaries of Chrétien
de Troyes and Marie de France were not sure. They were far from convinced that this world of fantasy dominance by the female and unquestioning service by the male provided a solution to the problems of power
relations and sexual relations which were the principal problems of their
society. Chrétien de Troyes, Gottfried von Strassburg, Peire Vidal, even
the author of the *Nibelungenlied,* all saw, though from different points of
view, the ineffectiveness of the Arthurian ethic. But they were all clever
enough to see that the most effective way to present their own ideas was
to write works which moved in the frame of Arthurian convention and
whose ideas thus reverberated against those conventions. In considering
Lanval, we must think rather of these reverberations than the "fairy-tale"
elements or the analogues in Celtic and other mythology. No one would
deny the existence of these elements and analogues nor the fact that they
often impart to the work an increased richness of texture by providing
anthropological and mythological elements of great importance. But I find
it hard to escape the conclusion that, in writing *Lanval,* Marie's purpose
was to question the fashionable assumptions of the courtly romance. Her
hero does receive his reward in the form of mutual love and material happiness but not within the Arthurian context, which is shown as hostile
to all noble aspirations. He who desires true love should clearly avoid it.

The matter of the Arthurian ethic is important. Not less so is the choice
of form. The use of the form of a Breton *lai* for an Arthurian topic di-

minishes that topic. As we saw, the verbal reminiscences, even reminiscences of whole passages, of the works of Chrétien de Troyes are very clear. It is highly probable that the more sophisticated of Marie's contemporaries would recognise them. The use of such material in a form devoted to pleasant tales comes close to mocking the genre from which it derives. Marie is doing very much the same as the Archipoeta, who refused to write an epic on the deeds of Friedrich Barbarossa but did write a short "lyric" on his prowess which proves to be an ironical criticism of his desire to be God's vicegerent on earth in both the secular and spiritual sense. Marie, by her neat use of the *lai* to parody the romance would make it clear to an audience which was very conscious of the limits of genre what she thought of romance conventions. One does not put battle scenes on cameo rings.

NOTES

1. *Les Lais de Marie de France,* Jean Rychner, ed., CFMA No. 93 (Paris: Champion, 1973).

2. Chrétien de Troyes, *Le Chevalier au Lion (Yvain)*, Mario Roques, ed., CFMA No. 89 (Paris: Champion, 1968).

3. Chrétien de Troyes, *Le Roman de Perceval,* William Roach, ed., Textes Littéraires Francais No. 71, 2d ed. (Geneva: Droz, 1959).

14

The Progress of Parzival
and the
Trees of Virtue and Vice

NO READER OF THE Wolfram criticism of the last two decades needs to be reminded of the impact upon it of theological ideas. Indeed, a vary large number of the recent studies of *Parzival* have concentrated upon the ethical and religious problems raised by the work and the relation between these and the theological ideas of his own time or the tenets of a vaguely defined heresy. Such studies assume, as they must, that Wolfram had considerable acquaintance with theological writing, the kind of acquaintance which could be gained only by detailed and informed reading, not by mere second-hand knowledge. Such an assumption is a far cry indeed from the days when Wolfram's "ichne kan deheinen buochstap" was interpreted by respectable scholars as a statement that he literally could not read. It may well be that such criticism, in its desire to open fresh fields of inquiry, has lost touch with reality. No one would deny Wolfram's interest in moral and spiritual problems or his sense of the deep meaning of life and its dependence on God's guidance but there is little or no evidence of systematic theological method, of an attempt to put into poetical form the subtleties of the thinking of the schoolmen. Wolfram's whole attitude would appear to make such an assumption unlikely. It is surely more probable that Wolfram's theology, if his ideas may be so designated, was rather a general attitude towards good and evil which was compounded, quite unsystematically, from ideas current in his day, ideas which originated indeed in the schools but which had become popular and were expressed in a form easily understood by the layman.

When we are considering the religious thought of Wolfram, taken in the broadest sense of the term, there are two main concepts which we should keep in mind: first, that Wolfram was drawing on sources of ideas which were generally available to an educated man and not merely to a student of theology and second, that the really essential feature of the Parzival story is progress, movement towards a goal, an attainable state of grace. By this I do not mean that we should return to the idea of *Parzival* as a *Bildungsroman*—the medieval conception of character and character development is not, in my opinion, consonant with the generally accepted conventions of that genre—but rather that we should realize that Parzival the man is born, like other men, with certain potentialities for virtue and vice. He can struggle to gain virtue, he can fall prey to vice. For him, progress means the defeat of the vices which beset his path and the full use of the innate virtues with which he has been endowed by God. Only by learning the application of these virtues can he hope to attain such a state as will qualify him to be Grail King. This progress is in fact that of any Christian man but the epic presents it on a heroic scale because Parzival had to reach here on earth a state of grace not granted to normal men. Once we realize this point we shall be less surprised at Parzival's failure to attain the Grail kingship on his first visit—he was not ready for such an honor—nor at the almost automatic way in which he finally achieves his goal, for the question on the second visit, like the baptism of Feirefis, was a mere formality, since Parzival had already demonstrated his fitness for the office.

It would be pointless to search for any one author or system of theology which would provide the key to the understanding of Wolfram's thought or Parzival's actions. But it may be permissible to call attention to a method of depicting progress in virtue and vice which was well-known in Wolfram's time and which conforms in essentials to Parzival's own progress. This system is the trees of virtue and vice described in detail by Hugh of St. Victor. It is perfectly possible that Wolfram may have known something of the work of the Victorines, but there is no need to assume this knowledge. The depiction of the virtues and vices as trees was widespread and the form given by Hugh is discussed here merely because it is a convenient and full treatment by an author whose work was likely to be widely diffused and well known.

In his work *De fructibus carnis et spiritus* (Migne, *P.L.* CLXXVI, 997 ff), Hugh examines the virtues and vices as the fruit of trees, each upon its branch and with progress from roots to tip. The idea was not, of course, original with Hugh. The story of the Tree of Life had led at an early period to numerous progressions of virtue and vice in the form of trees, a concept reinforced by such biblical statements as "no good tree bringeth forth bad fruit" and "pride is the beginning of all evil." More important than the general concept for our purposes is the order of the arrangement of the virtues and vices on the tree, the roots, the branches and the fruit, for these became matters of tradition and were well known even to laymen. The cardinal virtues and the seven—or eight—deadly sins had been isolated and discussed at an early period in patristic literature and the progress from one to the other had been established with only minor variations before Hugh's time.[1] We are very probably justified in taking Hugh's scheme as typical (it corresponds closely with the frequent depiction of the trees of virtue and vice in medieval art). His scheme will therefore be compared with the apparent progress of Parzival.

Progress in sin begins with the basic root vice of *superbia,* pride. From it spring all other sins, first those connected with *vanagloria* and *invidia,* then *ira* and *tristitia,* followed by *avaritia,* which lead in their turn to the sins of the flesh, to *ventris ingluvies* and *luxuria.* No doubt the topmost fruits of the tree, the sins of the flesh, were placed there to show the triumph of the flesh over the spirit. With such temptations in a literal sense Parzival has little concern (in spite of his bad manners at the bedside of Jeschute). It may be noted, however, that after the encounter with Condwiramurs, Parzival consciously abandons all sensual pleasure, even the legitimate embraces of his wife, until after he has attained the Grail. His progress in virtue is therefore begun by a denial of the flesh, a denial made even more explicit by the scene with Trevrizent on Good Friday.

It is rather to the lower sins of the spirit that we must turn in our investigation of Parzival's ascent to the Grail. That *superbia* is the basis of these sins, no one, I think, will deny. For Parzival believes that he has been badly treated by God. He had been told by his mother that God will help those who cry out to him but he had not been told that such an appeal must be made in complete trust and humility. Consequently, when he does not obtain results from his appeal, he is angry. He is in fact guilty of that type of *superbia* which believes that it alone is responsible for all prowess, refusing to believe that the qualities which have made that prowess possible are entirely the gifts of God. He demands fair pay for his efforts:

> Mac ritterschaft des libes pris
> und doch der sele pardis
> bejagen mit schilt und ouch mit sper
> so was ie ritterschaft min ger.
> Ich streit ie swa ich striten vant,
> so daz min werlichiu hant
> sich naehert dem prise.
> Ist got an strite wise,
> der sol mich da benennen,
> daz sie mich da bekennen.
>
> (472.1 ff.)

This pride bears fruit in *vanagloria,* the boast that he has done all that could be expected of a knight, and in the accompanying *inobedentia,* a refusal to submit to the will of God. Because of his failure to obtain "recognition," Parzival envies other mortals who are not in his sad position and thinks himself the most unhappy of men. It is, however, in the next two fruits, *ira* and *tristitia,* that we see most clearly how far he has fallen. Gregory the Great had described how *invidia* led to *ira,* which in its turn, being frustrated, led to *tristitia.*[2] A glance at the fruits of *ira* well illustrates Parzival's condition. For he is guilty of *blasphemia* (in his abuse of God), of *luctus* (in his bewailing of his fate), of *temeritas* and *indignatio* (in his challenge to God to help him), and of *furor* in his whole attitude before the meeting with Trevrizent. This stage gives way to one which, of all Parzival's conditions, has called forth the most comment—that of *tristitia.* Recent studies, such as that of Wapnewski,[3] have called attention to the similarity between the state of *zwivel* and that of *desperatio.* There is no doubt in my mind that *zwivel* is intended as an equivalent but it should be pointed out that *desperatio* itself is part of a larger complex, that of *tristitia.* The principal features of this state are all characterized by a desire to give up, to abandon the struggle—*torpor, timor, querella* and, most important of all, *acedia,* the sin of being no longer willing to fight for God. Parzival says:

> ich diende eim der heizet got,
> e daz so lasterlichen spot
> sin gunst über mich erhancte:
> min sin im nie gewancte,

> von dem mir helfe was gesagt:
> nu ist sin helfe an mir verzagt.
> (447.25 ff.)

When Parzival throws his reins over his horse's neck, he is not demonstrating a belief in the power of God to help him but rather challenging Him to prove that He is capable of helping. What Parzival expects is a reward for virtue and his conduct is in remarkable contrast to the behavior of Sigune, whom he has just met, and who, in spite of "provocation" far exceeding that suffered by Parzival, remains humble and meek. She it is who makes clear that each action, even each characteristic, has two sides. Her love was sought by Schionatulander with shield and spear. In the world's sense he died and thus lost his love. But in a spiritual sense he gained it by his defeat. "Even though I am still a maid, before God he is my husband," says Sigune. Parzival has up to now believed that the worldly method of gaining glory, so clearly stated by Wolfram at the beginning of this book, must necessarily impress God too. But the desire springs from the low motive of *superbia*—to be real, it must spring from *humilitas*. The road Parzival has set for himself can go only from *superbia* through *invidia* and *ira* to *tristitia*. It is while Parzival is in this state that the conversation with Trevrizent takes place. In that conversation, Parzival admits his search for fighting and battle and still worse, his hatred of God *(ira, blasphemia)*, and follows with a complaint *(luctus)*. Trevrizent recognizes the symptoms—he describes Parzival's state with the words *zorn, Gotteshass, klage* and points out that nothing can be wrung from God by anger, adding by way of example the fall of Lucifer *(superbia, invidia, ira)*. He demonstrates the futility of fighting when that fighting is based only on worldly considerations. But Parzival is unsatisifed. He still finds it hard to believe two things, firstly that God can or will help him, secondly, that the sins he has already committed can be forgiven—and that he can still attain the Grail. This general attitude is what is meant by *tristitia*, and it shows Parzival at the lowest point of his spiritual career.

Hugh's definition of *desperatio* is as follows: "desperatio est ad vitae statum vel virtutum reditum fracta spei gubernatio vel est spei de salute aut venia obtinenda abjectio." It would be hard to find a definition more accurately describing Parzival's condition—a lack of belief in God's ability to help him to his earthly goal or to his spiritual salvation. With the highly problematical methods of Trevrizent in "taking away" Parzival's guilt we are fortunately not concerned. He is probably speaking only for the family and altogether too much stress has already been placed on the details. More important is the inducing in Parzival of a state of *humilitas*. The scene has been set very carefully—the humility of Sigune and Gabenis, the ultimate humility of Christ on Good Friday, the physical misery of the cave, the sparse fare, the winter cold even in Spring. For, if *tristitia* is the lowest point in the pilgrimage of Parzival, the turn to *humilitas* is the beginning of the ascent. The significance of this turn to humility and rebirth has been frequently commented upon. I would only quote Hugh of St. Victor again, this time his definition of *humilitas:* "Humilitas est ex intuitu propriae conditionis vel conditoris voluntaria mentis inclinatio. Eius sunt comitatus principales prudentia, iustitia, fortitudo, temperantia, fides, spes et charitas." The definition includes two important changes in Parzival's attitude; he must *voluntarily* subject himself to God, not only because of his own condition but by contemplating (and thus recognizing) God himself.

The way now lies from humility to charity and this is the way Parzival must ascend in order to reach the Grail. Many of the virtues he already possesses but until now he has used them only in a worldly sense and in worldly pursuits—courtesy, bravery, truth-telling, loyalty, and self-control. These are qualities indeed but they are manifestations of the true virtues, learned as part of a courtly code. When based upon humility, they become parts of the tree of virtue, they are the fruits of the spirit, not of the flesh and they lead to *charitas* which, in its widest sense, Parzival must experience in order to attain the Grail. Here again we may quote Hugh: "According to their nature, all urges of love *(amor)* are alike but they are separated according to their direction. If love is not properly directed, that is, if it desires what it should not desire, it is covetousness; if it is properly directed and is turned to God and to what is holy, it is called love in the highest sense, that is, charity." The idea is not, of course, peculiar to Hugh. It is found also, for example, in Guillaume de Conches.[4] This idea of the proper direction of virtues is basic in *Parzival* and accounts, among other things, for the sudden conversion of Feirefis.

Having attained humility, Parzival can and does demonstrate those virtues innate in him which qualify him to become Grail King. His sense of justice and truth, his self-restraint, prudence, and bravery, already evident in his behavior but wrongly directed, now act as stages on the way to earthly and spiritual fulfillment. A couple of examples must suffice to show this change. One of the fruits of *fortitudo* is *perseverantia,* determination in the face of odds, a virtue rightly directed and therefore different from, though very similar to, *pertinacia,* a fruit of *vanagloria,* obstinacy or stubborness. One of the fruits of *temperantia* is *taciturnitas,* the avoidance of idle babbling. A misunderstanding of what Gurnemanz had meant had led Parzival to misdirect this virtue and hence it had become, not a vice indeed, but an act harmful to one's neighbor, a negation of *charitas.*

The "new" Parzival can attain the Grail when the three greatest virtues are clear to him and when he realizes that the greatest of these, charity, must guide all his actions. For in these three virtues are contained all those features which must characterize the Grail King. These are the ultimate fruits of the spirit in Hugh's tree of virtues, the qualities to which those already demonstrated are subsidiary, but which, without the humility taught him by Trevrizent, are impossible of attainment. In realizing the true meaning of *charitas* Parzival at one stroke attains the two objects which he had mentioned to Trevrizent:

> min hohstiu not ist umbe den gral;
> da nach umb min selbes wip.
>
> (467.26)

Charitas, says Hugh, "est mentis affectus et purus amor ad Deum et proximum ferventer et ordinate porrectus." With *charitas,* Parzival realizes the meaning of *compassio* (one of its fruits) and the celebrated question becomes a matter of form. Parzival is genuinely sorry for Amfortas, as he had not been at the first meeting (his main emotion was curiosity) and the reunion with Condwiramurs and the children reinstates Parzival's marriage on a higher plane of love than before. We may note especially that hope, the reverse of doubt, brings *gaudium, modestia, patientia, larganimitas,* while faith (*fides,* "triuwe" in the full sense) brings *castitas, oboedentia, continentia,* and *affectus,* and *charitas* brings *pietas, concordia, compassio, misericordia, pax, indulgentia, mansuetudo, benignitas, liberalitas,* and *gratia.*

This progress of Parzival has been sketched in general agreement with the scheme of virtues and vices drawn up by Hugh of St. Victor. I am far from insisting that Wolfram had read Hugh's work or that he was consciously following his scheme. The work of the Victorines had become widely known by Wolfram's time and the idea of progress downward and upward had become part of the common stock of knowledge of any educated man. What I do believe is that Hugh set out clearly what Wolfram felt and what he strove to express in his romance, that is, a definite progression in man, during which only failure can result from the wrong direction of virtues, however great they are, and attainment of the highest good of *charitas* can come only from *humilitas*. This is the lesson which Parzival had to learn and the question of his failure to ask the question on his first visit to the Grail castle becomes academic. His failure to ask reflects a state of mind, a spiritual immaturity. Only when he has passed through the fire can he realize the meaning of *charitas* and hence of *compassio*. It is here that Wolfram rises far above his model Chrétien. For whatever the theological background of his ideas may have been, he sets out to show a spiritual pilgrimage in accordance with a definite plan of descent from innocence through half-understood instruction to despair and thence an ascent firmly based on humility to the glory of full participation in God's purpose and of charity to all men.

Notes

1. E.g., in Gregory's *Moralia* and the pseudo-Aristotelian *De Virtutibus et vitiis*. See Morton Bloomfield, *The Seven Deadly Sins* (East Lansing: Michigan State University Press, 1952).

2. Gregorius Magnus, *Moralium Liber XXXI,* cap. xlv, section 88 f (Migne, *PL,* 76: 621).

3. Peter Wapnewski, *Wolframs Parzival* (Heidelberg, 1955), pp. 15 ff.

4. The reference here is to Heinrich Ostler, *Die Psychologie des Hugo von Sankt Victor,* Beiträge zur Geschichte der Philosophie des Mittelalters, (Münster, 1909), 6: 117. Hugh's actual words are: "et dicitur aliquando cupiditas; quando scilicet ad mundum est, quando vero ad Deum, est charitas." This distinction appears in the *De sacramentis,* 2: 13 (*PL,* 176: 527 ff.) but is implicit in many other passages. Guillaume de Conches calls attention to the problem in the *Moralium dogma philosophorum,* in the section *de cautione:* cautio est distinguere a virtutibus virtutum speciem praeferentia (John Holmberg, ed., Arbeten utgivna med understöd av Vilhelm Ekmans Universitetsfond, Uppsala, No. 37).

15

The Literary Views of
Gottfried von Strassburg

LITERARY CRITICISM of any sort is unusual in medieval writing. When works are cited or discussed, it is usually to help a student to formalize his own endeavors, and the authors used for the purpose are those beyond criticism, that is, the classical writers who have long been canonized. Any mention of contemporary authors is rare and when it occurs at all it is usually inspired by either affection or rancor and does not constitute literary criticism in any real sense of the term. Style or even poetic method is never discussed. There were, of course, numerous "Arts of Poetry" in Latin and in some of the vernaculars but these are works written with the express purpose of providing rules of poetic composition. They are prescriptive, not critical.

In view of this absence of even the most rudimentary literary criticism in the work of contemporaries, it is surprising to find embedded in a courtly romance an apparent digression which seems at first sight to be a review of the present state of the poetic art, complete with all the touchiness and prejudice which one associates with artists talking about their rivals' work. The passage has actually been called "Gottfried's literary criticism" and it is, of course, best known for its caustic references to a writer who is almost certainly Wolfram von Eschenbach. But does the passage in fact constitute literary criticism? Gottfried was not the kind of artist who dropped his theme to make asides, particularly asides of 456 lines. Nor, when the passage is inspected closely, is there much literary criticism in it. Very few authors are mentioned, and, as I hope to show, they are mentioned in a specific order with a very definite purpose in mind. The whole passage is an organic part of the romance, a carefully integrated discussion of the means of telling Tristan's story within the story itself.[1]

There is no need to spend very long in discussing the reasons for the description of a formal ceremony of knighting. Gottfried says that the subject has been treated ad nauseam (although there are no such descriptions in the works of Hartmann and Wolfram), but that is not his real reason for avoiding the subject. Tristan is, for Gottfried, a literary figure or, as I have shown elsewhere, an artist.[2] It would have been perfectly suitable to show his father Riwalin going through the ceremonies of investiture but to do so for Tristan would have been an offense against his nature. Here is the very point on which Gottfried and Wolfram disagreed most violently, for Parzival is the literary representation of a true knight, while Tristan is a literary figure, an artist who assumes the form of a knight because the chivalric romance was the principal literary genre of the day. If Tristan is to be made a knight, he must be made a literary knight, and it will be necessary to endow him not with the sword and spurs of the fighting man but with the qualities needed in a romance and furthermore in a romance of a very special kind. Here we must observe very closely. We are told that thirty other young men are to be knighted with Tristan, and their clothes—that is, their vestments, their new acquisitions or, allegorically, the qualities they take on when they become knights—are these:

> daz eine, daz was hohe muot;
> daz ander, daz was vollez guot;
> daz dritte was bescheidenheit,
> diu dise zwei zesamene sneit;
> daz vierde daz was höfscher sin,
> der naete disen allen drin.[3]
> (ll. 4567–72)

[The first was noble spirit, the second material goods, the third, discretion, which tailors these two into one. The fourth was courtly sense, which sewed for them all.]

Now all these are so-called courtly virtues, the qualities we associate with Hartmann's heroes. They have no special relevance to Tristan in his principal role in the poem. Gottfried makes this point perfectly clear by his (unnecessary) introduction of the other thirty young candidates for knighthood. The qualities listed are those which Tristan shares with all knights in all romances. Gottfried does not condemn them. In the spirit of his own prologue, he accepts them as desirable and praiseworthy—but they are simply not sufficient for Tristan. In his description of the way in which these qualities are applied, Gottfried indicates his feeling that they are superficial:

> der hohe muot der gerte,
> daz volle guot gewerte,
> bescheidenheit schuof unde sneit,
> der sin der naete ir aller cleit
> und andere ir feiture,
> baniere und covertiure
> und anderen der ritter rat,
> der den ritter bestat.
> swaz so daz ros und ouch den man
> ze rittere geprüeven kan,
> der geziuc was aller sere rich
> und also rich, daz iegelich
> einem künege wol gezaeme,
> daz er swert darinne naeme.
>
> (ll. 4575–88)

[Noble spirit desired, material goods fulfilled the desire, discretion created and tailored, sense sewed all their garments and other accessories, their pennants and their cases and all the other chivalric trappings that go with a knight. Their accoutrements were all very rich in respect to horse and man, so rich that each would have been fit for a king's knighting.]

The stress on externals is obvious—*cleit, covertiure, rich*—and the point is made that these were trappings for "ritter." This is what a normal literary investiture would be like but it is not for Tristan. The candidates are all ready with "bescheidenlicher richeit," but how is Gottfried to accommodate the description to what he wants in *his* story? Twice he stresses the necessity of suiting his words to this type of narration (ll. 4596, 4599) and points out that many authors have described "werltliche zierheit, von richem geraete" and also "ritterlichiu zierheit." This is precisely what Gottfried does not intend to do. But it is what Hartmann von Aue can do perfectly.

Now let us try to find out what it is that Hartmann is so good at. It is not that he tells the story of Tristan, for there is no evidence that he ever did, nor is there any reason for regarding him as an expert in describing knightly ceremonial, for we have no such descriptions in his works. He tells a relatively uncomplicated story, the knightly comedy of which Gottfried speaks in his preface. His words are clear—the well-known "cristalline wortelin"—and his "sense" is irreproachable:

> swer guote rede ze guote
> und ouch ze rechte kan verstan
> der muoz dem Ouwere lan
> sin schapel und sin lorzwi.
> (ll. 4134–37)

[Anyone who can understand fine writing with the right attitude and with judgment must grant the man of Aue his wreath and laurels.]

The correspondence with the words of the first two sections of Gottfried's preface is unmistakable:

> Der guote man swaz der in guot
> und niwan der werlt ze guote tuot,
> swer daz iht anders wan in guot
> vernemen wil, der missetuot.
> (ll. 5–8)

[If a good man does anything with good intentions and desiring only to benefit the world, then anyone who takes this in any spirit but that of fairness is doing wrong.]

Hartmann is one of those good men who write good stories with happy endings, whose sense is clear, whose language is pleasant and polished— and whose work is shallow. This description of Hartmann von Aue is not perhaps as flattering as many of his admirers believe. He is placed first in the list of writers, nearest to the thirty candidates for knighthood, because his work corresponds most closely to their characteristics. He also bears another of the stigmata by which Gottfried indicates half-approval—all the epithets referring to his style are visual—*durchverwet, durchzieret, figieret, luter, reine, cristalline* (dyes, ornaments, fashions, clear, pure, crystalline) and constantly the references to flowers. We are reminded of the description of Riwalin and the impression he made on the court, and especially on the ladies of the court, when he arrived in Cornwall. That impression was purely visual, as Gottfried's images show:

> "seht," sprachen si, "der jungelinc
> der ist ein saeliger man:
> wie saelicliche stet im an
> allez daz, daz er begat!
> wie gar sin lip ze wunsche stat!
> wie gant im so geliche in ein
> diu siniu keiserlichen bein!
> wie rehte sin schilt zaller zit
> an siner stat gelimet lit!
> wie zimet der schaft in siner hant!
> wie wol stat allez sin gewant!
> wie stat sin houbet und sin har!
> wie süeze ist aller sin gebar!
> wie saelecliche stat sin lip!
> o wol si saeligez wip,
> der vröude an im beliben sol."
>   (ll. 704–19)

["Look," they said, "that young fellow is *divine!* How *divinely* all his actions become him! What a perfect body he has! His legs are positively imperial and how smoothly they move together! His shield stays glued to his side all the time, his spear looks so beautiful in his hand—his clothes suit him so well and look at his head and hair! How sweet his whole bearing! His person is really divine—and fortunate the woman who can have her joy of him!"]

For courtly ladies enjoyment of details through the eye leads inevitably to speculation about Riwalin's potentiality as a lover. There is strong evidence throughout the poem that Gottfried associates visual imagery with the court of which Mark is the ruler and hence with literary courtliness.

Gottfried does, however, stress that within his sphere Hartmann is supreme. Furthermore, he is classical in his clarity and simplicity, in contrast to Wolfram, who is muddy and complex. It should be emphasized that Gottfried regards Wolfram as competing with Hartmann, not with himself. Hartmann knows how to write a perfect, classical, courtly romance. Wolfram does not. Furthermore, in his use of unclassical diction and imagery Wolfram attracts the untaught and inexperienced and makes them reject the pure classical tradition. Obscurity, in this type of writing, is the cardinal offense. It is obvious that Gottfried is not prepared to admit that Wolfram is attempting anything but a straightforward courtly romance, even though he was too intelligent not to have realized that

Parzival was a different kind of work. In particular, he will not admit that interpretation is needed to understand the poem. The work is obscure and in need of explanation not because it is subtle but because its author has no sense of style, unlike Gottfried's own work, which needs interpretation because it has several levels of meaning. Gottfried thus takes up a somewhat intransigent position—that the chivalric romance reaches perfection in a clearly presented story in classical diction and that the values presented in such a story are to be taken at their face value. The opinion is of interest to all who study medieval romance and one wonders whether Chrétien de Troyes was of the same opinion and if this is the reason for his frequent use of irony in handling the genre.

The passage on Bligger von Steinach is remarkable in several ways. It describes him as a narrative poet, a "dyer," a user of color imagery. Once again we are concerned with the poetry of description and visual imagery. Yet there are differences. The ideal of clarity and translucence gives way to that of rich stuff of embroidery. The fringes are Greek—perhaps Byzantine—and the words are not pure and clear in themselves but are made pure by fairies who dip them in their well. This must mean that some process of transmutation is needed before the "sin" is apparent. The stress is still on "wort und sin," as it was in the description of Hartmann, but in the exact middle of the description of Bligger, at a point which marks exactly one third of the length of the excursus, a new element is introduced which I would like to think is significant, namely sound imagery. Typically, Gottfried uses stylistic devices to call attention to the new element:

> sin zunge, diu die harpfen treit,
> diu hat zwo volle saelekeit:
> daz sint diu wort, daz ist der sin:
> diu zwei, diu harpfen under in
> ir maere in vremedem prise.
> (ll. 4705–09)

[His tongue has a harp in it and possesses two perfect delights—his words and what inspires them. These two between them play out their tale upon the harp with rare quality.]

The midpoint of the description of Bligger and the one-third point of the excursus falls at *saelekeit*. Pivoted about it are repetitions of "harpfen" and "zwei," in slight variation. The two elements are still "wort" and "sin" but the additional element of harmony has been added. The fact that the harp appeared on the family escutcheon of Bligger von Steinach merely enhances the allusion. The rest of the discussion is perhaps best described as a eulogy of Bligger's poetic technique, a subject which is never raised in connection with Hartmann von Aue. The final image is that of flight, not the flight of a singing bird, the nightingale, but of an eagle. The progression toward soaring and music is clear. Hartmann, although limpid, is earthbound. Bligger is borne by his own words in eagle's flight. Heinrich von Veldeke is carried aloft by Pegasus, the true classic inspiration, from whose hoofmarks there sprang the stream of Helicon.

With Heinrich von Veldeke we move into a new phase. Bligger von Steinach is known to us only through a few doubtfully ascribed lyrics; we know nothing of the narrative poem mentioned by Gottfried. Yet it is clear that, like Wolfram and Hartmann, he was both lyric and narrative poet. Heinrich, as we know from his extant work, was active in both fields, and Gottfried chooses to stress the fact, although he had ignored the lyric efforts of Hartmann and Wolfram. In the description of Heinrich the words "wort" and "sin" have become adjectival—"rederich" and "sinnic"—not by any means the same thing, and for the first time there is definite mention of the *Minnesang*.

> der sprach uz vollen sinnen;
> wie wol sanc er von minnen!
> wie schone er sinen sin besneit!
> ich waene, er sine wisheit
> uz Pegases urspringe nam,
> von dem diu wisheit elliu kam.
>
> (ll. 4727–32)

[He spoke from complete inspiration. How well he sang of love! How well he brought measure to his inspiration! I believe he drew his poetic skill from Pegasus' spring from which all such skill comes.]

Wisheit here is surely not wisdom but poetical skill. Once again there is strong stress on the classical origin of all true poetry, but this time the element of singing, of music is introduced. Gottfried clearly regards Heinrich as an innovator, as the man who had introduced into German literature the true forms of poetry. Is he alluding to narrative or lyric? The last line of the description gives the clue:

> . . . daz die den wunsch da brechent
> von bluomen und von risen
> an worten unde an wisen.
>
> (ll. 4748–50)

[. . . and they break off whatever flowers and blossoms they want, in words and music.]

The combination "wort und wise" is used so frequently in lyric poetry that it is almost impossible to escape the conclusion that *Minnesang* is what is meant here. As if to confirm this, Gottfried moves, without further comment, to the discussion of "nightingales."

Thus Gottfried has taken us from a eulogy of Hartmann von Aue, whom he regards as a narrative poet of pure courtly romance, through a vicious aside on the subject of Wolfram, whom he chooses to regard as a Hartmann *manqué*, to Bligger von Steinach, mainly narrative but with lyric possibilities, to the man who indeed wrote narrative poetry but whose fame rested on having introduced into German literature the lyric tradition of Provence and the *langue d'oil* which itself derives from classical sources. The movement from word to music, from the visual to the aural, is very clear. The description of the poets is in accordance with Gottfried's normal pattern of coupling the visual with courtly narrative and music with the higher faculties which transcend the courtly.

Gottfried begins the talk of nightingales and promptly rejects many of them, for I read the couplet

> der nahtegalen der ist vil,
> von den ich nu niht sprechen wil.
>
> (ll. 4751–52)

[There are many nightingales of whom I do not wish to speak now.]

as excluding the majority, not as a mere statement that there are many nightingales and that he will not talk about them. What he is saying is that most lyric poets are not suitable for inclusion in his literary discussion and in fact he selects only two, Reinmar von Hagenau and Walther von der Vogelweide. The selection from the point of view of a modern critic would be rather odd. Heinrich von Morungen would seem a better choice than Reinmar and Walther is a hardly a conventional *Minnesanger*. But we must remember that Gottfried is not discussing the words of the lyrics, which constitute the only part of them still extant, but rather the combination of words and melody, *wort und wise,* which to him and his contemporaries together formed the true *Minnesang.* If either of the parts could be regarded as more important than the other, it was probably the melody. His reason for the exclusion of many lyric poets is very similar to his reason for making courtly narrative inferior to his own:

> durch daz sprich ich niht anders da,
> wan daz ich iemer sprechen sol:
> si kunnen alle ir ambet wol
> und singent wol ze prise
> ir süeze sumerwise
> ir stimme ist luter unde guot
> si gebent der werlde hohen muot
> und tuont reht in dem herzen wol.
>
> (ll. 4754–61)

[Therefore I shall say of them only what I always have to say: they all know their trade and sing their sweet songs of summer in praiseworthy fashion. Their voices are clear and good, they give the world inspiration and spread warmth in our hearts.]

Note the repetition of the words "ambet," "luter," "guot," etc., which we found in the description of Hartmann von Aue and in particular the expression "ir sueze sumerwise." This and the statement "si gebent der werlde hohen muot" indicate the connection between these lyric poets and the group mentioned in the preface:

> ine meine ir aller werlde niht
> als die, von der ich hoere sagen,
> diu keine swaere enmüge getragen
> und niwan in vröuden welle sweben.
>
> (ll. 50–53)

[I don't mean the world of all those people of whom I hear it said that they cannot stand any hardship and wish only to float along in bliss.]

They are the poets of the joyous, unthinking love, the Maytime love of Riwalin and Blanscheflur in its first stages. Yet there is a difference. The emphasis is on music, not words, and this heightens the artistic effect, as the repeated *guot/muot, vogelsanc/gedank* motif shows.

These nightingales are differentiated from the named *Minnesänger* by

a rather unusual device, the introduction of an assumed listener who in-
terrupts Gottfried with the line:

nu sprechet umb die nahtegalen.

(l. 4774)

[Now tell us about the nightingales.]

The word *die* should here be regarded as a demonstrative rather than a
mere definite article. The author intends to talk about *the* nightingales,
the ones that matter, not merely about all nightingales, for Gottfried has
been doing that ever since he first mentioned the subject. *The* nightingales are the poets who sing of a love which is not pure joy:

die sint ir dinges wol bereit
und kunnen alle ir senede leit
so wol besingen und besagen.

(ll. 4775–77)

[They are all well trained and can express their yearning pain in words as
well as music.]

The important word is *senede,* which has not appeared in the previous
references to lyric poetry or indeed in any of the discussion of narrative
poetry. Its appearance marks the first time that the theme of mixed joy
and sorrow, Gottfried's professed main theme, has been associated with
poetry. In both the description of Reinmar von Hagenau and that of
Walther von der Vogelweide the stress is entirely on music and the imagery is aural. Words are mentioned very rarely. Gottfried uses a line
reminiscent of Walther von der Vogelweide in describing the activities of
these poets, "so wol besingen und besagen," compared with Walther's
"ze Osteriche lernte ich singen unde sagen" but after that he mentions
only melodies:

(ich meine aber von ir doenen
den süezen, den schoenen),

. . . .

ich waene, Orphees zunge,
diu alle doene kunde,
diu doenete uz ir munde.

(ll. 4785–86; 4790–92)

[(I mean their sweet, their lovey sounds) . . . I really think that Orpheus'
tongue, which was master of all music, sounds forth from her mouth.]

It is clearly music which conveys the joy and sorrow of love. Two other
features are worthy of note, the stress on love and the repetition of the
idea of mixed joy and sorrow. Gottfried leaves no doubt in the mind of
his audience that the lyric poetry he is referring to is love poetry only and
furthermore love poetry which is in the direct classical tradition. In his
praise of Walther von der Vogelweide, he explicitly excludes all lyric which
is not in this tradition:

> (ich meine aber in dem done
> da her von Zytherone,
> da diu gotinne Minne
> gebiutet uf und inne)!
> (ll. 4807–10)

[I mean in that mode from Mount Cithaeron where the goddess of love
holds power both within and without)!]

Presumably he is excluding both Walther's *Mädchenlieder* and his political
songs. Only love poetry is worthy of true melody:

> diu wiset si ze wunsche wol,
> diu weiz wol, wa si suochen sol
> der minnen melodie.
> si unde ir cumpanie
> die müezen so gesingen,
> daz si ze vröuden bringen
> ir truren unde ir senedez clagen:
> und daz geschehe bi minen tagen!
> (ll. 4813–20)

[She gives them exactly the right directions, she knows where to look for
the melody of love. May she and her company sing in such fashion that
they turn their sadness and yearning complaints into joy—and may it happen in my time!]

Thus the hope of the perfect combination of music and words to express
love lies with the company of lyric poets but it is not apparently realized
as yet. The goddess love is to guide them, the same goddess who appears
as the guardian of the *Minnegrotte* later in the poem.

There are several important implications in Gottfried's judgments on lyric poetry. Reinmar and Walther are the highest practitioners of the art; they lead a company which is devoted to love poetry; they are musicians rather than writers of verse; they approach the true classical concept of love more closely than any other poets. Yet it is also made clear that neither of them is capable of the expression of the highest type of love, Tristan love. It is hoped that Walther will be able to inspire his company to attain the goal of successful combination of melody with the joy and sorrow of love but there is no certainty that he will be able to do so.

What has Gottfried said about the poetry of his day? The narrative poets have shown great skill in the presentation of love at court. The lyric poets are charming in the same way and two of them show promise that one day lyrics will be written which will attain the ideal of combining fine music with the understanding of the true nature of love. Yet it is clear that the picture is imperfect. None of the poets reaches the highest goal. Music stands higher than words, but no contemporary form is truly capable of the expression of love as Gottfried understands it. Literature, in other words, has failed. And this is the reason for the relatively sudden transition to the person of Tristan and not only to his person but to a clear statement that all of this literary preparation is insufficient to make a literary knight of him:

> Nu han ich rede genuoge
> von guoter liute vuoge
> gevüegen liuten vür geleit.
> ie noch ist Tristan umbereit
> ze siner swertleite.
> (ll. 4821–25)

[Now I have presented my kind audience with enough talk about the skill of these good people. But Tristan is still not ready for his knighting.]

In other words, even though I have produced all the accepted literary devices and types of today, this is still insufficient to make a knight of Tristan in the sense that I would like it. As so often in the poem, the depiction of the character or place—for example, the *Minnegrotte*—is far less important in the literal than in the allegorical sense. We may note in passing that the *vuoge/gevüege* compounds are often uncomplimentary words for Gottfried, as may be seen in the bitterest passage in the whole work, the trial by hot iron:

> da wart wol goffenbaeret
> und all der werlt bewaeret,
> daz der vil tugenhafte Crist
> wintschaffen alse ein ermel ist:
> er vüeget unde suochet an,
> da manz an in gesuochen kan,
> alse gevuoge und alse wol,
> als er von allem rehte sol.
> .   .   .   .
> daz wart wol offenbare schin
> an der gevüegen künigin.
>   (ll. 15733–40; 15745–46)

[Thus it was revealed and testimony given before the whole world that Christ,
that most virtuous man, will flap in every breeze, just like a sleeve. He will
fit in and cling on in any way you wish Him to, as close and tight as you
please. . . . This was made perfectly clear by the example of the subtle
queen.]

The kindest translation would be "pliant." There is at least a suspicion
here that Gottfried means that he has provided enough conventionalities
for courtly people.

If, then, the accepted literary means are insufficient, what is Gottfried
to do? At first sight he seems to doubt his own ability to do more:

> ine weiz, wie in bereite:
> der sin wil niender dar zuo;
> son weiz diu zunge, waz si tuo
> al eine und ane des sinnes rat
> von dem sir ambet allez hat.
>   (ll. 4826–30)

[I don't know how to prepare him. My inspiration fails, and thus my tongue
doesn't know what to do, all alone and with no advice from the inspiration
that gives it its task.]

At first the passage seems to be a conventional humility formula, but why,
at this stage, would he introduce such a passage, particularly when we
consider at the point where such a formula might be in place, that
is in the preface, he was neither humble nor formulaic. Closer examination reveals that his words are not conventional. He once again uses the
word/sense combination and gives the reason why the combination does
not function properly here.

> dem man, der niht wol reden kan,
> kumt dem ein redericher man,
> im erlischet in dem munde
> daz selbe, daz er kunde.
>
> (ll. 4835–38)

[When a man who cannot speak well encounters a fluent speaker, even what he could say dies on his lips.]

Who is this "redericher man"? Not one of Gottfried's contemporaries but almost certainly Tristan himself. Gottfried is deprived of the power of speech when faced with the necessity of presenting such a fluent and talented individual as his main character and in the end he can think of nothing better than to write smoothly as the best of his contemporaries do. I have little doubt that these latter remarks are intended ironically. After all, Gottfried has made it clear on several occasions that he regards his work as unique. It is in the matter of making Tristan into a literary knight that his invention fails, not in the telling of Tristan's love story.

He now turns directly to Apollo and the classical Muses for inspiration. Again he ironically underestimates his abilities. Many men have been granted the full meausre of the Muses' inspiration—we may well ask who they are, for Gottfried does not tell us—but Gottfried asks for only a tiny drop to restore him to the path of rectitude.

> und mag ouch ich den da bejagen,
> so behalte ich mine stat da wol,
> da man si mit rede behalten sol.
> der selbe trahen der eine
> der ist ouch nie so cleine,
> ern müeze mir verrihten,
> verrihtende beslihten
> beidiu zungen unde sin,
> an den ich sus entrihtet bin.
>
> (ll. 4880–88)

[And if I can obtain that drop, I shall be in control of the situation so far as that can be done in words. That same single drop, small though it may be, will put straight again both my tongue and my inspiration, in respect of which I have strayed, ordering them and smoothing them as it does so.]

Poor Gottfried! He has lost his verbal skill and to show us how completely it has vanished he produces some neat plays on *verrihten* and *entrihten* but does not tell us what is the right and the wrong way.

I am not, of course, implying that Gottfried is being ironical at the expense of the Muses or the stream of Helicon. Throughout his work he makes it quite clear that he regards all true poetry as originating in the classical tradition. What is conspicuously absent here is the constant reference to music which we find, for example, in the references to classical poetry made in the *Minnegrotte* scene. It is words which are like gold, words which are like gems—all of them visual, not aural, images. The words they inspire are those of courtly poetry.

It is worth noting that the poets of the high Middle Ages, both French and German, regarded their poetry as directly descended from classical and even preclassical times. It is significant that the earliest courtly romances in the French vernaculars are the *Roman de Thèbes* and the *Roman d'Énéas,* followed by the *Roman de Troie.* These are all earlier than any extant Arthurian romance. An even clearer statement of the position is made in the German poem *Moriz von Craun,* where it is explicitly stated that the courtly virtues came from Troy through ancient Greece to Rome, where they were temporarily submerged by the wicked Nero to emerge again under Charlemagne. Gottfried may well be referring to this tradition in his references to classical inspiration.

The conjecture is perhaps strengthened by his next observation. He has now received everything he asked for, a small drop of inspiration from the Muses and the power to use words, and he tells us what the result will be:

> Nu diz lat allez sin getan,
> daz ich des allez si gewert,
> des ich von worten han gegert,
> und habe des alles vollen hort,
> senft allen oren miniu wort,
> ber iegelichem herzen schate
> mit dem ingrüenen lindenblate,
> ge miner rede als ebene mite,
> daz ich ir an iegelichem trite
> rume unde reine ir straze
> noch an ir straze enlaze
> dekeiner slahte stoubelin,
> ezn müeze dan gescheiden sin,
> und daz si niuwan ufe cle
> und uf liehten bluomen ge . . .
>
> (ll. 4908–22)

[Now let us suppose that all this has been done, that I have been granted all that I have asked for in respect to words and that I have a full supply; that my words please every ear, give shade to every heart with the deep green linden leaf; if it goes along at the same pace as my speech and clears and smooths its path and leaves not a speck of dust in its way that has not been removed and that it never moves except on clover and bright flowers . . .]

This passage should be compared carefully with the earlier one which deals with Hartmann and Wolfram. It will be noted that the same visual imagery is present. Wolfram can provide—or tries to provide—shade with the bare stick instead of with the "meienblat." In other words, he is incapable of using the style which will delight the audience for courtly narrative. (Gottfried constantly connects the linden tree or the flowering May with courtly poetry.) Even the dust of which Wolfram makes his "mergriezen" is carefully swept out of the way by Gottfried. The inspiration of the Muses and the stream of Helicon will, in other words, enable him to write courtly comedy, the happy ending, the type of poetry at which Hartmann excels—but there is still no evidence that it will allow him to treat adequately the story of Tristan and Isolde. He has already used such techniques to the full in telling the story of Riwalin and Blanscheflur, whose love was precisely of that character. It would seem that Gottfried is stating that he will need the help of the Muses in writing in the style of Hartmann.

Yet this way is already well trodden—and so is the next possible way, even though it is of a totally different kind. The preparation of a warrior's arms by a god, Hephaistos or Vulcan, is a *topos* in classical epic, and the most famous example of it is the description of the shield of Achilles. I know of no way in which medieval writers could have had direct knowledge of this passage, since it does not appear in the *Ilias Latina,* but there are plenty of similar descriptions in Latin poems, of which by far the most accessible to medieval writers was the description of the arms of Aeneas. The arming of the hero marks an important stage in his career. The gift of arms of divine origin sets him apart from other warriors, however brave, and he is shown as a person far superior to all contemporaries.[4] According to this system, we would have to assume that Tristan now stood before his greatest test, the conflict with Duke Morgan, and that his characteristics were indicated by the wild boar on his shield, the mark of courage, and the fiery dart of love on his helmet. These would be the normal characteristics of the knight-in-love, and every author would use these or similar symbols for his hero. Gottfried does not in fact say that he is doing or will do this but merely that he would do so if he were to adopt the classical convention. The reference to the production of clothes by Cassandra has puzzled generations of commentators, for no classical author ascribes to her any special skill in weaving. Her gift was that of prophecy with no one believing what she said. If Gottfried is not simply making an error here—and that is quite likely—he must be referring to the interpretation of the hero's future through special wisdom, that is, allegorical interpretation. In fact the matter is of little ultimate importance, for the author makes it clear that this system too is inadequate:

> was haete daz iht ander craft
> dan alse ich die geselleschaft
> Tristandes e bereite
> ze siner swertleite?
> (ll. 4961–64)

[What other effect could this have (than the one I produced) earlier when I was equipping Tristan's company for knighthood?]

All of the devices would be excellent to describe Tristan's company but not Tristan himself. The best the poet can do is to fall back on his earlier description and endow his hero with the four qualities of the literary knight which he has already mentioned—*muot, guot, bescheidenheit, höfscher sin.* So Tristan, so far as his literary knighthood is concerned, is back with his companions and we may well ask why Gottfried has gone to all this trouble to reject every literary possibility of describing adequately how his hero became a knight. The key, surely, lies in the following passage:

> sus si Tristan geleitet
> ze hove und ouch ze ringe,
> mit allem sinem dinge
> sinen gesellen ebenglich,
> ebenziere und ebenrich:
> ich meine aber an der waete,
> die mannes hant da naete,
> niht an der angebornen wat,
> diu von des herzen kamere gat,
> die si da heizent edelen muot,
> diu den man wolgemuoten tuot

und werdet lip unde leben:
diu wat wart den gesellen geben
dem herren ungeliche.
ja weizgot der muotriche,
der eregire Tristan
truoc sunderlichiu cleider an
von gebare und von gelaze
gezieret uz der maze.
er haetes alle an schoenen siten
unde an tugenden übersniten.
und iedoch an der waete,
die mannes hant da naete,
dan was niht underscheidung an;
des truoc der werde houbetman
in allen geliche.

(ll. 4986–5111)

[So let Tristan be led to court and to the joust exactly like all his companions in all his accoutrements, with the same trim and the same richness. I
am talking, of course, about the clothes sewn by human hands, not about
those he was born with, the ones that come from the wardrobe of the heart,
the ones called "nobility," which make a man of spirit and dignify person
and life. *These* clothes were not the same for the lord and his companions.
God knows, Tristan, spirited and ambitious as he was, wore quite unusual
clothes and in bearing and ease of manner he was quite unusually distinguished. He was far superior in fine manners and qualities. But in the clothes
that were sewn by human hands there was no distinction. The superior wore
the same clothes as everyone else.]

Tristan is exactly like his companions in matters pertaining to the court
and to fighting. Exactly like them indeed—there are three compounds with
eben—except that Gottfried is using one of his favorite stylistic devices,
repeating words within a line and over successive lines to show harmony
in one way and conflict in the other. Tristan is like his companions only
in externals, the qualities which can be imparted by human agency and
those which can be and have been adequately dealt with by the accepted
literary types. Only in things which are not visible, the indescribable
qualities, was he different. Gottfried uses the words "sunderlichiu cleider" in the sense that they are special and apart, peculiar to Tristan. Yet
obviously they cannot be seen, since Gottfried stresses the fact that in
outward appearance Tristan was indistinguishable from his fellows.

The imagery is extremely complex. We should not forget that the *descriptio ad vestitum* was a rhetorical commonplace—Chaucer's squire is an excellent example of its use—and the figure depends on the assumption that a man's character may be observed from his clothes. Yet Tristan's clothes reveal only a part, and that the least important part, of his character. Even the other candidates have allegorical as well as material clothes, the four qualities in which they are dressed. Thus their appearance is allegorized in terms of their milieu. As a Christian puts on the whole armor of God, so they put on the whole armor of literary courtliness. They are, we may say, in the courtly mainstream. This, I believe, is what Gottfried means by "wort und sin," and it is clear that he regards it as conventional enough. Tristan looks like his companions and so far as his visible trappings are concerned, he can be allegorized in the same way. He is, after all, the hero of a romance whose external form follows that of Hartmann and others. He fights in tournaments and wins a lady.

It is the invisible clothes which distinguish him from all other heroes. Since "invisible clothes" is a contradiction in terms, we must understand a third level of meaning, qualities which indicate character and which are purely his own. The rhetorical commonplace itself has been allegorized and now we have a *descriptio ad vestitum sin vestitu.* If this were the only example of such a proceeding in the poem, I might be accused of far-fetched interpretation, but surely Gottfried's famous mention of his own visit to the *Minnegrotte,* even though he had never been to Cornwall, falls into the same category. He is not allegorizing the *Minnegrotte* at that point—all the allegorizing has already been done—but allegorizing his own allegory in terms of the Christian allegory of the church. To understand the true significance of the *Minnegrotte,* the reader must be aware of the Christian allegories and make a comparison between the Christian understanding of the church and Gottfried's reference to it, in other words, allegorize an allegory. Only thus can the *Minnegrotte* experience have the same meaning for the *edele herzen* as the church building has for a Christian.

Gottfried is always most careful to show the different levels at which Tristan appeals to different audiences. I need only mention the contrast between his impact on the Irish court when he is introduced in his own person in order to reveal the falsity of the seneschal's claims (ll. 11102 ff.), which is conveyed entirely by visual imagery, and the impression made on Mark's court, which is intellectual, and on Isolde, which is musical. It is worth noting that the very similar techniques are used to show Isolde's varying impact. The audience at the knighting ceremonies could not see what Tristan's real qualities were. They were perceptible only to those who could see beneath the externals. They could not be imparted by any human agency or ceremony.

Thus the literary excursus proves to be literary criticism, and the humility formula far from humble. Gottfried has selected two topoi of literary narrative, the knighting found in some courtly romances and the arming which is found in classical epic. Each of them, properly used, should throw some light on the character of the hero. Yet a study of the leading narrative poets reveals that they are capable of description only when they rely on visual imagery. Brilliant though their surfaces may be they can reveal only those qaulities which make for chivalric prowess. They cannot depict a Tristan in his full stature. The lyric poets have different powers and a day may come—but has not come yet—when the combination of words and music will be able to render the complexion of a Tristan in its full terms. Nor is the classical arming adequate. Even with all of the powers of the Muses to aid it, it still can do no more than represent a hero who will succeed in gaining victory at a decisive point in his career.

Thus, so far as literary forms are concerned, there is nothing that can be done. The best of contemporary writing will show Tristan to be just like his companions and the audience will think he is just a polished knight. (Most critics and readers before Ranke and Schwietering fulfilled this prophecy of Gottfried's very neatly.)

Yet Gottfried is, after all, writing a poem about Tristan and Isolde, and there is no reason to think that he believed himself incapable of the task Like Horace, he dares to enter new regions to do things previously unattempted. He will use new and intenser forms of imagery, particularly musical imagery, to show the different qualities (the *tugenden* of l. 5006) which Tristan possesses. These will not be those of a knight, so there is no point in stressing investiture, but of an artist—hence the literary excursus. It is the artistic method we are discussing here. Then why bring up the question of knighting at all? Because Gottfried was well aware that he was writing a knightly romance. He could use no other genre, for without the ironic contrasts between Tristan and the normal knight many of his effects would be lost. He deliberately underrated or refused to recognize the originality of the work of Wolfram von Eschenbach. His own purpose was to show the inadequacy of the genre, to indicate that he could find none better, and then to take the reader into his confidence and ask him to look carefully at what he found in the *Tristan* and thus appreciate in what ways the poem differed from the work of contemporaries. The poem is, after all, written for *edele herzen* who live in courts but are not of them. Tristan and Isolde too live in courts but are not of them. As he had indicated in his prologue, Gottfried writes in the genre of the romance but his work is not of it. The literary excursus is an organic part of the poem, for it shares with the preface the task of indicating to the audience how the whole work must be read.

NOTES

1. There have been several articles recently on the literary excursus: Herbert Kolb, " 'Der ware Elicon.' Zu Gottfrieds Tristan vv. 4862–4907," *DVLG* (1967), 41:1–26; Hans Fromm, "Tristans Schwertleite," *DVLG* (1967), 41:33–50; Ingrid Hahn, "Zu Gottfrieds von Strassburg Literaturschau," *ZDA* (1965), 96:218–236; Louise Gnaedinger, "Musik und Minne im Tristan Gottfrieds von Strassburg," *Wirkendes Wort*, Beiheft, 19 (1967). None of these concerns itself specifically with the points raised in this essay.

2. "Tristan the Artist in Gottfried's Poem," *PMLA* (1962), 77:364–72.

3. I cite Ranke's text as revised in Gottfried von Strassburg, *Tristan*, Gottfried Weber et al., eds. (Darmstadt: Wissenschaftliche Buchgesellschaft, 1967). All translations are my own.

4. Homer, *Iliad* xviii and xix, and Vergil, *Aeneid* viii. 370 ff. and 608 ff. Both in Homer and Vergil the shield offers an opportunity for the poet to comment on society and Homer's highly sophisticated use of it shows that it was already a well-known device. The need to connect the shield of Aeneas with the theme of the greatness of Rome makes Vergil's description appear much more forced. It is made clear in the *Aeneid* that the provision of arms by a god assures victory. Tristan, of course, receives only the same type of arms as those given to his companions and is thus by implication differentiated from classical heroes. The spiritual values which actually distinguish him from them cannot be expressed, allegorically or otherwise, in terms of arms and clothing. Gottfried thus breaks with the very classical tradition that he has imported into the literary excursus.

HIEBERT LIBRARY

3 6877 00133 9174